JAN   2003

One Last Shot

One Last Shot

ONE LAST SHOT

THE STORY OF MICHAEL JORDAN'S COMEBACK

Mitchell Krugel

THOMAS DUNNE BOOKS
ST. MARTIN'S PRESS ⚹ NEW YORK

THOMAS DUNNE BOOKS.
An imprint of St. Martin's Press.

www.stmartins.com

Design by Susan Yang

ISBN 0-312-30354-8

First Edition: November 2002

10 9 8 7 6 5 4 3 2 1

For my wife, Teresa. Always.

CONTENTS

ACKNOWLEDGMENTS

When Pete Wolverton called to suggest taking one last shot at another book about Michael Jordan, he gave me the chance of a lifetime. Write *your* thoughts, Pete said, about the greatest athlete of the past century—and, who knows, maybe this one, depending on how many more comebacks. *One Last Shot* could not have come to life without Pete's vision and inspiration. St. Martin's Press is lucky to have an editor and publisher like Pete Wolverton. I am thankful to have worked with him for the past sixteen years, and my unending thanks for everything you did for *One Last Shot*.

My esteemed thanks to Thomas Dunne and everybody at Thomas Dunne Books. You have given me opportunities most writers only dream about. A special tip of my cap to John Parsley, who helped nurse me through this work. And, as always, Madeleine Morel, I couldn't have done any of this without you. Thank you for being the best literary agent in the business.

My girls—my wife, Mary, and my daughter, Brittany—are the backbone of this book. We wouldn't have made it without your love, inspiration and sacrifices—and your yogurt pretzels. My family is the best—so understanding, so supportive. To two of the smartest people I know: my mother and father.

Frank Scandale, the editor of *The Record* in Bergen County, New Jersey, was worried about whether I would survive this but never stopped pushing me to go for it. And for propping me up on those sleep-deprived days, I thank John Balkun, John Rowe, John Connolly, Rob Tanenbaum, Chuck O'Donnell and the sports department at *The Record*. Steve Adamek and Al Iannazzone, *The Record*'s NBA writers, were kind enough to share their insights, and to my sports columnists, Adrian Wojnarowski and Bob Klapisch: You both put more into this book than you will ever know. Rich Gigli, Joe Gigli and the photo department at *The Record* were a huge help.

Any time spent with Doug Collins continues to be the most rewarding I have ever had as a sports writer. You are an eloquent genius. The NBA is better for having you back on the bench.

Chicago Sun-Times sports columnist Jay Mariotti was more than gracious with his insights. You have taught me so much. I am proud to call you my friend.

One last thanks to Ben, Michele and Pauline.

And finally to Michael Jordan, whose Third Coming has put us all in awe of the possibilities. Although you were not involved in the writing of this book, the anticipation of seeing something we have never seen before every time you touched the ball provided the inspiration for this work.

WHY

1

MICHAEL JORDAN WON'T SUCCUMB TO TIME, TO AGE, TO PAIN, TO HIS OWN management gambles of the past eighteen months, and definitely not to expectations. Not tonight. Three months from now, he will reluctantly but exhaustedly admit he's not that player, the one known worldwide as the Greatest of All Time. But not tonight. Sure, his side aches where the broken ribs he suffered last summer while getting ready for this are still healing. His back spasms from time to time. He looks eerily older in the unfamiliar, almost traitorous blue of his new team, the Washington Wizards, and his right knee swells to a tormenting reminder that he is now thirty-eight years old. He was wrapped in so many ice packs this morning that if somebody put a swoosh on them, he would have been sporting a new line of Nike apparel. He says he will eventually get to the point where we will see plays "similar to what we're used to seeing." But not tonight.

Tonight, Madison Square Garden in New York buzzes with Red Carpet anticipation. Opening night of this National Basketball Association season, not coincidentally, matches Michael's Wizards against the Knicks, for where else would the Third Coming of Michael Jordan premiere but around the corner from Broadway? Woody Allen is here and so is Spike Lee and Kevin Kline and Diane Sawyer and all of the other renowned Garden partiers who saw Michael score forty-two points when he supposedly made a farewell visit here in 1998. Up in the Bronx, the Yankees are playing the Arizona Diamondbacks and struggling to make a run at their fourth consecutive World Series championship, but that is no more than an opening act tonight. Tonight, Bill Bradley and Joe Frazier and Kevin Bacon and David Spade would rather be at the Garden. So would Heidi Klum, even though she whispers that she's not really a basketball fan. And Jessica DeRubbio, a twelve-year-old sitting next to Spike. Spike auctioned off the courtside seat usually reserved for his wife to an anonymous person, who paid $101,000 to the fund for the victims of the September 11th terrorist attack. Jessica is one of those victims. Her father, Dave, and several other firefighters from Engine 226 in Brooklyn were lost in the attack. More than six hundred media men and women, including the usual suspects from Japan, France, Brazil and Israel, have also come here to make this event more of a spectacle than any of the NBA Finals Michael Jordan ever played. The BBC is here to televise the game live back to London. It might be 7:30 P.M. on October 30 in New York, but it's the middle of the night in England. Still Michael Jordan's return to active duty in the NBA after more than three years marks the first time the BBC has ever televised an NBA game live.

Approximately ninety seconds into the season, Michael Jordan lets us know what to expect in what will be revered and maligned as his Third Coming. Wizards center Jahidi White steals a pass and springs Jordan on the runway toward the Knicks' basket. He slips past New York's Latrell Sprewell, leaving only 6-foot-11 Felton Spencer as a 300-pound heavy bag standing in the way of a poster-perfect beginning to this Third Coming. Michael takes off, the Garden expecting him to strike the Air Jordan brand pose, arm extended, legs spread, a reassurance that he still hovers above all this. But he finds only enough lift to duck under Spencer and scoop the ball "up" to the hoop, a shot that bounces three feet above the rim and wiggles into the basket. For a moment there is hope—wishing really—that this breath of Air can be the start of one of those Garden nights when Michael scores fifty, that the next five or six months won't be an embarrassing egocentric stumble for a man who struggles to find other places besides the basketball court to define his worth. Another three minutes pass before Michael tries his next shot, after faking his way through the double-teaming defense of Sprewell and Mark Jackson. That the Knicks are doubling Michael should be a sign the NBA considers him the Jordan of old. But right now he says he feels like the old Jordan. His shot over this double-team leaves the Garden echoing "Air Ball, Air Ball." Only once on this night will he make back-to-back shots. He spends more time looking to set up Chris Whitney, Tryone Nesby, Popeye Jones and a bunch of guys who could never be confused with Scottie Pippen. He goes the entire third quarter without scoring a basket. In the final thirty seconds, Michael throws away a pass when Washington has a chance to take the lead.

Yet with sixteen seconds left in the game, Michael has the ball and the game back in his hands. He has just hit a jumper from the foul line, the first time tonight when the shot had some lift and the play ended with a bounce to his step, and now Michael is setting up for a three-point shot that can tie the score and pick up where the Second Coming left off. Like the nearly twenty thousand fans here at the Garden tonight, Wizards coach Doug Collins flashes back to the Jordan of old. Collins, who at the request of Washington's director of basketball operations, Michael Jordan, is starting his own third coming, remembers the first game he ever coached Jordan. Opening night of the 1986 NBA season brought Collins, the rookie coach of the Chicago Bulls, and Jordan to the Garden. With two minutes left in that game and the score tied, Collins called a timeout.

"I remember I had a splitting headache just from the pressure of the game," Collins related, perhaps fully understanding that part of his role this season will be official Jordan storyteller. "I was drawing up a play, obviously to get the ball to Michael. And he handed me a cup of water and said, 'Take a drink of this. I'm not going to let you lose your first game.' I think he went out and scored the last ten points of the game. We won. He ended up with fifty. That was my first taste of Michael Jordan."

Like the packed house here at the Garden tonight, Collins figures the aching knees, the one thousand, two hundred and thirty-three days since Michael's last game-winning shot and the previous forty-seven minutes and forty-four seconds provide no reason to think he won't make this one. Knicks coach Jeff Van Gundy speaks for an entire basketball universe when he says, "I thought it was in. I think we were all surprised when it didn't go."

Talk of the missed shot afterward brings a cat-that-swallowed-the-canary smile to Michael's face. He has fallen into this expression the few times during his career when he has been relegated to human, to less than savior. Like this is one time he didn't take everybody in the shell game. The big shot isn't going down. Not tonight. Who knows when it will? Maybe when the ribs have healed, the knee feels better and the expectations aren't so overwhelming. Michael says, "This is the beginning of a long season." Tonight, it looks like the beginning of a long struggle that leaves the world asking:

Why?

Why is Michael Jordan here?

2

WE ARE HERE LOOKING FOR THE RABBIT. GEORGE KOEHLER, WHO FOR eighteen years now has alternately served as being Michael Jordan's bodyguard, chauffeur, valet, caddie, confidant and surrogate big brother since MJ first set foot in the NBA, has this theory about watching for the rabbit. You have probably seen George sitting behind the Wizards bench or clearing Michael's postgame path to the locker room or the team bus, the guy with the mop top and mustache who could pass for the fifth Beatle. This conversation with George has turned into Jordanology, and there are four, five, six, maybe a dozen mavens inclined or equipped to probe Michael Jordan as a science. Michael Jordan is still popular culture, an economy, a soap opera inspiring us to analyze him with *National Enquirer* curiosity. Still that way, even though he hasn't commanded a double-team for more than three years. We have listened to the rhetoric and rationalizations Michael has fabricated up to this opening night, that he is here because of his love for the game and to make winners out of a motley crew of Wizards, who threaten to expose his basketball operations inferiority. But those who know Michael have once again seen him back under that spell, that what's driving him again is the opportunity to put obstacles so mountainous out there that if he can overcome them, then his legacy might grow large enough to match his ego and to justify the whole endeavor.

George is talking about the rabbit as the root of all this, reminding that every time we went to a game in Chicago we saw Michael pull the rabbit out with that raise-the-ball-in-one-hand, switch-it-to-the-other-hand, flip-it-in-the-basket sleight of hand. Now that Michael has come back to pro basketball for a third go-round at age thirty-eight—thirty-eight in human years but really about one hundred and twelve in NBA years—George issues a warning, a manifesto that could define what very well could be the greatest comeback in the history of sports. Keep looking for the rabbit. For what all this pomp and circumstance tells us on the very first night of another Michael Jordan comeback is whether Michael Jordan still has *it*. Not the *it* of the hang-time dunks. Not the *it* of last-second, game-winning shots. Not even the *it* that can win championships. The *it* that makes a Sunday in Toronto or a February night in Sacramento worth a five hundred-dollar ticket because he will do something that will enable future generations to hear about "the night when Michael Jordan . . ." The Third Coming will be a chase for *it*, as much as anything else. And for the first time in eighteen years Michael Jordan begins a season not really sure if *it* happens. Anymore.

"The skill level has changed, obviously," he reveals, "but I've compromised with the mind. I think I'm more strong-minded now, far more so than then, but all that equals success. So, yeah, I guess I still have it."

Just not tonight. Michael Jordan finished the first game of his third go-round with nineteen points on 7-for-21 shooting and one big missed shot. His team lost by two points. Flash back for a moment to March 19, 1995. At Market Square Arena in Indianapolis, Michael Jordan returned to the NBA after an eighteen-month sabbatical, hit just seven shots and finished the first game of his second go-round with nineteen points and one big miss. His Bulls lost in overtime. Not that we need to be reminded, but by the time he ended that stint, he had another three championships and an ending that confirmed Michael as The Greatest Player of All Time.

So if Michael Jordan left us with the Greatest Drama of All Time when he flicked his wrist, extended his arm and dropped the shot to knock out the Jazz in the 1998 NBA Finals, then is the first game of his new life as a Washington Wizard one electrifying rabbit test? With one three-point shot—a missed shot no less—Michael Jordan has again become the greatest soap opera in sports. Unless Tiger Woods can win every major golf tournament or the Williams sisters can win every major tennis tournament, Michael Jordan returning to the NBA for a two-year encore is, as noted Chicago sports writer and thirty-year follower of the NBA Lacy J. Banks surmised, an even greater feat than Muhammad Ali's return from his five-year conscientious objection to the Vietnam war to regain his heavyweight boxing title. Michael's comeback is continuous nights of the kind of drama that followed Jack Nicklaus as he won the Masters at forty-six years old, or the game-winning, extra-inning home run the Yankees' Derek Jeter hit in Game Four of the 2001 World Series the night after MJ's Magical Mystery Tour began in New York.

Whether it was late December in Charlotte or mid-February in Sacramento, the drama would follow Jordan every night like the fans who lined up after the game just to watch him get on the team bus. Added melodrama surfaced shortly after Michael officially confirmed his comeback on September 10. The terrorist attacks on the United States the next day obviously put Jordan fervor on hold, but there are those who theorized that his comeback could actually aid the relief effort, and not just because he was donating his entire one million dollar salary for the 2001–2002 season to the September 11 relief fund. "In our lifetime, no athlete has symbolized American domination more than Jordan," *Chicago Sun-Times* columnist Jay Mariotti wrote. Michael's fifty-point nights and gluttoning for championships and multimillions of dollars in earnings on and off the court symbolized an era of unprecedented superfluity for America, a time that was in the process of slipping away when Michael came back to the game. Could Michael Jordan reestablish American domination, or at least add fuel to a post–September 11 American comeback? And if he could at thirty-eight years old, carrying a group of players that included Tyrone Nesby, Popeye Jones, Hubert Davis, Richard Hamilton and Christian Laettner—a group far less talented than many he played with in Chicago—wouldn't that make for a tale that could elevate the Jordan domination well beyond his last-shot-in-Utah legend?

Here lies the drama within Michael Jordan's Third Coming. Those close to him had heard Jordan talk for the eighteen months prior to his return about how he had not hit his last shot yet. He was chasing one more, and the reason he always made for the greatest theater in sports was because of his relentless push to validate "it," it for Michael being the will or the mystique or the rabbit. So you can fathom how Jordan can look at all this commotion over his return and less than a month into his comeback boast, "Nothing has changed since I've been gone."

What has changed, however, is that for the first time in the history of Michael Jordan, not everybody is so sure he can hit that last shot, and that those who insist he has set the obstacles higher than even he can overcome include those closest to him. Magic Johnson and Charles Barkley, Jordan's two best friends in the game and really the only two who have always been truly honest with MJ the past eighteen years, expressed their doubts publicly and privately. Magic perhaps spoke for the masses by watching the first few games of the Third Coming and saying, "This is not the Michael Jordan I want to remember." And the one person who was Michael's greatest enabler in all his championship seasons added his reservations about whether there is still mystique in Michael.

"I don't think we're ever going to see that person who elicited those responses of, 'I've never seen this before,'" Phil Jackson related after watching Michael roller-coaster through the preseason.

Opening night does little to change that perspective. The reviews include commentary describing Michael as looking more like a burly traffic cop than a lithe shooting guard and calling his play a slower, smarter game played way below the rim. One observer notes, "Once able to defy gravity, he never got twelve inches off the ground against the New York Knicks." For Michael, this night ends having to answer his critics with dark glasses covering his eyes—and who can forget the last time he dressed like this: that interview during half-time of Game One of the 1993 NBA Finals when he tried to spin-doctor gambling forrays that supposedly cast him betting up to one million dollars on a round of golf. When Michael states the obvious, you know he's hiding something behind the Foster Grants. His first answer, in which he admitted, "Obviously, I'm a little older than the last time I shot the basketball," is the first whiff of self-deprecation he will use this season to defray talk of deterioration. More revealing of just how uncertain Jordan is about the season comes with his con-cluding statement about what he expects from here. "No one knows," he says. "Everyone speculates. But no one knows."

The consensus on opening night argues that the road ahead is not only beneath Jordan's legacy but beyond his grasp. Even if he expected to be as good as that most valuable player/all-defensive team/scoring-leader season of 1991–92 when he turned twenty-eight, the greatest obstacle of all would be how Michael could fit his game, that was so Sade, so Anita Baker when he retired last, with some teammates whom Wizards assistant coach Johnny Bach described as products of the New-Jack generation. The talent on this team would make for punch lines all season. Whitney would be known as the guy leftover from the 1997 Washington team, the last one to make the playoffs. And then he was only a thirteen-minute-a-night mop-up man playing behind not just Chris Webber, Juwan Howard and Rod Strickland, but such household names as Jaren Jackson, Tracy Murray and Harvey Grant. Laettner was the prize Jordan reaped when he finally traded Howard and his hundred million–dollar contract the previous season. Yet here was Laettner, a former college player of the year and, like his boss, third pick in the NBA draft, ten years removed from that last-second shot he hit to lead Duke over Kentucky in the greatest NCAA Tournament game ever played, now with his sixth NBA team. Kwame Brown, the first overall pick in the most recent draft, was barely two weeks old when Michael hit his NCAA Tournament–winning shot in 1982, and the Jordanologists were looking at the offseason acquisition of Tyronn Lue and joking, "Can you say Dennis Hopson?" This assortment of vagabond free agents, rookies and second-round picks sported Hamilton as the front man, and he was into the fourth- or fifth-edition Air Jordans when his star first started to rise. The chasm here was so great that behind closed locker room doors you can imagine the rest of these Wiz kids standing behind Hamilton, pushing and whispering, "Go over and talk to him," like a group of sixth graders at recess. Michael wondered if they could handle the side of him they never saw in those posters on their bedroom walls, the wrath that would come with mistakes, the petulance that would dictate that no one show up the boss, the blame for failure that would be passed on to them. A locker room filled with more Dennis Hopsons than Dennis Rodmans left that same question about this comeback lingering.

Why is Michael Jordan here?

3

MAKE NO MISTAKE, MICHAEL JORDAN IS NOT HAPPY ABOUT HAVING TO ANSWER this question. If body language makes a statement, Michael is downright pissed about having to go through the third degree challenging why he is here. In a statement of another kind, he has come to the news conference officially announcing his return to playing status on

October 1, 2001, dressed in a red-and-black sweatsuit that could easily be confused with the colors he wore with his previous greatness. The outfit echoes a sentiment he expressed a couple of months earlier when asked about how his comeback could ruin the perfect ending to a perfect career that came with that game-winning shot in Utah. Yes, Pelé scored the winning goal in his final professional soccer game and Ted Williams hit a home run in his last at-bat and John Elway scored the winning touchdown in the Super Bowl on his last Sunday in the NFL and Cal Ripken hit a home run in his last All-star Game. But wasn't Michael even more perfect by hitting his last shot to win a championship?

"What perfect ending?" he told ESPN. "Who said it was a perfect ending?"

Now, Michael is intermittently falling into his defiant tone. There are some issues he cannot tolerate being pressed about. When Shaquille O'Neal made his first-ever visit to Chicago with the Orlando Magic during his rookie season, Michael slapped Shaq with a sixty-four-point outburst, the second highest of his career. But with time winding down, Jordan threw away a pass, a turnover that allowed Orlando to tie a game the Magic went on to win in overtime. After the mass media spent its usual thirty minutes after the game showering Michael with questions about his second-highest scoring monologue ever, a question came about the turnover. "Did you see the fucking game?" Michael snapped in a tone he rarely showed the public, a tone that boiled over when the ability to win at all costs he thought of as his manhood was challenged.

But he's showing that tone again at this comeback news conference on this first Monday in October 2001. More than two hundred reporters are peppering him with questions and citing how Magic and Barkley and Kareem Abdul-Jabbar and Red Auerbach, among so many others, have poo-pooed his comeback. Combine their opinions with the naysaying newspapers and Internet sites that have spread since word that Jordan might attempt another return first leaked out the previous April, and maybe Michael's reasoning insists he's doing this just because everybody says he shouldn't. How long, then, before stubbornness and defiance threaten to become the legacy?

"If I read every newspaper about negative things I was trying to do, I swear I wouldn't live in America," Michael explained when the questioning at the news conference turned not to why, but why he shouldn't. "America's supposed to be the free will to do whatever you choose, do whatever you want to do. That's all I'm doing. I'm not committing a crime here. I'm not afraid to take a step. If I fall, I fall, pick myself up and move on. If at the end of the day, I do it, great. If I don't, I can live with myself."

The idea of a comeback probably took root when Michael watched from his president-of-basketball-operations perch as the Wizards he put together in 2000–2001 stumbled to sixty-three losses, twenty more than he experienced in his last three years combined with the Bulls. The urge, as he called it, came from being around the players. The logic of a return picked up more legitimacy when he watched close friend Mario Lemieux leave his ownership loft to rejoin the Pittsburgh Penguins after thirty-six months away from the National Hockey League. Apparently, watching Mario made Michael realize, "There's an itch there that still needs to be scratched here, and I want to make sure the scratch doesn't bother me for the rest of my life."

Itch. Maybe more like a rash, which might truly explain why Michael is here. The only category Jordan measured himself by in 1998 was championships. Rings and trophies and Most Valuable Player awards, for sure, but the opportunity to command that whitest-hot stage and pull out the rabbit just when the entire world was expecting you to most defines what fueled Michael Jordan those three years of his Second Coming. When Charles Barkley submitted that Michael would be "chasing his own ghosts" in the Third Coming, MJ writhed with anger usually reserved for bad officiating and retorted by telling the *Chicago Sun-Times*, "Charles never won a championship. He doesn't know what it's like." Michael is not here talking championships, not yet. But he is here to recapture that endorphin of being the ultimate winner, the feeling he finally admitted was taken from him before he was ready to let it go.

"Obviously, when I left the game, I left something on the floor. You guys may not be able to understand that. After we won the last title, I didn't sit down, ready to quit the game. I didn't want to go through the whole rebuilding process at that time. If Phil had stayed there and the team had stayed intact, I would have still been playing."

Imagine the fury percolating inside Jordan if he's willing to be the hub of another rebuilding process in Washington, one with Jahidi White, Etan Thomas and Brendan Haywood forming a center triumverate that would have to improve to be as good as Luc Longley? For a city that had seen its team try to rebuild around Mitch Richmond and Chris Webber and Tom Gugliotta and Pervis Ellison and Bernard King the past fifteen years, Jordan's return had more newsworthiness than Monica Lewinsky. The talk around town positioned Michael coming back as a professorial move. He didn't hesitate to adopt the politically correct approach, saying his return was to help build the foundation for a perennial playoff-contending team. Teach this young team what he knows best: how to win. What better way for the first high school player ever selected No. 1 in the NBA draft to learn than to study at the feet of Michael Jordan? Brown, the six-foot-eleven high school kid from Georgia, would get a crash course from Michael. So would the others. And Michael would do what nobody else could do and lift this young bunch of losers to the brink of playoff contention, and he would try to convince the world—and himself—how that could be as great as any championship he ever won.

The company line sounded good. In moments like these, Jordan gets prone to rationalizing. How else could he return after telling the masses on January 19, 1999 that he achieved everything he set out to in the world of basketball, that he could live with the challenges of being a good parent and that he was fine with becoming the world's best carpool dad? But this time around, he was telling anybody who would listen basically that winning isn't always about winning championships, that turning the Wiz kids, this group with less skill and experience than any group Jordan ever played with, into a playoff threat very well might become the legacy of Michael Jordan's new millennium comeback.

Funny thing, though. Nobody was buying the company line from Michael. When *Sports Illustrated* asked the Celtics' Paul Pierce why he thought Jordan was coming back, Pierce responded without hesitation: "He's coming back to dominate." Shortly after Michael completed his first official question-and-answer session of the comeback, Doug Collins considered why Michael was here and the legitimacy of the learning experience approach he heard making the rounds the past few weeks. Eventually, Collins would have to determine if Michael's play was elevating the team or if his play was carrying this overwhelmed group to places nobody else could. Some nights it was one; some the other. Some it was both. But right now, Collins knows why Michael is here.

"People think Michael is coming back to be Socrates or something," Collins explained with a dissertational tone that will be called on so often this season. "Sure, he wants to teach. But Michael still wants to kick your ass while he's teaching. Believe me, his fire to win burns hotter than ever."

Michael Jordan is so calculated, so cold-blooded that perhaps he has only based this comeback on how far he can take his team. He has looked at the competition in the Eastern Conference and seeing no Shaq, no Lakers, no Sacramento, an old and injured Alonzo Mourning and an Allen Iverson still several spankings short of the maturation needed to be a winner and figured he had as good a shot at making the playoffs as he did with Granville Waiters, Dave Corzine and Earl Cureton. If he could get the Wizards to the playoffs, would you bet against him in a playoff series? In the three seasons he was gone, nobody staked a claim to his stature as the dominating player in the game. Well, maybe Shaq, but Kobe Bryant played an equally vital role in the Lakers past two championships. And nobody can really claim most-valuable-player standing until they can prove it against Michael Jordan. So for a guy who has always seen the game within the game, maybe he's back for the hunt. The Air Apparents have been tripping over each other the past three years, but now they have a shot at Michael, and perhaps taking them on is the only way for him to once and for all leave it all on the floor.

"The young dogs are going to chase me around," Michael acknowledged. "Well, I'm not going to bark too far away from them, either. I'm not running from nobody. I'm not saying I can take Kobe Bryant, that I can take Tracy McGrady. You guys are the only ones saying they can take me. All good and fine. I'm pretty sure they're sitting back, welcoming the challenge. Guess what? I'm sitting back welcoming the challenge, too. I'm not walking into the dark. I know what I'm capable of doing. I know everybody is putting my head on the block. Everybody's motivated to come out and play against me. Well, everybody was motivated to play against me when I left. So things haven't changed."

Maybe that is the real question here. From pretty much the opening tip on opening night, opponents were double-teaming Michael. And triple-teaming him when necessary. Michael said he realizes fans expect him to score fifty points every night. So, no, it seems things really haven't changed that much. Three or four years ago, he could walk onto the court after thirty-six holes of golf and drop forty or fifty on anybody. Now, to put it in Michael's words, no one knows, but the thrill of the hunt, the quest-quest-quest-until-conquer syndrome that drove Jordan more than he ever let on came no place else in his life—not on the golf course or at the blackjack table—like it did on the basketball court.

And that's precisely why he's here.

4

MICHAEL JORDAN IS HERE FOR NIGHTS LIKE NOVEMBER 7, THE SECOND WEEK of the Third Coming. We all are, actually. The fifth game of his comeback matches Michael against the Celtics in Boston and Pierce, the New-Jack star. Of all the young dogs purported to fill Michael's

son have already fostered a do-you-think-he-will-go-off-for-fifty buzz. But the fact of the matter was how long would Michael go on this season playing one night like the old Jordan, and the next like an old Jordan?

Questions, so many questions for Michael about this Third Coming. Why, for example, did he retire in the first place? Why couldn't he exist in the life of an NBA executive? When he retired in 1999 why didn't the Chicago Bulls offer him the executive privileges? How can he teach this ragamuffin bunch of Wizards that couldn't hold court with the Granville Waiters-Earl Cureton-Brad Sellers-Dave Corzine Bulls of 1986 to win? Can he add to the Airobatic days of his First Coming and the post-up terror of his Second Coming with yet another evolution of his game to define the Third Coming? Can he handle the showdowns with the Air Apparents, Kobe and Vince and Tracy and the others, who will force Michael to play much of this season as a High Noon? And the one seemingly everybody is asking: How much can Michael Jordan be the player he once was?

Doug Collins exacted the difference between Michael at thirty-eight and his previous versions on the very first night of the season. When the three-point shot wouldn't go down against the Knicks, Collins realized what the young Michael had that he wasn't sure the current one did. Michael rebounded from the missed three-pointer and the 7-for-21 shooting against the Knicks like the Michael of old. He hit the first shot of the next game against Atlanta. He hit his next shot. He scored eleven points in the first quarter. He dunked. He had nineteen points in the first half. And then the clock struck 2001. Collins said there would be nights this season when Michael would come out of halftime, wonder where his legs went and his game would feel thirty-eight years old. Jordan went on to miss fourteen of his last twenty-two shots. And though he finished with thirty-one points for the game, he missed five of seven fourth-quarter shots. Forget the fifty-point nights and the SportsCenter dunks and such. The question of whether Michael could re-establish himself as the game's ultimate closer came to Collins, and he realized early on the difference between Michael at thirty-eight and the previous version meant that, "One of the things I have to get Michael to understand is that he can no longer win games by himself anymore."

The more he tried, the harder he fell. Early in the season, he went off for three straight games of thirty or more points, but after scoring thirty-two in the last of those three—a third consecutive loss—Michael admitted he was missing "shots I normally make." Worse yet, NBA teams were doing something they had never achieved against Michael. They figured out how to play him, or more discouraging, how to stop him. After his first two seasons, Michael stated time and again how offended he was hearing the scouting report other teams had on him. "Play me for the drive, they said. Lay off of him and let him take the jump shot," was how he remembered it. So the next season, he went out and scored 37.1 points per game. Now, in 2001, opponents were giving Michael the 1986 treatment. See if he can hit the shot. Lay off and use the new NBA rules that allow zone defense to set up a wall ten feet from the basket. Suddenly, all the fears of those who begged Michael not to try this comeback were materializing.

Against Seattle he promptly missed twenty-one of the twenty-six shots he attempted. He didn't make his first shot of the game until the third quarter. Hitting seventeen of thirty-three shots—the first night in the comeback he topped the 50-percent shooting mark Michael always set for himself as a measure of a good night—against Utah seemed like a momentary return to yesteryear. He tied an NBA season high at the time of forty-four points and even scored six during a 10-0 second-quarter run over Jazz guard Bryon Russell, whose legacy, no matter the final verdict on this coming, would always paint him as the guy Jordan hit the shot over to win the 1998 title. But at game's end, Washington had lost its sixth straight of a streak that would eventually reach eight, the longest of Jordan's career. And this was the most devastating blow to Michael because this is not why he came back.

He did not come back for nights like November 27 at Cleveland.

Cleveland, of course, is where the legend took life. May 11, 1988: Sunday Silence as then Chicago Bulls coach Doug Collins called it. With two seconds left, Michael hit that hang-time, double-pumping jumper over the Cavaliers' Craig Ehlo to win the fifth and deciding game of a first-round playoff series. Cleveland is where Michael scored his career-high sixty-nine points in 1990. But on this November night, the Cavs are struggling with a 5-11 record, yet blow away the Wizards 94-75. In a fit of postgame rage, Jordan looks at his team and declares, "We stink." Afterward, he has to face the numbers: He has shot 32.4 percent in his last three games and for the first time in one hundred and twelve contests, he failed to attempt even a single free throw. Though nobody is saying it out loud like Mike, a tension seems to be cutting through the Wizards' locker room, assessing Jordan so far and charging, "You stink, too."

The temptation now is to measure this edition of Michael Jordan by the numbers of greatness: Fifty-percent shooting from the field. Thirty points per game. Fifty wins. A twelfth first-team All-NBA selection. A tenth first-team All-NBA defensive team selection. But the mistake now would be to measure this edition of Michael Jordan by the numbers. Lest we forget, we're here looking for the rabbit. George Koehler returns to his theory on the rabbit by pointing out that the rabbit doesn't show up as much as we're used to in the past. "But you know what," George continues, "the rabbit's there. You just have to wait and be patient. It could be coming every two or three minutes." We know the chances of Jordan leading the Wizards to a championship are remote. Though you would never bet against Michael in a playoff series, is he going to take down Kobe and Shaq with Rip Hamilton and Jahidi White by his side? So sure he wants to win, but he is here to show us—to show a whole generation that has never seen him play— the rabbit, for it is the rabbit that will always define Michael Jordan.

If this were the Michael Jordan of old, he would pull off the magic when the spotlight was the hottest and the stakes the highest. If he could do it on the 2001–2002 stage, well, then this is an acceptable way to measure Michael's comeback. And here he is, back in

Madison Square Garden on December 22 with another shot to win the game. The Wizards are riding an eight-game winning streak. One more victory will tie a franchise record. Prior to this game, Michael spent nearly an hour working on his shot, working into a pregame sweat he hasn't needed since the mid-1980s. Washington has recovered from a ten-point deficit in the fourth quarter and with 51.5 seconds left and the score tied at 83, Jordan pulls up for mid-range jump shot.

And misses.

Again.

Latrell Sprewell returns the miss and with twenty-four seconds left, the Wizards are maneuvering for another shot at victory. In the timeout huddle, Jordan promises Collins he'll make the shot this time. And with 3.2 seconds to play, Michael hits the shot over Sprewell to give Washington an 85-83 lead. Popeye Jones puts a bear hug around Jordan as he raises his right fist in the kind of one-armed salute Tiger Woods would show after dropping a birdie putt on the eighteenth green at the Masters.

Finally, we have come to as much of an understanding of why Michael has returned as he will give us, for now at least. Yes, he wants to teach this NBA version of the cast of *New Jack City* how to win. And yes, he does love playing basketball like anybody else loves their job. And, yes, he knows he can add a chapter to his legacy by pulling off the greatest comeback of his time. But he doesn't want to hear any of that perfect-ending talk about hitting that last shot over Bryon Russell to give the Bulls that sixth title. Those close to him have heard him asking that who's to say he doesn't have that one last shot in him. It might not be for a championship. It might be for that ninth win in a row. It might be for the eighth seed in the playoffs. When he announced on January 19, 1999 that he was retiring, Michael said he was 99.9 percent sure he wasn't coming back. This is why he left that one-tenth of one percent. Michael Jordan is still searching for that one last shot, and the 2001–2002 season is a chance to not only find out if it comes but whether he can still make it.

JORDANOLOGY 2

1

TO FULLY UNDERSTAND WHAT MICHAEL JORDAN ATTEMPTED AT THIRTY-NINE years old, we must remember what Michael Jordan accomplished at twenty-nine years old. Already by 1992, Michael confided that he was playing for only one reason. He had just come off winning his second consecutive NBA Championship, and he was venting about how a third would be the one to separate him from Magic Johnson, Isiah Thomas, Larry Bird and even Kareem Abdul-Jabbar. None of them had ever won three in a row, and Michael desperately wanted that ego trip. In the pursuit of the goal, Jordan manufactured the most cold-blooded, moneyed game in the history of the NBA. Whether he still had that game at thirty-nine, of course, made his comeback in 2002 so captivating.

To fully understand how even though he didn't have the elevation or the stamina, Michael still could have that game at thirty-nine years old, we must look at Michael at twenty-nine. On this particular November night in 1992, he is battling the Detroit Pistons, the opponent against which Michael developed the one-on-five stubbornness that made him believe he could always come through no matter how insurmountable the circumstances, the same stubbornness and confidence that made him such a moneyed player. With twenty seconds left and the game tied, Jordan is staring down Joe Dumars, who seems to know he's about to become a page in *Sports*

Illustrated or some other newsstand scrapbook, and his last defense against such humiliation is to bury a forearm in Michael's chest. A turn and a fadeaway and Michael will add another cold-blooded shot to his game-winning portfolio. That Jordan misses this shot only adds to the memory. The game goes to overtime and with eleven seconds to play, Dumars hits a jumper to put Detroit ahead by one. The clock is down to four now, and Jordan takes an inbounds pass at half-court, dribbles twice and hoists a shot from behind the three-point line. He is nearly down those stairs that bookended the main floor of the old Chicago Stadium and in the Bulls locker room before the ball hits the bottom of the net, once again like Elvis disappearing on a chorus of "My Way." Several minutes later, Dumars sits an arena and a world away in his locker room trying to interpret what just happened.

Like Mike, life after basketball for Dumars has been as an executive trying to rebuild a moribund franchise, a kinship that began in the late 1980s when Jordan found a one-on-one glare in Joe D that matched his own brutality. Throughout his career, Dumars was one of those opponents to whom Michael gave unlimited respect. When Michael bitched and moaned about the cactus patch the Pistons always seemed to be back then, he knew that Dennis Rodman's stalking, John Salley's linebacking and Bill Laimbeer's piling on would have been just WWF stuff if Dumars had not been the hub of that defense customized for Jordan. The 1989–90 season best chronicled the jousting of this relationship: Michael going off for forty and thirty points in the two games at the Stadium that season; Dumars holding MJ to twenty-two one night and twenty or less on two other nights in the meetings at the Palace of Auburn Hills.

Joe D can be considered one of the most knowledgeable Jordanologists of his era, a man who reportedly studied tape of Michael in slow motion and undeniably one of those truly qualified to explain the yin and yang of Michael Jordan. On that last shot, Joe said he played textbook defense, that he stayed in front of Michael, made him use up time looking for an opening to get off a shot and forced him to fire while fading away from the basket. So how, Joe, can you explain Michael making the shot? He paused, seemingly to rewind through all the tape for the answer, regained the defensive glare of a few minutes ago, pounded a bench and in a high-pitched, soft-spoken voice that made him sound a little like Michael Jackson, Dumars replied, "Don't ask me to explain Michael Jordan."

To fully explain why Michael Jordan can come back to the NBA at thirty-nine and, after three years off, still be the player about whom Allen Iverson said it would take the rest of the stars in the league to fill his shoes, we must look at Michael Jordan at nineteen. As a sophomore at North Carolina, Michael was less than a year removed from hitting the winning shot in the 1982 NCAA Championship game, his debutante ballgame as he preferred to remember it more than the defining moment he hated hearing it called in and around the state. North Carolina was playing at Maryland when Michael took an outlet pass from Sam Perkins and accelerated on an open break to the basket. Instead of the standard one-handed flush, the one dunk shot that was actually in Dean Smith's Tar Heels playbook, Michael invented on the fly. "I kind of turned sideways while rising to the basket," he began. "Before you know it, I'm cranking the ball back, rocking it left to right, cuffing it before I put it down." On this January night of 1983 in College Park, Maryland, Air Jordan was born. Launched, actually. "Every breakaway after that seemed like a chance to try something new."

The rest of Michael Jordan's prodigy was hatched through a series of events that read as coincidental, but really make you wonder if this latest comeback was truly pre-ordained. Growing up in Wilmington, North Carolina had such a profound effect on Michael that when he took over as basketball operations chief for the Washington Wizards, he moved the team's training camp to this hardworking town by the Atlantic Ocean. Perhaps Jordan was thinking that the bunch of underachievers he inherited with this team could learn the single-mindedness, the intensity of focus and the absolute demand for nothing but excellence he did in Wilmington.

The lore of Jordan's life tells that Michael's childhood included being a baseball star in Wilmington who once pitched his team to the Eastern Regional Finals of the Little League World Series and that among other goodies he worked one summer as pool boy at Whitey's Hotel on Market Street. But the incidents that contributed most to what he would become come down to Michael's repeatedly hanging on the monkey bars in his backyard trying to make himself grow, and the ordeal of being cut from the Laney High School varsity basketball team as a sophomore. Never mind that Michael spent the following summer on the cutting edge, waking at 6 A.M. every morning to develop the skills and fundamentals and work ethic on which he built his game. During the travels of his NBA life, Michael often checked into hotels under the name Leroy Smith, the player Laney coach Clifton Herring decided to keep on the varsity instead of Jordan. Leroy Smith became Michael's imaginary friend, a haunting reminder he never wanted to let go, a specter that made him believe that missing any of those game-winning shots would be like being cut from the team again.

Maybe every play since the day he was cut from the Laney varsity has been a chance to prove himself. For sure, the doubts he faced in trying to come back to the NBA for the third time were nothing he hadn't heard more than twenty years before. Even when Michael became a star power forward at Laney in his junior season, some were skeptical of his future. Among those was North Carolina coach Dean Smith, who needed a telephone call from Mike Brown, the athletic director of the Wilmington school district and a UNC alum, to be convinced Jordan could be a Tar Heel. And yet as a freshman, he's in the North Carolina starting lineup, playing against Georgetown in the national championship game, getting the word from Smith during a timeout with fourteen seconds to play that when the time came to take the game-winning shot that he—not James Worthy or Sam Perkins—should "knock it in," as the coach related afterward.

But of all the defining moments he would have in becoming the national collegiate player of the year in 1983 and again in 1984, the shot to beat Georgetown, the dunk against Maryland and everything else he did in a Carolina uniform, none made Michael believe he had the caliber of game that would redefine basketball. That moment came in the summer of 1982 when the hype that goes with hitting a shot to win the national championship began to bubble. In August, about a month before school was set to reconvene, Jordan was playing a pickup basketball game at Carolina. His Tar Heel teammate, Matt Dougherty, was on the floor. Mike O'Koren and Walter Davis, former North Carolina players who had matriculated to the NBA, were partaking of the ritual of coming back to get in shape by playing pickup games against the current UNC players. The first game on this day began with Jordan soaring over Davis to dunk, tongue out and wagging, eyes wide, a play that Dougherty said made everybody on the floor realize "The guy had something special."

Something special. Michael had been hearing it for so long. Back at Laney, he would sneak out of class for his own personal street corner, otherwise known as the school gym, where he would shoot away his truancy. Happened so many times one year, he had to be suspended. Michael called these his "bad boy" days, and eventually James Jordan had to put it to his son in no uncertain terms. You can't continue this behavior, James told Michael, "because you have something special and you're gonna blow it." When all of North Carolina celebrated Michael's first Miracle and a picture of him launching the shot became the cover of the *Chapel Hill* phone book, Smith grounded Jordan, telling him that if he worked hard over the summer on his defense, he could really become something special. Dean didn't win like a thousand games—more than any other coach of his time—only by dreaming up gigs like the four-corners offense. He saw what made Jordan special and tried to develop it as much as Michael's jump shot. In some practices, Smith played Jordan with four non-starters to let him feel the desperation of getting blown out in scrimmages, and through it all Michael built up that utter disdain for losing, the foundation of that killer will. Perhaps Smith never figured his mentoring would manifest in that dunk against Maryland, or the one a year later against Virginia, the first time he was seen taking off from the foul line on a fast break and soaring to a slam, or the time against North Carolina State when Michael jumped over Wolfpack guard Sydney Lowe to score. What seemed special to Smith were situations like February of 1984, the home stretch of Michael's college career. North Carolina was ranked number one in the nation and undefeated when Arkansas sneaked in under the glare of one of those made-for-television nonconference matchups and upset the Tar Heels. In the next two games, Jordan responded with fifty-seven points, grabbed fourteen rebounds and added nine steals to right Carolina on a path that continued through the rest of the regular season without another loss.

Michael always preached a theory of evolution about his success. A few weeks before his thirty-ninth birthday and more than three months into his Third Coming, he admitted that he wouldn't change anything about his life, even though at the moment he was trying to fend off a divorce and had conceded three, maybe four of the best years of his basketball prime to compulsive decisions to walk away in fits of anger. As he was confessing this peace, he was thinking more of nights like March 22, 1984, when Michael started to fully realize his powers.

North Carolina faced Indiana in the NCAA Tournament's round of sixteen, a game in Atlanta that figured to be little more than a brief layover in the Tar Heels' route to the Final Four. Jordan had already confirmed his national player-of-the-year status, so stopping him would probably take one of those gimmicks coaches always seemed to claim they drew up on a napkin during lunch at a Denny's. Indiana coach Bobby Knight conceived his own machination, calling for little-used guard Dan Dakich to match up with Michael. Dakich gave up size, speed and athleticism—and a few pounds after reportedly finding out about the assignment and returning to his room to throw up. The story is part of Jordan lore, the night when he was *held* to eight points in a shocking loss. Foul trouble slowed Michael as much as Dakich, and though Jordan never copped to playing the rest of his life to make everybody forget this game, he never denied it either. This was that something special in Jordan, the something Knight saw during the trials to pick the 1984 U.S. Olympic basketball team. When he wanted to get a sense of a player's ability and more importantly his heart, Knight would match him one-on-one against Michael. This was something special that then North Carolina teammate Brad Daugherty explained by saying, "If Michael is laying in bed, ready to go to sleep and you tell him you can beat him in pool, he'll get up, go downstairs and play until he proves you wrong."

That something special would eventually be measured by championships, Most Valuable Player awards, scoring titles, and by all the other accomplishments like having the highest regular-season scoring average in NBA history (31.5 points per game), highest career-playoff scoring average (33.4 points per game), highest career All-Star-Game scoring average (21.3 points per game) and being the only guard in the history of the game to record 200 steals and 100 blocks in one season. There was no statistic to measure what Michael Jordan felt was the most critical aspect of his game. Doug Collins called Jordan the greatest practice player to ever play the game, single-minded when it came to preparation.

When he was a Bulls rookie, Michael admitted that he never let up in practice primarily because he was the highest paid player on the team and he wanted everybody to understand, "I was worth it." When he first started with the Bulls, then coach Kevin Loughery invented a ploy that would make Jordan's practice blood boil with game-winning fire. At the end of every practice at pretty much every level of basketball comes the scrimmage, in which the best five players take on the next-best five in a simulated game. When Jordan's team would run up a lead—usually eight to one or nine to two on the way to the eleven baskets needed to win—Loughery would switch Michael to the losing team. He would find a way to get his team back in the scrimmage game, and he looks back on those challenges as "the time when my confidence grew the most."

And his venom. During one scrimmage in his third season, Collins recalled, there was a discrepancy over the score. Jordan insisted his team had one more point than what was declared. Collins disagreed. Jordan fumed and stormed out of practice. Over one point. Made Michael so mad that he didn't show up for the team's flight to an away game the next day until less than a minute before takeoff. Collins also remembered times during his stint as Bulls coach from 1986 to 1989 when he would take Jordan out of a practice scrimmage, only to look away and a minute later see Michael check himself back in, replacing Charles Oakley at power forward. Collins figured Michael would pull such ploys to work on his defense or he would play center to get a chance to practice his post moves. But he also reasoned that Jordan was so relentless during practice because, "Every day he had this need to show you he was the best. It's like, 'I'm the best today, and I'm going to show you, and tomorrow I'm going to show you, and the next day I'm going to show you.' That's the only way he could do it one hundred and ten times a year. Throw away all the talent. The way he practiced put him on a level above everybody else."

2

THE ENERGIZER BUNNY BINGEING ON ENTENMANN'S DISGUISED AS MICHAEL Jordan glared at Dennis Johnson, Larry Bird and the rest of the Boston Celtics on this April Sunday in 1986. Jordan combined between-the-legs dribbles like a Globetrotter doing a halftime show with the Ali shuffle, leaving Johnson frozen and Bird catatonic as Michael drilled a bank shot from the right wing. Energy pent up from missing sixty-three regular-season games with a broken bone in his foot spilled out on this playoff stage at Boston Garden as Jordan blew past Bird again, floated under Kevin McHale and threw in an over-the-shoulder, no-look reverse layup. This, of course, was the day when Michael stopped all the mall traffic in Chicago with his sixty-three-point concerto, the one after which Bird sent up the famous remark, "He was God disguised as Michael Jordan." Michael remembers this day like nobody else does, a double-overtime marathon loss that wiped away any feeling of achievement. His first three seasons repeated this refrain. The Bulls never won more than forty games in any of those seasons, never finished with a winning record and won just one playoff game. Michael scored an average of 37.1 points per game in his third season, the highest since Wilt Chamberlain scored 50.4 in 1962. Still, his critics kept asking during this time whether Michael could take his skill sets and raise them to Bird's sanctuary.

To get there Michael knew he had to add to his game. He couldn't, for example, be just a high-flying act. Dominque Wilkins had tried that and never won anything. So Michael invented a method of takeoff that made him hard to guard in the air. His bunny-hop jump, as he called it, enabled Jordan to spring into the air and to defenders it appeared as if he was floating. To that, he added an ability to move the ball once in the air. Magic Johnson explained the residual value of this: "A guy on defense would think, 'I got him now,'" Magic explained the day after Michael used such talent to score the decisive basket and finish off a fifty-five-point show to defeat Phoenix in Game 3 of the 1993 NBA Finals. "But he would just hang there and hold the ball back. With one left-handed move he could get three guys to jump and then hold it back. Then, at the last second, he could swing the ball way out to his left and spin it in off the glass. You see, there's nobody else who can do that."

Collins said that Michael also learned the value of watching game tapes of upcoming opponents, taking them home to search for holes in the defense. He became a gluttonous student of tapes, something he tried to impart to Wizards teammates before games in his come-

back. He would beckon Popeye Jones, so much a student of the game
that Doug Collins projected him as an NBA coach some day, and
Popeye would describe his amazement at how Jordan could tune into
pregame film study and turn oblivious to the world going on around
him. This had been habitual for Michael for a long time, now. Before
a game against Indiana at Market Square in 1993, Jordan sat in a
folding chair, rocking back and forth, lathering as he scouted Reggie
Miller. "This guy's a fucking joke," he revealed before going out and
scoring forty points on his Indiana counterpart that night.

As for the mentality of a winner to go along with the game he
had put together, well, maybe he started grooming that on those
afternoons in his backyard when as a nine-year-old he actually
thought hanging on the monkey bars would make him taller. By his
third season, he was developing the know-how to reach back for that
mentality when he absolutely needed to, like in his last three games
of the 1987 season when Michael scored fifty-three, fifty and sixty-
one points to lift the Bulls to a 40-42 record, their best since 1981.
Eventually, this became his sixth sense, a sensation Jordan felt
nobody understood about him and the one that made it hard for him
to accept why a teammate couldn't hustle for a loose ball or make an
open shot or see the bounce pass that would lead to the back-door
layup. When he was coaching the Pistons, Chuck Daly believed this
mentality led to what he called astro points from Jordan, astronomical both in numbers, like that three-game stretch in 1987, and in the
elevation of both mind and body put into such play. Michael himself
might have never fully understood it, though he explained it this way
during a postgame chat with a couple of Jordanologists one night in
1992: "Whenever we needed a win, it was one of those moods I could
get myself into. It just kicked in, like a fourth gear. Maybe the fifth,
sixth or seventh. It was the last gear, let's put it that way."

A ten-game stretch in November of 1986 epitomized what some
people might call Jordan revving up. Michael scored an average of
41.1 points per game. He hit a low of 37 points in the first game of
the stretch at Denver and a high of 45 points midway through the

run at Utah. And the Bulls, then including such NBA transients as Darren Daye, Brad Sellers and just one player—John Paxson—who would be around for the first three championships, lost seven of those ten games. Herein became the toughest challenge Michael faced in growing into a champion. The time he spent working to bring his skills to new heights and the time he spent studying to gain an edge he might not be able to create with his physical attributes empowered his ego. Michael could score and score and score and will his team to victory. Usually. But his teammates had to learn to stand up to his relentless will. And he had to learn to let them.

When he did, and they did, it presented best-seller moments like the fifth and final game of the 1991 NBA Finals. After missing the critical shot with time running out in the one-point Game One loss to the Lakers, Jordan seemed determined to personally vindicate himself for the rest of the series. In leading the Bulls back to a three-games-to-one lead, Michael had the up-and-under as part of forty-two points in Game Two, the length-of-the-court shot to force overtime in Game Three and the courageous Game Four effort, playing on an excruciatingly inflamed big toe. In Game Five, Jordan was on his way to a thirty-eight point soliloquy that would confirm his Most Valuable Player status, but the Bulls were having trouble shaking the Lakers. Paxson, however, was trying to make a stand, hitting a streak of open jumpers, when the ball actually found its way to him. After urging the Bulls to ride Paxson, Jackson supposedly had to call a time out to challenge Jordan, asking, "Who's open, Michael?" No response forced Phil to let out a fatherly shout: "Who's open?" Though Jordan never raised his head, he finally answered "Paxson," and the Bulls had a 108-101 championship-clinching victory that featured twenty-two points from Pax.

Eventually, the same approach imposed on the Wizards in 2002, a season reminiscent for Michael of 1987, 1988 and 1989 in so many ways. During the 1986–1987 season, Michael Jordan scored forty or more points in thirty-seven games. The Bulls went 22-15 in those contests, but in the pre-championship seasons the more Michael tempered his scoring soliloquies, the more his team won. No game was more indicative of this conundrum than March 28, 1990, in Cleveland's Richfield Coliseum. This was one of those nights when Cavaliers coach Lenny Wilkens walked down his bench every couple of minutes, looking for somebody to guard Jordan. As the game wore on Cleveland's Winston Bennett and Craig Ehlo refused to make eye contact with Wilkens in hopes that they would not be sacrificed to Michael. He hit twenty-three of thirty-seven shots that night, a Jordan variety that equaled a career-high sixty-nine points. The Cavs came into this night four games under a .500 record; the Bulls were sixteen over. Yet with Michael at his career best, the Bulls needed overtime and a series of Jordan free throws to escape with a 117-113 victory. Because the Bulls blew an eleven-point lead in the game, Jordan would have to listen to Scottie Pippen comment that even though Michael had the hot hand, "it disrupted us and allowed the other team to get back in the game. It's not that we don't want MJ to get points, but it makes it tough for others to step up when they have to." Even at thirty-nine years old, Michael was still stamped by his ability to throw up astro points, but by twenty-nine he learned that being able to score astronomical numbers was not the legacy of a winner.

So finally Michael Jordan began to understand what would make him Michael Jordan. His scoring could only get the Bulls to a certain level. When they defeated Cleveland in the opening round of the 1988 playoffs, the Bulls' first postseason series win in seven years, Michael scored fifty-five, fifty and forty-four points in the three victories. In the next round of the playoffs, however, Jordan learned that it wasn't about his scoring. In this round, the Detroit Pistons were waiting with a strategic battle plan for defending Michael. Never leave one man to defend him, Daly explained, use a forearm in his back and always be physical. These became known as the Jordan Rules, and when the Bulls went down to defeat in the final game of the series Michael spent the afternoon like a quarterback under a constant blitz, finding defenders at every corner and forever having to reverse his field just to squeeze out a career-low eight shots. During the next season Michael scored forty or more in fifteen games, twenty-two less than in the 40-42 season of 1987. The Bulls were 7-8 in those games, perhaps the first sign that Michael was on the verge of becoming more than a scorer. The next sign came on May 7, 1989, a Sunday in Cleveland.

Two days earlier, the Bulls, seeded sixth in the eight-team Eastern Conference playoffs, were on the verge of upsetting the third-seeded Cavaliers, holding a two-games-to-one series lead that gave Jordan one of the greatest I-told-you-sos of his career. Worldwide media forecasted the Bulls to be swept out of this series in three consecutive games, but when he felt the Game One victory was secured, Michael ran past press row in Cleveland yelling, "Sweep, my butt." Now, however, he had missed a key free throw of Game Four, the Bulls lost in overtime and the fifth—and deciding—game of the series provided a memorable stage at Richfield Coliseum. The day before, in the one hundred and twelfth running of the Kentucky Derby, a horse named Sunday Silence unexpectedly ran away with the roses. Perhaps he didn't know at the time that the whole upset concept came when a thoroughbred named Upset unexpectedly won a horse race, but nevertheless, Doug Collins remembered telling his team on the flight to Cleveland that silence would indeed come on this Sunday. By now, few people don't know what happened with two seconds to play on that Sunday. Michael took an inbounds pass with his team trailing by one, put his head down, eluded two defenders, dribbled to the foul line, elevated and floated just long enough to regather his shooting posture and outhang Ehlo before draining the series-winning jump shot. That image of Jordan reloading before scoring is page two in the scrapbook of Michael Miracles, second only to the freeze-frame of Michael hitting the shot to deflate Utah ten years later in the NBA Finals.

But this Sunday silence in Cleveland may have been far more important. On this Sunday, the fifty-point games became mere pages in the record book. On this Sunday, one of the game's greatest scorers moved downstage to make room for the emergence of perhaps the greatest closer in NBA history, in the history of all sports. Air Jordan gave way to his Air for the dramatic. The most moneyed game in the history of the Game began to show up on nights like February 17, 1989, when Michael celebrated his twenty-sixth birthday by scoring twenty-seven fourth-quarter points, including a sixteen-foot, game-winning jump shot against Milwaukee, and became his reputation, his signature. His record would always be a number like the twenty-three consecutive points he scored against Atlanta in 1987. But his legacy would become nights like May 17, 1992, Game Seven of the Eastern Conference Finals when he finally broke the shackles of the New York Knicks' Jordan Rules Eastern Style that accentuated the bumping and grinding with a forty-two-point carving. Or the sixth and deciding game of the 1993 NBA Finals when Michael scored nine of the Bulls' twelve fourth-quarter points to beat Phoenix. Or that June 11 night in Utah when he overcame food poisoning to score thirty-eight points and deliver a victory in the pivotal fifth game of the NBA Finals. Or that June 14 night in Utah when he hit the last shot of his second go-round to win the sixth championship.

Whether Michael, at thirty-nine years old, could get his game back to what it was at twenty-nine years old was mostly about that last shot. He added to his resume of cliffhanging endings during the 2001–2002 season with yet another game-winner in Cleveland and one in Phoenix in February that even his rickety knee, on the brink of surgery, couldn't stop. But could he ever become the same serial killer at thirty-nine that he was at twenty-nine? Jordan went through a transformation in those situations. Those who marveled at how many times he finished off an opponent used the jumping-into-a-nearby-phone-booth analogy to describe the transformation. But to hear Michael describe the feeling, it seemed more Dr. Jekyll-to-Mr. Hyde than Superman. "When I got into the situation where it's the fourth quarter, the game is on the line and we needed to win," he explained, "I started talking to myself, 'This guy can't guard me.' And I believed it."

The clock winding down to the last shot made Michael's eyes turn almost bone white. On any given night, you could be in row ZZ of the upper bowl and see how the sweat pouring down from his bald head would nearly turn to steam by the time it dripped off his chin. His protruding tongue—the signature of coming drama—extended. He chewed his gum with the metronome-like precision of a man feeding off his anger. His first pass coaching Michael made Doug Collins realize that Jordan had a mean streak, that "he could be vicious. You played one-on-one with Michael, and he was not going to let you score. A lot of guys will play, it will get to game point, and they will win. Michael wanted to shut you out, like you didn't belong there." He still had this during the Third Coming, using it during training camp to slap down the ego Kwame Brown had built up all summer since becoming the number-one pick in the draft. Collins also professed that Jordan couldn't control this feeling, that if he went out on the golf course with a pro like good friend and suburban Chicago neighbor Chip Beck, Michael believed in the recesses of his mind he could actually beat Beck if he had a great day. Collins said he didn't think there was anything Michael did just for fun, and he wasn't alone.

The night before one of Michael's most memorable closing nights, he was playing cards with Magic Johnson, Quinn Buckner and Ahmad Rashad. Two nights earlier the Bulls had lost Game Three of the 1993 NBA Finals to the Phoenix Suns in triple overtime. He scored forty-four points that night but missed a free throw in the first overtime that could have sealed a victory and took forty-nine shots in the game. After Michael ran a series of Suns defenders ragged, Kevin Johnson shadowed Michael through the fourth quarter and the overtimes, when Jordan missed fifteen of his last twenty-four shots. Johnson spent the next two days answering questions about how he had finally become the one to stop Michael Jordan. Now at the card table, Magic saw Jordan look like a teapot coming to a boil.

"He's saying, 'OK, OK MJ'—he calls me MJ, I call him MJ—and then he starts breathing heavy and kind of rocking back and forth," Magic recalled. "'OK MJ, they think he stopped me. Well, let's see if he can stop me now.' His eyes are getting a little bigger, and he's got that look of determination on his face."

The next night, Michael scored his career NBA Finals high of fifty-five points. In the final minute, he drove past Johnson, around Charles Barkley and as another defender grabbed him, threw a shot over his head into the basket. The resulting three-point play sealed a 111-105 victory that gave the Bulls a 3-1 series lead and all but guaranteed a third championship. Such Jordan heroics—Michael Miracles, as a select few in Chicago began calling them—would do better on those highlight videos that define Michael Jordan rather than the ones with all the dunks and other Big Air moves you get at Blockbuster.

3

TO FULLY UNDERSTAND WHETHER MICHAEL JORDAN COULD MAKE A GO OF THIS comeback at thirty-nine years old is to know where Michael Jordan was at twenty-nine. He is dashing out the side door after a Chicago Bulls practice, slipping a full court of press that has been trying to put a damper on the first-ever NBA championship he celebrated several months ago. The only real difference between Michael now and before he won a title is the CHAMPS vanity license plates adorning the Jeep Cherokee he was awarded for being the NBA Finals Most Valuable Player. The motor is running and Michael is clutching the steering wheel so tightly that the soft leather bulges out between his fingers. For the first time in perhaps his professional career, Jordan is questioning himself, wondering where he's going to find the passion to meet the challenge of being a champion, of meeting the feeling that he—in his own words—can't have any off-nights now. Here, Michael admitted that if he doesn't win another championship the first one won't mean a whole lot. Bulls assistant coach Johnny Bach has already noticed that winning the first championship has made Jordan more uptight than relaxed. Michael feels this way, too, and before he speeds away he confesses that the lasting impact of winning the first championship means, "I must work like hell."

At thirty-nine years old, he was still working like hell. At twenty-nine, this was Michael's personal hell, a mania to win championships even he never understood until after he had three of them. The images of Michael after winning each of the first three championships tell so much about what was going on at this point of his career. When the Bulls finally disposed of the Lakers to win the first one, a champagne-and-sweat-drenched Jordan sat in the locker room, hugging Juanita and crying on the NBA championship trophy. Finally, he said, he would not be known as just a high scorer or high flyer. When the Bulls finished off Portland in 1992 to win the second title, Michael jumped on top of the scorer's table at Chicago Stadium and danced for all the world to see, twisting and shouting a personal validation. Proving the first one was no fluke meant more to Michael than anybody would ever know, which might explain why even two hours after the game he was still running around Chicago Stadium wearing his uniform and a cigar-and-champagne induced buzz. And then there was the third championship. No public displays of tears or cheers this time. After defeating Phoenix, Michael ducked into the chapel at America West Arena and prayed. Throughout the 1993 playoffs, Michael had repeatedly talked about how another championship would put him a step above Magic, Larry and Isiah, whom he tagged as his contemporaries because they won multiple championships, too. But none of them won three in a row, which is what Michael worked like hell to achieve.

Now, Michael Jordan had what he wanted most, a legacy to overshadow Magic, Bird and Isiah and one which all future winners would be measured against. Sure, Magic had five titles to Michael's three, but Magic's came with him and Kareem and James Worthy forming perhaps the most imposing threesome in the history of the game. Bird won his championships with future Hall of Famers Robert Parish and Kevin McHale on his flanks, and as for anybody else who dares to compare, does Isiah win his two rings without Joe Dumars playing NBA Finals Most Valuable Player? Such was Michael's rationalization as he sat in the chapel at America West Arena telling his father, James, that he thought he had finally made history.

Truth be told, Michael was only starting to make history. The three titles, during which Michael also became the first player in league history to win three consecutive Finals Most Valuable Player awards, formed the first winning streak of its kind in the league since the 1960s when the Bill Russell/Bob Cousy Celtics dominated an NBA that had all of twelve teams.

Jordan had also changed the game in other profound ways. Collins remembers running a clinic in Chicago's impoverished Marquette Park in the summer of 1991. His son, Chris, who would go on to play in an NCAA championship game for Duke University, put on a shooting exhibition during that clinic in which he hit eleven consecutive three-point shots. A no-big-deal hush came over the crowd, after which Doug Collins recalls somebody asking Chris, "Can you dunk?" Everybody wanted to dunk like Michael Jordan, Collins reasoned, because that's what they thought they needed to do to be successful. In effect, those kids in Marquette Park could have become the top dogs of the next-millennium NBA, who made soaring and scoring the way of life in the league.

By 1993, Michael had also elevated the NBA's star system commissioner David Stern used to build his league into top-dollar entertainment. Jordan had become the game's most identifiable brand, a marketable commodity so big that Chicago cable television station WGN sued the NBA and eventually won a U.S. Supreme Court ruling to be allowed to increase the number of Bulls games it televised. The Jordan brand was worth so much that companies such as Gatorade, Nike and Hanes underwear contracted with him to be lead endorser until Michael would turn forty. When Michael came back to an NBA in 2001 that was suffering through waning popularity and was on the verge of renegotiating its multibillion dollar network television contract, Stern realized he needed Jordan's Q Rating as his last shot. All of this was validation that by 1993 the NBA had become Michael's league.

Still, one more thought emanated from Jordan's hideaway prayer group the night he won the third title. "Once that was done," he said, "I knew I had nothing left to prove." What Michael was really saying, what he had been telling some of those close to him for several weeks, confirmed that his life was wearing him out. On the court, he had taken more shots during the 1992–93 season than any year since 1987 when he averaged a career-high 37.1 points per game. The Bulls needed every one of his 35.1 points per game in the 1993 postseason to endure the title run. And every game was ending like this: He would answer to media scrutiny for up to forty-five minutes postgame or until one of his team of security guards would tell Michael, "Your car is ready." That was code for time to go. One guard would pick up his bag and cover Michael's rear. Another would take the lead. Still another would pick an exit route from the five they had set up, the one that would enable Jordan to evade a public that was not willing to allow him even a few minutes of peace. Off the court, he was having too many nights like this: He would go to Chicago mall to buy a pair of shoes when a girl would shout, "There's Michael Jordan." Eventually, George Koehler would have to get a manager to lock the doors, call mall security and form a human circle around Michael to get him to his car. As George explained, "He couldn't even have car trouble without an article appearing in the newspaper saying Michael Jordan was seen fixing a flat tire."

Michael's life was also generating the kind of supermarket tabloid juice that made him feel like his privacy was always being invaded. When a check he wrote for $57,000 wound up in the possession of a convicted drug dealer, the ensuing investigation called into question his gambling lifestyle, what some even described as an addiction. Michael said the check paid a gambling debt, but it was dated the day his teammates were visiting President Bush at the White House, a day he said he was off relaxing with friends and family. For him, though, this was relaxing and that it made for headlines presented an opposition he could never find a way around. During the 1993 playoffs, Michael's trip to Atlantic City to play blackjack on one of the nights between Games One and Two of the Eastern Conference Finals sparked a media inquisition far more contemptuous than anything the Jordan Rules put him through. And when a report surfaced a week later that Michael had been betting up to a million dollars on a round of golf, he privately confessed to teammate Cliff Levingston that he would give a million dollars if only he could walk down a street with nobody recognizing him. Eventually, Michael had to close off the entire outside world when he was on the road and vulnerable to the public. James Jordan said he could not remember the situation getting much worse for his son than it did in New York during the 1993 Eastern Conference Finals, when Michael wasn't even safe in his hotel suite because the telephone would not stop ringing. "We blocked all the calls, but they still found a way to get through. I mean we had relatives calling, or at least people claiming to be relatives, saying, 'This is an emergency. I'm a cousin. I've got diabetes, and I've got to talk to him.' What are you supposed to do?"

Michael did what he always did. Play harder. Win. Move on, hoping the next day would be a little more free than the last. But as James Jordan said, Michael couldn't control it. After news of the Atlantic City incident spread, Michael took a vow of silence with the public that he didn't break until an interview during the NBA Finals NBC televised at halftime of Game One. Michael wore dark glasses during that interview, the look of a burnt-out star more than a man on top of the league. So when it was all over, when he had provided one last fifty-five-point soliloquy to win Game Four, when he had scored all nine of the Bulls' fourth-quarter points prior to John Paxson's title-winning jump shot in Game Six, Michael found his way into that chapel in America West Arena not just to be alone but perhaps to contemplate his calling.

Nearly four months later, Michael confessed publicly how on that night he first thought about retiring. He could pull off the one move Magic and Bird and Kareem and pretty much nobody else in American sports ever had. He could walk away from the game on top, on the absolute top. On his own terms, as athletes say. And when James Jordan was murdered in August of 1993, Michael probably made his decision to walk away.

Or storm away. During his farewell address circa 1993, Michael made statements in his defiant, curt tone as if he were scolding one of his kids. Or one of his teammates. He said he would stay in Chicago if the media would stay away from his house and give him "some peace and quiet." He admitted that the relentless scrutiny had gotten on his nerves. When asked in the end what his special contribution to the game was, Michael teased. "The tongue," he said. "You never saw anything like it, and you might never see anything like it again." Michael Jordan was leaving the game on top, but leaving with a snub, sticking his tongue out in a hissy fit.

Clearly, he wasn't walking away on his own terms. Clearly, he was missing something.

THE SECOND COMING

1

WHEN MICHAEL JORDAN BUGGED OUT OF THE NBA, RUNNING FROM THE BAG-gage that came with three championships, Terry Boers and Dan McNeil, the afternoon drive-time hosts of a new game in Chicago known as sports talk radio on WSCR (820 AM), spoke for an entire city by arguing that the end had not come, not this way. Michael never gave a reason to think otherwise. He still hasn't. Maybe he was still here at thirty-nine years old nursing a basketball Jones that has never been satisfied. Maybe he's still looking for that perfect ending. Maybe he's Jonesing for the spotlight, which would be a better expla-nation for his dilly-dallying with baseball in 1994 than any rationale Michael ever provided.

Following a summer of playing minor league ball in the Chicago White Sox farm system—during which he reportedly tiptoed away for occasional Sunday morning pick-up hoops with his Birmingham Barons teammates—the basketball addiction chased Michael again. Scottie Pippen was hosting his annual charity basketball game to benefit Operation PUSH/Excel. The game was set for September 9, 1994 and was to be the last played at Chicago Stadium, with the House that Michael Built—otherwise known as the United Center— ready to open for the next NBA season. Michael never really had flushed basketball out of his system. About a month before the invita-tion to play in *Scottie's Game*, Jordan was quoted in the *New York*

Post as saying he could come back to the NBA and with just two weeks of preparation still average thirty-two points a game. "Eight points a quarter," he explained. "How hard could that be?" Michael rarely dropped these statements as mere braggadocio unless he was sitting around a card table with Magic and Ahmad Rashad, and if he indeed found no more challenges as he said when he retired in 1993, well, here he was creating a new one.

Still, he rationalized that this cameo would be a farewell performance at the beloved Stadium and went about preparing for the game with a week of heated but secret practices at the Berto Center with Scottie and some other former Bulls teammates. Then, on the first play of the game, Michael dribbled the ball off his foot and out of bounds. But for the next two hours, Jordan reminded fans why they had paid two hundred and fifty dollars per ticket for this game, why they would still pay that price. He dribbled into a triple team, hung in the air, faked a shot then swished a rainbow jumper. He fooled Ron Harper with the one-handed, yo-yo fake, making Harp look like a volunteer from the crowd in a magic act, then vanquished him with a fallaway jumper. He flashed some of the old vertical leap by catching a wild alley-oop pass from an incoming rookie point guard named Jason Kidd with one hand and dunking. Michael scored fifty-two points by hitting twenty-four of forty-six shots. He argued with officials after being called for what he termed "questionable" fouls. In the waning minutes, he went one-on-one against Pippen, who opted to play against him. For an encore, Michael threw down a dunk off the drive and hit a fifteen-foot fallaway over Scottie. "Judging from the last seven years of playing him in practice, it didn't seem like he has lost anything," Pippen observed.

In his most memorable move of the night, Jordan waved off one last go-round with Pippen. And with six seconds left to play in the game, he kneeled at center court and kissed the Bulls head that adorned the floor right between the eyes. Then he walked off the court. In the ego-inflating world of pro sports, this move would have passed for the type of farewell drama that makes for perfect endings. Except Michael wasn't talking that way afterward. "I didn't go out there to mess around," he began. "I didn't want you guys to say, 'He lost this, he lost that.' I wanted to show that if I want to do this, I can still do this." If he hadn't opened his mouth, his career would have been sealed with a kiss, an even more perfect ending than the one in Phoenix. But, just like in 2001, he was a man not sure if he was coming or going, and this night left nothing to confirm that Michael was done with basketball forever.

Nothing he did playing baseball let on that basketball would become an occasional one-night stand. When Michael announced his retirement in the fall of 1993, he said he wanted to spend more time with his family, recapture his privacy and have a life away from media dissection. But in early February 1994, Jordan played the role of lab rat when the Chicago White Sox invited the media in to get a look at Michael the baseball player. This was a true made-for-television spectacle in which Jordan and several White Sox players walked through fielding drills on the hardwood of the Illinois Institute of Technology basketball court, a small college across the street from Chicago's Comiskey Park. When he finally went to spring training with the White Sox, Michael had to face two hundred and fifty reporters showing up on the first day to watch him take batting practice. Jordan did have one memorable day when the White Sox called him up from their Class AA affiliate in Birmingham to play in the annual Crosstown Classic against the Chicago Cubs at Wrigley Field. Pre–interleague play and post-threepeat, this was the biggest moment of the summer in Chicago. A double, another hit and two runs batted in not only bathed Michael in one more standing ovation but made him realize what he was missing by going through a minor-league season in which he struck out 114 times in 436 at-bats, hit for a paltry .202 average and made a league-leading eleven errors.

Off the field, baseball didn't do much to hook Michael. When he traveled the NBA, he was used to a suite at the Plaza, where he could order a seventeen-dollar room service cheeseburger for lunch. As a minor-league baseball player, he was relegated to room 212 at the La Quinta Inn just like everybody else and getting a peanut butter and jelly sandwich in the clubhouse was dream cuisine. As he was playing through this Hee-Haw country, one night the team pulled into a Holiday Inn. Maybe it wasn't the Plaza, but surely Michael could find a suite to his liking. Right this way, Mr. Jordan, and he was led to a second-floor conference room that included a hideaway Murphy bed. A double. Even though the Waffle House served as his four-star restaurant, Michael returned for a second season in 1995 a better player, actually hitting batting practice pitches out of the park instead of rolling them to the outfield fence like he had the prior year. But the baseball strike that began the previous August did to Michael what no other sport, no other defender ever had. When major league baseball owners decided during spring training of 1995 that they would use scabs to start the season, Michael was forced to declare himself a strike breaker or become a minor leaguer. A minor leaguer in spring training is forced to use a clubhouse roughly the size of a jail cell. With similar plumbing. In other words, Michael had to become just another player and no way was Michael Jordan ever going to consider himself just another player. He promptly quit baseball and ultimately rationalized this endeavor as a tonic or a therapy to realize what he was missing. "The new players who were ten years younger than me had an attitude that they truly loved the game," Michael explained. "It was a dream they were fulfilling. I kind of lost that in what was happening to me two years ago with basketball. I was on a pedestal for so long that I forgot about the steps it took to get there."

All this to find his way back.

2

IF MICHAEL WAS DESTINED FOR THE PERFECT ENDING, THIS COULDN'T HAVE been it, the night of November 1, 1994. The gathering at the United

Center was called the "Michael Jordan Retirement Party." Almost thirteen months after he quit basketball, this celebration came together supposedly to honor a legend—and raise money to build the James Jordan Boys and Girls Club, a lavish facility Michael was bequeathing to Chicago's impoverished west side to honor his father with a legacy and give himself one more tax shelter. The evening played out more like a church bazaar—albeit a celebrity-filled one—than the closing night for the greatest basketball player ever. Magic and Larry weren't even there, sending in their tributes by video. In between Woody Harrelson singing and Sinbad and Craig T. Nelson telling jokes, Larry King unveiled the bronze statue of Michael soaring over a figure that vaguely resembled old Detroit Piston Bill Laimbeer and now stands as one of Chicago's treasured landmarks. Michael's kids helped him raise his No. 23 jersey to the United Center rafters by pulling a string somewhat similar to a clothesline. All anybody saw was that they hung a piece of laundry that Michael could easily slip back into when ready.

Between laundry night and the last day of Michael's visit to the Chicago White Sox Fantasy Camp, rumors of his return to basketball took on a *National Enquirer*-like presence. And they circulated about as often. But when he officially announced he was paroling himself from baseball on March 3, the immediate conclusion came blaring across sports talk radio. *This is Bob on a carphone, and I just saw a white Jeep Cherokee with* CHAMPS *vanity plates turning into the Berto Center*. Reports sounding something like that made the rounds, and some reporters actually staked out Michael's house as the sporting world awaited evidence of his Second Coming. One fan anticipated Michael's return with a deification of sorts, holding up a sign during a Bulls game at the United Center with the message, "Michael 3:16," a reference to the date he might rise again in the NBA. On March 18, 1995, the Chicago Bulls' public relations staff let out an all-points bulletin, telling reporters wherever you are, get to the Berto Center ASAP. A roomful of cameras and reporters waited, and Michael re-entered pretty much as he left, literally stick-

ing his tongue out at the press. Jordan made his return by proxy, fax-
ing in his confirmation via press release. The communiqué simply
read, "I'm Back."

Back with a clang. But don't be fooled by Michael missing
twenty-one of twenty-eight shots when he returned to the NBA on
March 19, 1995 against the Pacers in Indianapolis. Don't be fooled
by Michael going dunkless or by Michael not coming through in
overtime when the Bulls coughed up a 103-96 defeat. One of the stories hidden among the comeback fervor supposedly had Michael
telling Phil Jackson as long ago as 1993 that if he could just find a way
to play the last twenty games of the season and the playoffs, that
would be perfect. After the loss to Indiana, the Bulls were treading
slightly above a .500 record and, with sixteen games left on their
schedule, had just enough terrain to make a push that would position
Michael as savior. He would ride in to get them into the playoffs, and
as Steve Kerr said, thoughts of winning a championship suddenly
were not so absurd. The way of life that made Jordan crave the
absurd, that could only be fulfilled by a series of adrenaline rushes,
first manifested in the Second Coming. His internal roadmap pushed
his Porsche to seventy miles per hour on back streets and three-lane
cuts across midday traffic to exit a Chicago expressway because he
played like the world had one plane for Michael Jordan and one
plane for everybody else. The fourth game of the return ended with
his length-of-the-court sprint to a fifteen-foot, buzzer-beating jumpshot to defeat Atlanta, 99-98, and the next turn led Michael through
Madison Square Garden where the jumpers started falling like it was
1993, the spring in his step belied a man who dressed daily in baseball
spikes less than a month ago and the fifty-five points he scored fueled
his urge to continually build the wall higher and higher. So take every
turn at seventy for, just like the 2001–2002 season, he never anticipated any bump in the road.

Just like in the Third Coming, the world was waiting to see the
same old Michael in the Second. The Bulls sprinted to the end of the

regular season with a 13-4 record and put together a pair of six-game winning streaks, their longest of the year. No, this wasn't the same old Michael. Not yet. For openers, he was wearing uniform number forty-five, perhaps content to leave number twenty-three to hang in peace or perhaps part of a plan to invent a whole new Michael Jordan. James Jordan once said his boy was not beyond "laying in the weeds," letting an opponent—letting the world for that matter— think he had lost a step or he couldn't go to his left as strong anymore or he didn't quite have the same Airobatics as he once did. Maybe that was going to become his next greatest advantage. Yes, Michael Jordan comes back older, but he comes back wiser, playing more to his venom than his Air raids. In the opening round of the playoffs, the Bulls faced Charlotte. When that matchup was inevitable a week earlier and the Bulls hosted the Hornets the last weekend of the season, Michael struggled to nineteen points, the lowest output of his comeback. Then, in the first game of the postseason he went off for forty-eight points. As irony would have it, the game went to overtime and this time he scored a Jordanesque ten of the team's sixteen points in the extra period, delivered a 108-100 victory and told his critics afterward, "Well, maybe my step is not as slow as some people think."

As he reminded then and reminds us now, the intrigue of Michael Jordan is that we never really know how he's going to pull it off. The Second Coming perpetuated a common Michael denominator. Before he would find ecstasy, he had to find a certain degree of agony. In 1995, he found humiliation, too. After hitting a pair of game-winning free throws to finish off the best-of-five series with Charlotte in four games, the Bulls moved on to face the top seed in the Eastern Conference. The Orlando Magic represented the new breed in the NBA. Shaquille O'Neal began to realize his enormous potential. Anfernee Hardaway was never going to be the Air Apparent, but he had become in the Jordanless era one of the league's top five players. Nick Anderson was actually the Jordan clone on this team, having grown up in Chicago when Michael was first coming to power. And Horace Grant had defected to Orlando where his years of jealousy over the double standard that came with playing with Jordan made Horace feel like he was finally good enough to run with the cool kids. In the first game of the series, Horace and his buddies kicked sand in Michael's face. He had victory in his hands. Three times. But Jordan missed a free throw that would have sealed a victory, watched Anderson steal the ball from him with seventeen seconds to play and threw it away on the final possession of Orlando's 94-91 victory. After the victory, Anderson proclaimed, "He didn't look like the old number twenty-three out there." From Nick's perspective, number forty-five was some lesser version of the number twenty-three, MVP edition. Herein lies the drama that has us chasing Michael Jordan today. How would he respond to Anderson's premature evacuation? Could Michael reach into his bag and pull out yet another miracle?

Before Game Two of the series, Michael reached into his bag and pulled out the old number twenty-three. Bulls equipment manager John Ligmanowski had put the jersey there thinking Michael was going to need this prop sometime. And with the jersey, out came the Jordan of old. He hit eleven of his first thirteen shots in the second half, an in-your-face response that led the Bulls to a series-tying victory. As the explanations oozed out for such a transformation, Phil Jackson put it this way: "That's the mystique of Michael Jordan. I can't really tell you I was surprised by it."

No, the surprise of this season came when Michael failed in the end. In Game Three of the series, twenty-three showed up to score twenty-nine points in the first half. But forty-five returned in the fourth quarter when Jordan missed nine of thirteen shots. Facing elimination in Game Six, the Bulls held a 102-94 lead with 3:24 to play but went scoreless the rest of the way. Michael Jordan was shut down during the time of the game on which he built his legend, and as he answered questions afterward for more than forty-five minutes, he talked of how much improving he needed to do, how absurd it was for him to think he could come back for twenty games and win a championship. Here was a side of Jordan never seen before, him sending a potential perfect ending the way of a Sinbad joke.

3

MICHAEL JORDAN CAN NEVER ENJOY JUST A TASTE OF BASKETBALL. HE CAN never just play in a pickup game at the YMCA. He can only play for one last shot, and everything we have seen in three championships, the pre-return and even *Scottie's Game* is no more than preparation and pursuit. He knows nothing other than lacing 'em up tighter, which leads to obsessions like the one during the summer of 1995. Prior to his comeback, Michael had booked a summer job to star in his first major motion picture. Ironically, the plot had Michael coming out of retirement to team with Bugs Bunny for what became a cult film known as *Space Jam*. On the Warner Bros. studio lot in Hollywood, Michael held court with Charles Barkley, Reggie Miller, Shawn Bradley, Mugsy Bogues and Nick Van Exel among other NBAers for after-hours, get-back-in-shape pickup games in a gym Jordan had fashioned out of a sound stage. Magic even came by a couple of times for games that rivaled the summer workouts Michael used to endure annually at North Carolina, the boot camp he would push himself through to measure his NBA worthiness. If he could declare himself fit after one of these regimens, Michael felt there was no limit to the possibilities on the NBA court.

He needed all of opening night of the 1995–96 season to reach the outer limits. In a 105-91 defeat of the Charlotte Hornets, Jordan went off for forty-two points. He scored nineteen in the third quarter alone. The day after his best opening night since 1989, the headline atop the *Chicago Tribune* sports page took a shot at Michael rarely seen in print by musing: "Now, He's Back." Michael apparently saw the humor in it all, joking after the opening-night hit, "I'm not old. I can still play." The season then progressed like the I'm Back redemption tour, Michael finding more energy and venom from those who said he couldn't or shouldn't, leaving landmarks along the way that looking back read like road signs to how the third act might play out. The Bulls were in the middle of an eighteen-game winning streak when the tour pulled into Philadelphia. The Bulls, who added rebounding maniac Dennis Rodman in the offseason and moved Ron Harper into the starting lineup to give Jordan the best talent that ever surrounded him, would eventually build a 39-3 record at the midpoint of the season en route to an NBA-record seventy-two victories. But in Philadelphia, Michael had to deliver some I'm Back–talk to one of those NBA young punks he thought was scarring the league he built. Philadelphia's Jerry Stackhouse was one of the Heir Jordan hopefuls hanging about, a North Carolina disciple with the air in his game to make him try to be Jordanesque. Stackhouse thought so, too, pronouncing early in the season that nobody in the NBA could stop him. Michael did, slapping a fifteen-point first quarter and a season-high forty-eight points on Stackhouse, who finished with twenty. And Michael sat out the final nine minutes.

The comeback included many such High Noons. By the numbers, it would not be wrong to think these were what MJ missed most, and that the only perfect ending could come when he took down a Fab Five of Magic, Bird, Kobe, Doctor J and Jerry West. In early March 1996, Michael met up with the presently anointed Air Apparent, Grant Hill. The Detroit Pistons star had been the only one all season to outscore Jordan, that is if you count the voting for the NBA All-Star Game. Michael hit fourteen of his first sixteen shots, dumped another NBA season-high fifty-three points on Hill and was fast on his way to regaining the league's Most Valuable Player status. Not that this season had anything to do with a tenth scoring title or any of the other road signs of success. No, this season—this comeback—was all about a means to an end.

Michael, you see, is all about having the last word. Perhaps he's so fastidious with the last shot because it leads to the last word. One of the classic Michael Jordan stories comes from the 1988 season when the Bulls were playing in Utah. Michael lined up a drive to the basket, wound up dunking on John Stockton and when backpedaling to defense was greeted by a challenge from a Jazz fan who asked, "Why don't you pick on somebody your own size?" Next possession, Michael takes off, dunks over Utah's seven-foot center Mel Turpin, finds the fan as he's running back and asks, "Was he big enough?" Looking back, it's not unreasonable to think the motivation for the record-setting 1995–96 regular season, a fourth Most Valuable Player commendation, and a return to the NBA's All-Defensive Team all came from getting a last shot at Nick Anderson and the Orlando Magic. The Bulls cruised through the first two rounds on the 1996 playoffs, barely breaking a sweat in sweeping Miami in the first round and ousting the Knicks from the Eastern Conference semifinals in five games.

Orlando wasn't going to have any better shot at the Bulls even though the Magic had the second-best record in the East. In the series opener the Bulls scored a franchise record thirty-eight-point victory. In Game Two, Orlando was on the rebound until the third quarter, when Jordan outscored the Magic by himself, 17-16. The Bulls held a 3-0 series lead when on the morning of Game Four Scottie Pippen said he saw that look in Michael's eyes. Many of Jordan's extraordinary or extraterrestrial feats can be attributed to irony or instinct. Throw in his standard venom, and that explains a dark side of Michael Jordan that Magic Johnson says drives Michael more than he would ever admit. On the day of Game Four, observers probably weren't thinking too much about a little more than a year ago when Michael, clad in the No. 45 jersey, threw away Game One of the Eastern Conference semifinals to the Magic. They probably weren't thinking about Anderson's infamous "didn't look like the old number twenty-three out there" line. Michael, however, had never forgotten. In a victory that shouted "I'm Back" for all the world to hear, he dropped a crescendoing forty-five points on Orlando. Afterward, he whispered with that I-have-my-little-brother-locked-in-the-bedroom-closet gleam in his eye, "Sometimes, it's very ironic the way things happen."

That the Bulls had to play Seattle in the NBA Finals seemed almost anticlimactic. They won the first three games of the series, with Michael topping out at thirty-six points in the Game Three triumph. His streak of nine consecutive NBA Finals games scoring thirty or more points ended with twenty-eight in Game One. Seattle eventually pushed the Finals to six games, which only served up another helping of irony. The Bulls celebrated their fourth NBA championship on Father's Day, three years to the day after the Bulls celebrated their third championship. The difference between then and now was that James Jordan was alive to see the third one. So the man who hugged the championship trophy in one hand and his wife in the other after winning his first, who table danced after the second, who prayed after the third, collapsed on the game ball at the final buzzer of the fourth one and cried. A memorable ending to be sure, not to mention a climax to a season that saw MJ achieve the unprecedented accomplishment of being the regular season, All-Star Game and NBA Finals MVP.

Ironically, after he had regained his MVPs, had led the Bulls to their greatest single season ever and had authored the greatest comeback in the history of sports, Michael again heard the talk asking whether the end was near. When he returned for the start of the 1996–97 season, Jordan actually let on what would make him ultimately think about the end—then or now. "I might be slipping a little," he admitted at a media-day briefing, "but the double teams are still coming at me. And when they stop coming, that may be a sign that I've lost a step or two or whatever. And when I see that, I know it's time for me to go." Michael had also gained the other missing confirmation of his legend. For this season, Bulls owner Jerry Reinsdorf gave Michael a one-year contract worth thirty million dollars. A balloon payment, many argued, for years of mortgaging the future, for building Reinsdorf a new arena, but a payment that suggested it might be a buyout. The wrath always looming over the Bulls' success was Krause's ego repeatedly talking about building a champion post-Jordan. Post-Jordan now seemed to be a year away. Initially, Michael seemed worthy of a three-year deal worth somewhere around fifty million, but by settling on the one year, Reinsdorf would not be obligated to megabucks through the 1998 season when a free-agent class would be available that featured, among others, Kevin Garnett. "Certain things were important to Michael and certain things were important to me," Reinsdorf revealed after negotiating the deal via telephone with Jordan. Michael wanted the overdue money and acclaim as the highest paid player in the NBA, and Reinsdorf achieved his estate planning that also ensured him not having to guarantee long-term deals to Jackson or Rodman.

Michael took the money and ran, putting together a season that packed enough Michael Miracles to be his last. The first of these came four games into the 1996–97 season when the Bulls traveled to Miami. Pat Riley had supposedly assembled the new flavor of the month in the Eastern Conference, a group led by Alonzo Mourning and Tim Hardaway that could challenge the Bulls like Riley's Knicks did in the early 1990s. After Michael put up 18-for-33 shooting and dropped fifty points on the Heat in a 106-100 victory, Pat Riley wasn't having any of the Jordan-had-lost-a-step talk. In fact, Riley saw much of the old Michael come out on this night, saying, "You know Michael. In games like these, he comes for fifty. Even when he's forty, he'll want to make a statement."

Lasting statements, perhaps. Prior to a February rematch with NBA Finals opponent Seattle, Sonics coach George Karl submitted that Michael looked older, that he was settling more for jump shots rather than taking the beating that went with the Airodynamics. Jordan last-worded Karl with an assault of jump shots, hitting nineteen of twenty-eight en flight to a forty-five-point outing, after which Michael asserted, "I may be older, but I'm also smarter." In his dissertation before the start of the 1996–97 season, Michael also considered the idea of whether he had lost a step. He said that if he did, he would be the only one who would know it. Perhaps it's no coincidence then, that during the 1996–97 season Jordan went about reinventing the aspect of his game that might allow him to make statements until he was forty.

He still had the quicks and ups to get to the basket, but the second coming of Michael Jordan was one in which he became the best-ever post-up, turnaround, fadeaway jump shooter in the history of the game. On a team which featured such low-impact seven-footers as Luc Longley, Bill Wennington and forty-three-year-old former Boston Celtic Robert Parish, Jordan became the Bulls' best option in the post, the area where players plant themselves like tree trunks, catch the ball, back up to a defender and work to get a clear shot as close to the basket as possible. Michael's hidden strength that came from years of weight training with personal guru Tim Grover enabled him to hold off any defender with one hand, catch the ball with the other and use his tree trunk–strong legs to turn and elevate for a clear shot. To make the shot impossible to defend, Jordan would fall away from the basket just out of the defender's reach, the style Wilt Chamberlain used to average fifty points a game in 1962. Armed with this weapon, Michael put up nine games scoring forty or more points during the '96–97 season in the process of winning his ninth NBA scoring title.

Reinvention was the challenge here for Michael. Not just with his game, but his legend. Not just now, but always. The Second Coming, the Third Coming and every coming after would be defined by a matter of moments so unexpected, and perhaps so unexplainable, they had to be the result of irony. Or some greater force. But none until now—not the in-your-face forty-five against Orlando in the 1996 Eastern Conference Finals, the fifty against Miami, the jump-shooting embarrassment of George Karl—would put a face on the legend the way Michael did on June 11, 1997. The NBA Finals series against Utah was tied at two games each, and he had already left a wake of Michael's Miracles to get to this point. The Bulls breezed past Washington, Atlanta and Miami to ease to these Finals, and in Game One, Jordan provided one more miracle by hitting a nineteen-foot jump shot over Utah's Byron Russell to spell an 84-82 victory.

The series went to two games each, a sign that maybe an opponent had found common ground with Michael. A watershed game was coming, and it wouldn't be hard to figure out where that left Jordan. At 3:30 A.M. on the day of Game Five in Utah, Michael woke up with what he said were flulike symptoms: nausea, vomiting, dehydration. He spent the hours leading up to the game in bed, and he spent the pregame lying on the floor of the locker room with his head next to a bucket. As Longley described him, "He was just listless. He could hardly sit up."

Phil Jackson added, "Literally, standing up caused nauseating and dizzy spells." The Bulls were down by sixteen points early in the second quarter of this pivotal game of the series, and finally there was one opponent Michael seemed unable to beat: Mother Nature.

We know now, of course, that Jordan's kryptonite turned out to be some bad pizza that left him food-poisoned. *Mystic Pizza*, as the *Chicago Tribune* would call it the next day. We also know now that Michael revived himself to score seventeen points in the second quarter to cut the Jazz's lead to four. We know now that when Michael missed a free throw during the final minute with the score tied at 85, then pulled the rebound out of a scrum and hit a three-point shot, it wasn't even the legendary image of this game. After Utah called timeout to regroup, Jordan staggered toward the Bulls bench, Pippen eventually propping Michael up and carrying him off the floor. "I couldn't breathe," was how Michael described his feeling when he was finishing off a fifteen-point fourth quarter, a series-best thirty-eight-point night and a 90-88 victory. The fifth championship would be marked by this one moment, and if Michael had indeed been considering the end, well, why wouldn't this be the perfect stopping point?

4

MICHAEL JORDAN DIDN'T TAKE THE LAST SHOT OF THE 1997 CHAMPIONSHIP run. Steve Kerr became the shooting star, taking the ball from Michael when he passed out of a double team in the final minute and scoring the memorable basket from the top of the key in the 90-86 Game Six victory. Still, Michael might have wished it would have ended right there when he returned for training camp the next season. In the wake of the fifth championship, Phil Jackson had become a poster boy for the rift that threatened to defeat the Bulls before any Jazz, Knicks or Sonics could. Bulls owner Jerry Reinsdorf and his vice president of basketball operations, Jerry Krause, cast management as the evil empire for letting Jackson hang in limbo before giving him a six million dollar contract for one season, his last, it now seemed. Michael had to endure a similar wait before getting a new deal—this one for thirty-six million that Reinsdorf postscripted by saying another such payout could put the Bulls into ruin—and Rodman still wasn't re-signed when camp opened. Krause added to his Jabba the Hutt image during the media gathering that preceded the opening of camp when he answered a question about the prospect of rebuilding the Bulls without Phil and Michael in the imminent future by saying, "Organizations win championships. Players and coaches are parts of organizations." Krause furthered his diatribe by pointing out that Joe Lee, the organization's caricature locker room attendant, had won five championship rings just like Michael and Phil. Then, when Pippen failed to show up for the start of camp partly in a pout over the organization's having entertained trade offers for him during the summer and partly because of a foot injury that would require surgery and ten weeks of rehabilitation, Michael surveyed the future and sighed, "This will be my biggest challenge ever."

When he was told that Phil said wild horses couldn't drag him back to the Bulls after this season, Michael publicly admitted he would quit, too. Said it in those words, too, and so matter-of-factly that nobody believed him. "Totally," he reiterated. "If Phil doesn't want to be here anymore, or the organization doesn't want him to be here anymore, than it's hard for me to come and play." Michael went on to talk about trust, how it would walk out the door with Phil and if the rebuilding process was coming that everybody should realize that, "We're going to be together maybe for the last time and use that as motivation." When NBA commissioner David Stern came to town in November for his annual outing to award the Bulls their championship rings, the words coming from Jordan and Pippen and everybody else were more fit for a eulogy than a celebration. "I'd like to thank the city of Chicago for taking a guy named Michael Jordan into its arms in 1984." Pippen added, "I've had a wonderful career here, and if I never have an opportunity to say this again, thank you." Michael closed by guaranteeing a sixth—and final—championship, his pledge to fulfill what was inscribed in 14-karat gold on the championship rings just awarded: Team of the Decade. But as the events of the preceding summer told Michael, nothing was guaranteed.

We know that the end coming now was not Michael's idea. If he had lost a step, perhaps he would, as he said before the start of the previous season, be gone. But if he had a lost a step, it sure didn't show when a second-year Air Head named Kobe Bryant came to Chicago in December. Early in the fourth quarter, Bryant cornered Michael during a brief stoppage in play and asked his Airness about the intricacies of his fadeaway move in the post. "I felt like an old man at that point," Michael said. But not the rest of the night. He scored thirty-six points as the Bulls ran the Lakers out by a 104-83 count. Kobe did have thirty-three of his own, but twelve of those came in the fourth quarter after Michael had left the game and after the statements had been made. "Kobe is a young player who may someday take his throne," observed Ron Harper. "But I don't think Michael is ready to give up his throne yet."

As the 1997–98 season played out, it's easy to understand why Michael Jordan was not ready to quit. He led the Bulls in scoring in sixty-four of the eighty-two games, scoring forty or more points in twelve of those, three more than the previous season. Flulike symptoms hit Michael again the day before the All-Star Game in Madison Square Garden, but he recovered in time to score a game-high twenty-three points and win his third All-Star Most Valuable Player award. By season's end, the Bulls had the best record in the NBA for the fifth time and Michael had his fifth regular-season Most Valuable Player award. So, if the last shot was a fate awaiting, well, it had to be a good one.

After the Bulls breezed through the first two rounds of the play-offs, Indiana awaited as their sixth different Eastern Conference Finals opponent in as many appearances during the threepeats. Larry Bird had taken over as the Pacers' coach and appeared to be bringing his team to the level he once played at. But as Bird knew, that level was never good enough to match Jordan. At least without Parish, McHale and Dennis Johnson. Indiana extended the Bulls to a seventh and deciding game of the series, just the second one Michael played during the championship run. Jackson and several other Bulls players admitted that on the morning of the game, they went so far as to consider that they could be facing the end on this night. Michael's only thoughts, however, centered on guaranteeing victory. Then he delivered it by scoring twenty-eight points, grabbing nine rebounds and adding eight assists while holding longtime whipping boy Reggie Miller scoreless in the fourth quarter of an 88-83 victory.

When the 1998 season filtered down to its final thirty-seven seconds, Michael Jordan exhibited calm assurance, an endorphin enriching the usual last-minute, water-faucet sweat. Having missed six of his eight shots didn't seem to worry him, nor did John Stockton's three-point shot that obliterated Michael's previous several minutes of scratching for four free throws to make the score 83-all. Jordan figured he held a no-lose situation here, having reconciled the finality of all this long before the season ever started. As Bulls management let the future of Jackson and Pippen and Rodman spin like a pig at a luau, Michael responded to a question about the greatest obstacle to the repeat threepeat by raising his eyebrows to the second floor of the Berto Center, where Jerry Krause had his office, and then show-ing his practical joker smirk. Maybe he was about to show Krause in a way that only Jordan's arrogance and bravado could what made the organization a champion, but for some reason he admitted that the final thirty-seven seconds of the season unfolded almost in slow motion. Some argued it was fatigue setting in from compensating for Pippen, whose back was so sore he could barely walk, by scoring forty-one points through the first forty-seven minutes and twenty-nine seconds. If James Jordan were here, he would have said his boy was laying in the weeds until, with the Jazz leading 86-83, Michael drove the length of the floor, spun past Bryon Russell and floated a layup in over Antoine Carr. Why Karl Malone wasn't looking a few seconds later when Michael snuck up from behind and stole the ball from him on Utah's ensuing possession only illustrates the vast chasm between Malone's wannabeing and Jordan's superior being.

There are many pictures of Michael on that last drive, the one he didn't want to call time out for and let Utah set up its defense. An angle from Jordan's back as he ascended for the final shot shows Jazz fans standing, many with mouths open, 6.4 reading on the clock above the backboard. About twelve rows up, just to the right of the basket, a man appears to be talking on a cellular telephone. Who could he be calling? "Honey, listen to this, Michael is about to make one last shot."

Each Michael Miracle freeze-framed its own indelible memory. The Shot in Cleveland in 1989 culminated with Jordan punching air and woofing. The three-point shooting spree against Portland in the 1992 NBA Finals sent up the shoulder shrug. And just a year prior to this, Jordan needing Pippen to carry him off, food poisoning oozing out of his pores, became what Jackson called the lasting image of Michael. Until now.

Jordan jitterbugged to the left of the lane, threw a fake to clear Russell—though to this day many, including Michael, insist he threw a forearm to clear Russell—and struck one final pose, right arm extended for what seemed like an eternity as the last shot splashed into posterity. No gestures followed; no genuflecting. Michael said he held his right hand to make sure to get the ball over the rim, a compensation, he said, for heavy legs that had caused all the misses in the fourth quarter. Megalomaniacal Jordan held this pose for the world to get one last snapshot. Venomous Jordan held it to enjoy a last word for the now-silent Delta Center crowd and perhaps Jerry Krause to hear. Subdued by the moment, or by having to endure a final 5.2 seconds and one last Stockton shot, Jordan finally made his celebratory move and lit up a cigar.

Before he could return to a smoke-filled locker room, he was hearing the debate about this one last shot. Yes, this was his best shot ever because the single greatest player in the history of the game had conjured his single greatest shot in the history of the game to give the Bulls an 87-86 championship-winning victory. To put it in perspective, some argued this was like Babe Ruth hitting a game-winning grand slam in the final at-bat of his career. In the last game of the World Series. Or Jim Brown running for a game-winning touchdown on the last play of his career. In the Super Bowl. As for it being the last shot, well, Michael had to consider the significance after the game when he was asked if it was a satisfying ending.

"Yes," he said. "If that's the case, yes."

On January 13, 1999, one week after the NBA and its players settled a labor dispute that delayed the start of the season three months, Michael Jordan again announced he was retiring. So many lamented this passing, because as Frank Deford wrote for a *Sports Illustrated* tribute to Michael, he was the defining icon of a time when the United States ruled not so much as a superpower but a superculture. Jordan, Deford reasoned, turned sport into art, up to and including that one last shot. In his closing arguments that came right after Reinsdorf re-raised No. 23 to the United Center rafters, Michael insisted his physical skills were still as strong as ever, that his love for the game was a strong as ever and that he chose to walk away knowing, "I could still play the game." He admitted that the Bulls team of the first three championships was better than the one of the second three and that his most fond memories were of two shots: the one that beat Cleveland in 1989 and the one that beat Utah a few months earlier. But he hid behind the contention that the new challenge in his life would be parenting and that he was 99.9 percent sure he was done with the game forever. "I am not going to say never," Michael added. "I'm saying ninety-nine point nine and you take it for what it's worth."

Just like at the first retirement announcement, Michael never gave a reason to think the end had really come, never gave a reason to think he had fully flushed basketball out of his system. The tone here was solemn, tense, just like that first retirement announcement five years ago, even a little angry. Reinsdorf brought Jordan's championship ring to this ceremony at the United Center and re-hung his jersey in the rafters. There would be no Michael Jordan Night this time around. Take your ball and go home, Michael. And while nobody really wanted to believe he was gone, nobody wanted to believe he would come back.

EXECUTIVE PRIVILEGES

1

SO MICHAEL JORDAN SITS HERE AT ONE SIXTY BLUE, HIS NEW DOWNTOWN Chicago restaurant, picking over some pork chops and contemplating his Third Coming. It's not what you think, though. Not now. Eight months removed from being put out to stud in 1999, Michael is listening to a recruiting pitch intended to lure him back. Newly minted sports mogul Ted Leonsis has flown to Chicago from Washington on his private jet and put a deal on the table that would make Michael one of his partners. Leonsis is so kid-in-the-locker-room awestruck he can barely resist sneaking away from the table to call his wife and kids so they can tell everybody on their block about his dinner with Michael. Not that Leonsis isn't a big leaguer himself, having built this little Internet venture into an entity half the world uses daily and knows as America Online. In addition to AOL, his company, Lincoln Holdings, owns the Washington Capitals and a forty-four percent stake of Washington Sports & Entertainment, which controls the NBA's Wizards, the WNBA's Washington Mystics, the MCI Center, US Airways Arena and the D.C.-area Ticketmaster franchise. As the chefs at One Sixty Blue send out plates of steaks and chicken and lobster, Michael has suddenly regained his appetite for the NBA. Appetite, nothing. He hasn't felt a hunger like this since the Bulls trailed Utah by three points with thirty-seven seconds to play.

If Leonsis can make good on the critical part of his offer—getting Michael the power to run the Wizards' basketball operations—then it's to hell with the carpooling Juanita Jordan had planned for her husband's retirement. Yes, the Wizards are among the dregs of the NBA, their only playoff appearance in the past twelve years occuring in the 1997 season, when Jordan's Bulls swept Washington out of the first round. And yes, Michael's reputation in the realm of personnel evaluation rested on the embarrassing statement that the Bulls should have forsaken the deal that sent Charles Oakley to the New York Knicks for Bill Cartwright, who turned out to be the defensive cornerstone of the first three championship teams. But here was the chance to find a channel for his competitive energy that didn't include a twenty-dollar Nassau or a blackjack table. The ego that made him the greatest player ever now tempted Michael into thinking how great of a basketball operations guru he could be. Building the Washington Misfits into a success would also give him the vehicle to stick it to Jerrys Krause and Reinsdorf, at whom Michael is still seething for breaking up the Bulls and not giving him the management opportunities that simmer before him right now.

Imagine Michael sitting here, now breaking into that poker-table smile, rubbing the stubble on his chin and envisioning another stogie-lighting ceremony and David Stern handing him another gold basketball. The bright-eyed look he is wearing is not so much from the hundred-dollar bottles of wine they have been drinking, but the intoxication of finally finding a way to resurrect a franchise that has tried nearly a dozen rebuilding plans since its championship season of 1978. Surely he can do better than bringing in such "saviors" as Jeff Ruland, Michael Adams and Gus Williams, or getting stuck with Moses Malone, Bernard King and Mitch Richmond after their NBA warranties expired. Michael has flirted with this kind of opportunity at least twice already, unable to reach a deal with Milwaukee, which might have been more interested in his name as a marketing tool than his chief executive offerings, and Charlotte, where owner George

Shinn shortsightedly refused to part with control of basketball operations. Now, Jordan would want to meticulously assess the stakes. The Jordan brand name risks taking a hit. Not the one that goes with Nike and Gatorade and Hanes, but the brand for winning, the brand that even Stacey King and Craig Hodges and Will Perdue and Steve Kerr could slip into and find success. He is hesitant now because he knows he would stoop to anything to keep from being called a loser or a failure, and he knows the general managing world in the NBA has been filled with great players who have failed to make the transition to suit-and-tie sensation. The Wizards already had one in long-time franchise player Wes Unseld and other such luminaries as Willis Reed and Isiah Thomas suffered humiliation as chief execs.

No two all-time greats illustrate the extreme possibilities for Michael more than former L.A. Lakers teammates Jerry West and Elgin Baylor. While West built the Magic-Kareem champions and rebuilt the Shaq-Kobe edition, Baylor was behind the desk when the cross-town Clippers became the long-standing butt of the NBA draft lottery through a series of criticized personnel moves, and by 2002 had built a team of top picks renowned for its trade prospects, NBA drug policy violations and one more season of watching the playoffs. Of the all-time greats, Michael always admired West the most. Like Jordan, West built his legacy by making the big shots when they absolutely needed to be made. And the thought of matching West by rebuilding a team as woeful as Washington had Michael ready to let Leonsis fulfill his business plan of putting the Jordan brand atop the MCI Center marquee. Sure, Michael knew the Wizards wanted him to sell tickets and fill what had become a half-empty arena on most nights, but, he also knew he could use this to stack the deck in his favor. Wouldn't packing the house make Washington an attractive place to play, and couldn't Michael use that and his name to lure new players and a new image to a town he would need to West-ernize this franchise?

Now the grin had probably reached a jack-o-lantern–like hue as

Michael realized that the feast/famine laying before him combined his two greatest obsessions—addictions, from what we already know. Being a general manager was basketball and gambling in its most fundamental execution. And in exchange for being Washington's show pony, Michael could have a chance to play with house money. The game here was one his ego couldn't let Michael sit out, one he wanted a shot at more than anybody knew. Except George Koehler, maybe. In one of his many roles as the official Jordan personal assistant, George had seen Michael play the executive position in the process of running his own Fortune 500 of "corporate involvements," as he always called his endorsements, Internet ventures, real estate deals, stuff like that. George revealed that behind the desk Michael could find the same game face that always came with time running out and the ball in his hands.

So as with just about everything concerning Michael Jordan, we are now wondering why? Or more precisely, why here? Why now? Apparently carpooling his kids to school and the challenge of being a parent wasn't enough to keep him busy. Or maybe as *Chicago Tribune* columnist Skip Bayless put it, Michael couldn't bear being thirty-six years old and realizing he would never be as successful at anything else in life as he was at winning NBA championships. Bayless went on to contend that the greatest athletes of the twentieth century—Babe, Wilt, Mantle to name a few—lived out their days as sad or sympathetic figures because they could never quite figure out what to do in life without the athletic equivalent of trying to draw the inside straight. Retrospectively, Michael indicated he could have gone on playing at the level at which he left the game for another three years because his body had not told him it was time to quit. Yes, he was being put out to stud, but now he could take his achievements and his name and his relentless drive, perhaps even recapture the elusive exhilaration that only seemed to come with last-second shots and hot dice at the craps table, wheel and deal and generally manage an organization into a team of players that would Be Like Mike.

2

WHEN MICHAEL JORDAN WAS INTRODUCED AS THE WASHINGTON WIZARDS' president of basketball operations on January 19, 2000, he announced his involvement would include practicing with players as part of getting to know the hand he had been dealt. Wizards coach Gar Heard stood at the back of this news conference/coronation and said nothing, apparently a silent concession to whatever Michael wanted to do. Eventually, the question came to Jordan whether he thought Heard would mind or feel undermined by Michael's presence at practice, to which he responded by saying, "I don't know if Gar likes that or not, but I'm his boss." This is truly what Michael wanted from life after basketball. Absolute power. He would show Jerry Krause that he could dominate the Bulls' operations chief in his own arena, which might have more to do with Michael's eventual return to playing in 2001 than many people initially thought. He would show Jerry Krause it's not organizations that win championships. It's Michael's organization that wins championships.

And this was going to be Jordan's organization. The official introduction featured the trimmings of the receptions most heads of state enjoy when they come to Washington. New Wizards ticket brochures adorned with Michael's likeness were already spread through the MCI Center by the time Jordan arrived. Wizards president Susan O'Malley, who ran the business side of the organization, warmed up a packed room by reminding that season tickets were available and gave reporters the telephone number for readers and viewers to call for orders. Washington, D.C. mayor Anthony Williams served as master of ceremonies, and by the end of the day Michael would watch the Wizards' game against the Dallas Mavericks sitting in owner Abe Pollin's suite alongside that noted sports fan, Bill Clinton. For the time being, Michael had really found his next calling, leaving his first day in office with two resounding statements. First, he said he was not coming back to play. And second, he said he would evaluate the organization from top to bottom, but at this point in time, "everyone's disposable."

The rush for Michael here was that this job let him do what he loves best: keeping score. From the moment he stared across the table at Leonsis and his partners, he once again felt all the intensity of trying to beat the double team. When he first thought about making this play, Leonsis heard that his chance of landing Jordan was about the same shot the Cleveland Cavaliers had that night in 1990 when Michael went off for sixty-nine. But Leonsis didn't build AOL into a multibillion-dollar business by not thinking big. Four months prior to his first meeting with Jordan, Leonsis targeted Michael as the potential partner who could add some pop-culture appeal to the Internet venture he had planned to grow interest in the Capitals and the rest of his new holdings. Jordan had already delved into the online world with an interest in CBS Sportsline and another venture he created with Wayne Gretzky and John Elway known as MVP.com that eventually went the way of most of the other dot.coms not beginning with the letters A-O-L. Knowing that he had Leonsis posted up, Michael tried to back him down for the slam dunk. He wanted executive privileges with basketball operations in this package, and that's when the negotiations took on a fourth-quarter frenzy. As the One Sixty Blue cuisine went down, Leonsis and the partners he brought to this meeting questioned Jordan's hunger. They wondered whether he would be able to play forty-eight minutes a night at this job even though he maintained he would keep his home in Chicago.

That's when Michael detailed his previous attempts to become a basketball executive as an indication of how he would approach the job. He had briefly talked with Milwaukee Bucks owner Herb Kohl about an executive opportunity but backed off when he realized Kohl wanted the Jordan name more than the Jordan brain. A much more substantive discussion took place with George Shinn in Charlotte. Shinn was failing with the franchise he brought to town in 1988. The people of Charlotte had voted against funding a new arena Shinn desperately needed, and he was having other public problems after being named a defendant in a sexual assault suit from which he was eventually absolved. In the end, Shinn would not relinquish control of basketball operations to Jordan, a move that now might explain why his franchise packed up and moved to New Orleans during the summer of 2002. Michael made it known that he had to be able to run a team, that if he was investing the Jordan brand he would have the last word on all hirings, firings, trades, free-agent deals, coaching changes and everything else from socks to jocks. This was the only way he could conceive to again become the driving force behind an effort to win more championships.

After three hours of talking, Leonsis left the dinner table that September night knowing what Joe Dumars and Hersey Hawkins and Bryon Russell had been through. And Leonsis decided to play it like Dumars. He came right back at Michael. Leonsis put Jordan face to face with Pollin, the man who could make the deal by giving Michael control of the Wizards' basketball operations. The history between Pollin and Jordan made them about as unlikely a ticket in Washington as Jesse Helms and Hillary Clinton. When the NBA owners locked out the players over a collective bargaining agreement dispute in the fall of 1998, Jordan and Pollin reportedly screamed at each other during the negotiations.

Maybe that moxie drew them together, for in late December of 2000, they sat together in the living room of Pollin's home in Bethesda, Maryland, talking as if a corporate merger was in the works. Or a new deal. According to one report, Jordan would pay between twenty and thirty million dollars in exchange for a roughly five-percent interest in the Wizards and a ten-percent share of Lincoln Holdings. Another report indicated Michael would receive a thirty- to fifty-million dollar equity in Lincoln Holdings without paying a dime. Michael would yield final say to Pollin for budgetary approval, but the piece of control he gave up was worth enough of a better financial deal for Jordan to declare victory in this game. And he had what he wanted: direction of basketball operations and a piece of the team, a better deal than, say, Magic or any other former MVP-turned-chief executives had in the NBA. This new deal gave Michael a kid-in-a-toy-store feeling, and he said he was looking forward to putting his imprints and footprints on this team.

What Michael saw in the collection of Wizards he inherited, however, was the plague that turned too many teams into the Clippers. Richmond, Rod Strickland, Juwan Howard, Tracy Murray and Ike Austin packed the baggage of players who were in it for the money, who were looking for their shots more than their victories, who had spent—or were going to spend—their time in the NBA wandering from team to team. He knew the footprints would come before the imprints, kicking players, coaches, scouts and secretaries out the door. Washington had become an NBA Siberia, a place where careers went to die during so much of the past twenty-five years. If the Wizards traded you, you had to have technical difficulties, technical foul diffi-culties like Rasheed Wallace, or you had to be allegedly smoking dope and busting up strip clubs like Chris Webber. Not surprisingly, Michael announced on his first day: "If everybody is looking over their heads making sure their necks aren't going to get chopped off, then that is good." The joke making the rounds on this day punch-lined with the question of whether Superman could trade in his cape and begin rebuilding Metropolis with what amounted to some card-board cutouts. The office pool was about to become a game of who would be the first to go. Start the clock. Two years after he retired from the Bulls, Jordan was most definitely back, keeping score again.

3

A MONTH OR SO BEFORE THE WASHINGTON BULLETS DEFEATED THE SEATTLE Supersonics to win the 1978 NBA Championship, Clifton Herring, coach of Laney High School in Wilmington, North Carolina, cut a skinny sophomore from the varsity basketball team. When Michael

Jordan followed up his second NBA Championship by leading the United States to the 1992 Olympic basketball gold medal, the Washington Bullets were figuring out how to recover from a 25-57 season, their worst in twenty-five years. During the next nine years, the Washington franchise lost fifty or more games five times, including sixty-one in 1995, more than Jordan's Bulls lost in either of their three-year championship runs combined. Like water flushing down a toilet, Washington swirled to a 28-54 record the season Michael took over the bridge. He inherited a team that had not won a playoff game in twelve seasons and an organization that had to endure jokes that its best player might be Chamique Holdsclaw of the WNBA's Mystics.

What had he done, taking charge of the second-worst team in the NBA in 2001? His life would now be all about learning the collective bargaining agreement that dictated players' contracts and the intricacies of a salary cap, the NBA rule that limits how much a team can spend on its players. He would also have to deal with players' agents and be responsible for their lives in a league that was drafting increasingly younger and disturbingly less mature and less talented players than Michael ever shared a locker room with. He would have to set up a preseason training camp, travel internationally to scout players, travel cross-country to scout college games and tournaments—and high school games and tournaments—hire and fire coaches, scouts and office staff and deal with a media inquisition that would demand more than the twenty minutes a day he was used to giving. This is what his peers were doing, even Jerry Krause, who had the only team in the league worse than Washington. Would he give up the golf outings in Lake Tahoe and the gambling junkets to the Caribbean to keep up with peers like Orlando general manager John Gabriel, who had reportedly made fifty-one player personnel moves during a two-year period just to get the Magic out of NBA lottery land and into an ousting in the first round of the playoffs in 2001?

Some of his newfound competitors forecasted success for Michael. On the day Jordan was installed in Washington, Indiana Pacers president Donnie Walsh told *USA Today*, "Players who play ten years–plus have a Ph.D. in basketball. I expect him to be very good." Philadelphia 76ers general manager Billy King predicted Michael "will know the personnel in the league better than most general managers because he played against most of the guys." And Atlanta Hawks GM Pete Babcock might have broken this issue down to its most basic principle when he said in the *USA Today* report, "It doesn't take a great genius to do what we do. If it did, none of us would be doing it. You have to be willing to put in the time and do the work." But for the first time since he played little league baseball, Michael's commitment was being challenged. If he planned to live in Chicago and do his scouting by calling friends around the league, as George Koehler said Jordan would, how could he outwork the competition? Considering the illustrious but almost comical history of this franchise, would Michael need a more hands-on approach to being successful at this job? Eventually, he would have to use his own hands to turn things around because the Washington franchise he was running had become the laughingstock of the NBA.

The lineage of this conundrum reads as the Chicago/Baltimore/Capital/Washington Packers/Zephyrs/Bullets/Wizards and that wasn't even the punch line. If Kwame Brown had known what had transpired in franchise history during the forty years before he became the first player the Packers/Zephrys/Bullets/Wizards picked number one overall since Walt Bellamy in 1961, he surely would have rented an apartment in D.C. rather than going condo. No team oscillated between success and futility as haphazardly as this one, the one that gave life to that classic sports mantra, The Opera Ain't Over Until The Fat Lady Sings. A San Antonio newspaper columnist tagged the Bullets with that battle cry after they recovered from a three-games-to-one deficit in the 1979 Eastern Conference Finals to advance to the NBA Finals. Then a year later, the man who danced with the Fat Lady, head coach Dick Motta, resigned after a 39-43 record left Washington out of the playoffs. The franchise made it to the NBA Finals four times, but in 1978 when the Bullets won their only title, they did so after posting a 44-38 mark, the worst ever by a champion. In their best season ever, 1975, they went 60-22 but lost the championship round in five games to the Golden State Warriors in what many observers call the greatest upset in the history of the NBA Finals. The Bullets also made the playoffs twelve straight seasons from 1969 to 1981, a streak they started by fashioning the best record in the league one season after suffering through the worst record.

No other season defines the highs and lows of the Washington franchise more than 1988. The Bullets' team leader in blocked shots was a seven-foot-seven Dinka tribesman from Sudan who became one of the league's greatest novelty acts, playing under the stage name Manute Bol. The Bullets' team leader in assists was a five-foot-three former Washington-area high school star named Tyrone "Mugsy" Bogues. A picture of Bol and Bogues side by side might as well be the lasting image of the Chicago/Baltimore/Capital/Washington Packers/Zephyrs/Bullets/Wizards. Unless you remember that this could be the only franchise in NBA history to have two seven-foot-seven players on its all-time roster. In 1997, Russian import Gheorge Muresan played center on the Bullets' last playoff qualifier, though his career ended one year later due to foot injuries. Perhaps it's only appropriate that Muresan left the NBA to play the title role in Billy Crystal's *My Giant*, a flop spreading the same odor as the state of the franchise that had asked Michael Jordan to become its savior.

Not that the past was completely checkered. In addition to the four championship-round appearances, the team won five division titles in six seasons between 1969 and 1975 while changing from the Baltimore Bullets to the Capital Bullets to the Washington Bullets and relocating from Baltimore to Washington in 1973. Ironically, the one season in that stretch the Bullets didn't win a division title, their 52-30 record was better than either of the next two years. The Bullets' all-time roster would never be confused with the Lakers' or the Celtics', but NBA Rookie of the Year selections Walt Bellamy,

Terry Dischinger, Earl Monroe and Wes Unseld started their careers with the franchise. Additionally, all-stars Howard, Wallace, Webber, Moses, Jeff Malone, Elvin Hayes, Tom Gugliotta and Kevin Porter played here.

If you were picking the club's all-time team, Bellamy, Monroe, Hayes and Unseld would be a good place to start. (That group could even win with Bol as the other starter.) Phil Chenier and Jeff Malone might be worth considering for their tour of duty that overshadows all of the rest of the above, and even Bernard King, who resurrected his post-injury career in Washington. Bellamy was the first player ever drafted by the franchise and in his rookie season of 1961–62 he led the Chicago Packers, as they were known for one season, with 31.6 points and 19 rebounds per game. After the team floundered to a 20-61 record in 1967, Monroe came to the Bullets. Kareem Abdul-Jabbar once called "Earl the Pearl" the best player he ever saw after watching Monroe in Harlem's famous Rucker Park Tournament— the one parodied in the Nike commercial that introduced Vince Carter playing Dr. Funk during the 2001–2002 season. "Black Jesus," as Monroe was also called, scored fifty-six points in a game against the Lakers during his rookie year, a franchise single-game scoring mark that still stands. In 1969, the Bullets added Unseld, who became the only player other than Wilt Chamberlain to be named Rookie of the Year and Most Valuable Player in the same season. And when Hayes came over in a trade with Houston in 1972, he teamed with Unseld to be the foundation of the 1975 finalists and 1978 champs.

Yet what marks this franchise as much as those achievements is this: Bellamy, Monroe, Hayes, Dischinger, Porter—the all-time franchise leader in assists—Moses, Webber, Howard, Gugliotta and Wallace each were traded from the Bullets/Wizards. Bellamy and Monroe both went to the Knicks, where Monroe teamed with Walt Frazier to form one of the NBA's all-time greatest backcourts and win an NBA Championship. Porter went to Detroit for an aging

Dave Bing. Hayes was traded back to Houston for a couple of draft picks. After some off-the-court trouble, Webber was jettisoned to Sacramento in a deal that brought an aging Mitch Richmond and his ten million–dollar annual salary and marked the breakup of the 1997 playoff team. That team outlasted Cleveland, 85-81, in the final game of the regular-season to make the playoffs. The following year, Muresan missed the entire season with an ankle injury and even though the newly renamed Wizards won their last four games of the regular season, they missed the playoffs by one victory. Once Webber was dealt during the offseason, which was prolonged by the 1998 owners' lockout of the players, a slide began in which the Wizards went 66-148 the next three seasons and extended their measure of futility to making the playoffs only once in the previous thirteen seasons. In the 1990s, Bernie Bickerstaff was billed as a genius for reviving the franchise to a pair of winning seasons. Yet, Bickerstaff left the job in the middle of the 1999 season with a a 77-74 record.

When Michael Jordan looked at numbers he hadn't known since the Ennis Whatley-Quintin Dailey-Granville Waiters era of the Chicago Bulls, he really had no idea how bad this was going to get. Richmond's contract and the hundred million–dollar deal Howard signed in 1996 left Washington seventeen million over the thirty-four million-dollar NBA salary cap. When he took over, the team with the second-worst record in the league had its seventh-highest payroll, so even if Michael wanted to bring in some of the free agents he would need to remake the team in his image, he would have to pull off the equivalent of rehabbing a Hollywood Hills mansion using food stamps. Instead, he was left with what could have passed for the 1985 Bulls. Rod Strickland and his rap sheet, which had forced him out of New York, San Antonio and several other NBA cities, played the part of Dailey. Such household names as Austin, Aaron Williams, Jahidi White and Gerald King gave the Wizards as many backup centers as those Bulls teams. Richmond was about to turn thirty-five when he came to the end of his Washington run and he played like it, the mileage of playing forty minutes per game the past fourteen years rendering his knees irreparable. Howard's career seemed to be declining, too, from a 22.1 points per game average in 1996 to 14.9 points per game when Michael came on board. The only potential building block seemed to be shooting guard Richard Hamilton, who was less than a year removed from being the Most Valuable Player of the NCAA Tournament's Final Four.

To undo this disaster, Michael needs the general manager's version of the take-off-from-the-foul-line-ball-raised-high-in-the-right-hand-duck-a-defender-switch-to-the-left-hand scoop of 1991 NBA Finals fame. And he won't get much help. Privately, the basketball ops guys around the league are colluding to freeze him out of the transaction game and laughing because they know better than he does how bad it is in Washington. He quickly finds out, keeping his promise to practice with his new players, to look them in the eyes and find out what's behind those big contracts. Ironically, he sees the most substance in Strickland, but Jordan knows the practices and the team flights he has been missing make him too risky to keep. Otherwise, he sees none of the fiber of the Jordan brand: no allegiance to work ethic, no crisp commitment to fundamentals, no win-at-all-costs desperation, no heart. He has no more patience or tolerance in the board room than he did on the court, and he lays the blame on Heard, whose 2-3 record in the first ten days of the Jordan empire is not good enough to keep his job. Michael knows he's about to experience losing like he had never known before, a feeling perhaps even worse than being cut from the Laney High School varsity basketball team. And he had no idea what that feeling would push him to do.

4

MICHAEL JORDAN IS A RENOWNED SORE LOSER. THE NIGHT HE THREW THE Monopoly board as North Carolina teammate and roommate Buzz Peterson was building hotels on Boardwalk and Park Place is one of those legendary tales that illustrate just how much of a temper

Michael had, how violent and intolerant he could get when facing a losing hand. The season he sat out sixty-four games with a broken foot, he would watch the Bulls wither from his living-room sofa and throw soda cans at the television when they couldn't find the resilience to fight. There are other telling stories that cast Jordan as far more insolent than that time he stormed out of practice when he disputed the score of a scrimmage game with Doug Collins. During the 1990 Eastern Conference Finals, Michael was so upset at the way his team had played in the first half of a game against the Pistons that he burst into the locker room at halftime and kicked over a garbage can. Now, here it was happening to Michael all over again. A month into his first full season as the chief executive—a month into the season he predicted would be no worse than .500; a month into the season he asked his critics to judge his basketball ops expertise on—the team was 2-7 and playing the young and hopeless Los Angeles Clippers. Through three quarters, the Wizards seemed to be running like one of those Indy race cars at full speed, building a nineteen-point lead and not slowing down. Then in the fourth quarter, the proverbial rub against the wall came, and they started to break apart, one piece flying into another until they burst into the fireball. As L.A. recovered to win 93-88, Michael reportedly told those sitting around him in the owner's suite that he thought he was going to explode in anger right there for a half-full MCI Center to see. Good thing no Monopoly boards or garbage cans were within reach. He controlled himself until he reached the locker room, where he blasted his players, calling them a "disgrace to the fans because of their losers' mentality." When he saw no immediate reaction, nobody else exploding, Michael described his team as scared and added, "I can see why fans get pissed off and boo."

On this night, Michael realized that his initial plan to remake the Wizards had the same chance of succeeding as *My Giant*. That no player stood up during Jordan's post-game eruption angered him more. He would watch this team play, see it crash and burn and react by, "throwing shit at the television and cursing." But the only response he could get over this tirade came when one player anonymously responded in a newspaper story by describing Jordan as "sounding like an arrogant owner slamming everybody." Michael didn't concern himself so much with the talent level at this time. Yes, he knew he needed better players, but he would slowly upgrade the talent via trades until the summer of 2003 when Washington would finally be free of its salary cap straightjacket. Between now and then, Michael would focus his power on remaking the team mentally, building an attitude to take Boardwalk and Park Place at all costs, even if it meant knocking over garbage cans.

He had already tried the good cop approach, a dual role of Sigmund Freud and Apollo Creed. Initially, he offered some basic psychology, calling each player at least once each week during the summer after he took over for a status report and a prescription to prepare for the coming season. Then, he took the team to the University of North Carolina at Wilmington for preseason training camp in 2000, back to the place where he built his toughness—just like in *Rocky III* when Rocky went with Apollo to that gym in the filth-infested area of L.A., the place where he became a champion. "I just want to make sure we get out of the blocks with the understanding of the dedication to the game," Michael told the media in explaining his theory of relativity. He put on his Airs and practiced with the team, reasoning that the best way to evaluate a player was to look in his eyes, "and see how scared he is." He basically set one condition for running this team and that was to give each player, "very little rope," adding that, "I will make changes as quickly as possible."

In other words, be tough or be gone. Michael had already swept out the management team, and the way he did so indicated he wanted only a certain caliber of competitor at his side. By the time the Wizards reached Wilmington, he had made not one, but two head coaching changes. After dumping Heard, he called Darrell Walker out of a job in the Continental Basketball Association to be the interim coach. Michael absolutely loved having Walker as a teammate with the 1993 Bulls. With no real jump shot or offensive substance,

Walker carved a place for himself in the NBA by scratching and clawing to become one of the league's designated defenders. Jordan loved to show off the nicks and scars he incurred playing against Walker in practice, and Michael figured that was the type of defense and toughness that could give the Wizards a chance to win. Walker posted a 15-23 record finishing out the season in Heard's place, and his work there was done. Michael moved Walker to the player personnel department so he could bring in his best friend in the league to coach.

When Rod Higgins was in his second season playing with the Chicago Bulls, he befriended a rookie from North Carolina. He and Jordan bonded over playing cards, an occasional game of miniature golf on the road and basically their affinity to compete at anything. Everything. Jordan wanted Higgins from the start, but he couldn't work out a deal to pry him away from his assistant coaching position in Golden State. Michael eventually made Higgins the assistant general manager, then completed his front-office overhaul by bringing in Fred Whitfield, a onetime attorney for Jordan's longtime agent David Falk, and a former player and coach at Campbell University in North Carolina, to be player personnel director.

Finding a coach wasn't quite such an exact science for Michael. He needed toughness, but also somebody who could motivate like Phil Jackson and teach relentless competitiveness like Doug Collins. He also wasn't going to hand out one of those six million dollar per year coaching contracts like Jackson was getting unless it was to Phil. This more or less ended Michael's courting of Mike Jarvis, a onetime local coaching legend at George Washington, who had moved on to St. John's University in New York, and led Michael to hire Leonard Hamilton from the University of Miami, who had been coaching at the college level for some thirty years.

Now he thought he had a coach, a plan and a goal. All of which made Michael confident enough on the eve of training camp to announce, "My name is at stake. My credibility is at stake." And nobody was going to mess with that. After four training-camp practices, he cut loose Austin and Murray, who combined for nearly seventeen points per game the previous season. That same day—the second one of camp—he also waived onetime shooting star Dennis Scott, whom Michael acquired during the offseason only to realize that his laziness had become more developed than his jump shot. All three were escorted out of town by the famed "disgruntled" tag, cutting a path many more would follow. By the end of his first full season in charge, only three Wizards players—Richard Hamilton, Jahidi White and Chris Whitney—would be left from the group Jordan had inherited. Michael insisted he was looking for players who were "fresh, raw and ready to fight."

He had a method to his madness. Put the pressure on the players, provoke them publicly if necessary as he did on the night after blowing the lead against the Clippers and see who would fight back. White spoke up almost immediately, saying Michael's appraisal of the Wizards playing scared was "his opinion and he has a right to that." Others like Juwan Howard apparently took another approach. Howard said in a story in the *Chicago Sun-Times* that Michael's comments made him feel like "It's really us against the world. And that includes us against the management that put this team together."

After his team stumbled in the season he asked to be judged to a 5-25 record—the worst start ever in franchise history—Michael apparently figured he could no longer sit and watch the misery and throw soda cans at his television set after every turnover. He had attended very few games in Washington at this point, and when he did fans would look up to the owners' box and yell for Michael to come out and play. He was listening to mounting criticism for trying to run the team by cell phone while still living in Chicago. Unseld and Higgins said they heard from Michael up to four times per day. "More than I wanted to," Unseld said, given the state of the team. Finally, on February 22, Jordan had seen enough. Howard would never be fresh, raw and ready to fight and his contract would continue to submarine any hopes of improvement. Taking advantage of new Dallas owner Mark Cuban, a man who figured he could run his team like it was part of some Playstation game and who couldn't wait to run out and tell everybody on his block he was making a deal with Michael, Jordan dumped Howard on the Mavericks. In the biggest deal in franchise history, Michael sent Howard, Calvin Booth and Obinna Ekezie to Dallas for Christian Laettner, Courtney Alexander, Loy Vaught, Hubert Davis and Etan Thomas. Thomas and Alexander were each lottery picks in the 2000 NBA draft. Alexander went on to win Rookie of the Month honors in April when he topped twenty points in seven games. Four of these five would be part of the supporting cast success of the next season. Michael also got Cuban to throw in three million dollars in cash.

This was not exactly West stuff. Not that he expected instant gratification, but when Washington limped through the last two months of the season with 6-16 record Michael made up his mind about what had to be done next. Seeing the handwriting on the wall—and probably the soda stains on the TV—Leonard Hamilton resigned after the worst season in franchise history. But it was Michael's name and credibility taking a huge hit, and he was beginning to hear the I-told-you-sos from the other basketball ops guys about his belief that wayward moves would be like missed shots and that he could always follow his personal my-way mentality and keep shooting. The decision to hire Hamilton made him look more like Baylor, for Michael apparently miscalculated that his collection of misfits and petulance needed somebody with professional exposure to grow them into pros. Salary-cap relief still wasn't coming until the 2002–2003 season ended and with the way Jordan was blowing the budget, with gambles on players like Scott that forced Washington to absorb an extra two million to its payroll, the cap might become stuck on permanently.

In considering all options to turn around the Washington Misfits, word of one leaked to the media. A report that first appeared in

Sports Illustrated indicated that Michael was thinking about returning to play. His thinking went something like this: Play for two years. Teach his players how to be mentally tough in the process by getting in their faces at practice every day. Show them the glory and the toughness needed to play every night in front of sold-out arenas against teams gunning for you at all costs. When he won the NBA draft lottery in May of 2001, he had the No. 1 overall pick he could groom to be the centerpiece of the future. Add Vince Carter, Antawn Jamison or another one of the Air Apparents in 2003 and then he might have the foundation of a championship contender. And as this prospect of one more shot registered, Michael realized he hadn't felt a hunger like this since the Bulls trailed Utah by three points with thirty-seven seconds to play.

BREAKING POINTS

1

LOWER YOUR VOICE, RON ARTEST SEEMS TO BE SAYING WITH A MOTION EASILY construed as air dribbling. This is also the universal sign for sit down before anybody else realizes what's going on. Artest fights back a smile that is part Hannibal Lecter, part class clown, knowing history will not treat him like the Pacino character in *Dog Day After-noon* for what he did on that June day last summer. In his third season as a Chicago Bulls guard, the six-foot-seven, tree-trunkish Artest represents much of what many purists believe has gone wrong with the NBA. He is renowned for having a personal staff of nearly forty friends, brothers, cousins, girlfriends and boys from the hood on his payroll. The pop culture of the NBA labels this Artest's entourage, and with the money they're paying even a mediocre player on a bad team can have an entourage. At times, Artest has objected to fouls being called on him by dropping his pants at referees or punching the official scorer's table. Not the scorer, but the fiberglass table in front of him where sponsors hang their advertising signs, furniture hard enough to easily break a hand. Now as he sits hunched over in the Bulls' locker room at the MCI Center on this January night of 2001, Artest has taken on a villainous whisper, as if he's about to tell the story of the latest victim he tied to the railroad tracks.

"We were playing hard," Artest begins.

We included Antoine Walker, Michael Finley, Juwan Howard,

Courtney Alexander, Penny Hardaway. We included a former Bull (Dickey Simpkins), two other current Bulls (A.J. Guyton and Marcus Fizer) and a future Bull (Tyson Chandler) and a former/future Bull (Charles Oakley). And Charles Barkley. Howard likened this pickup play to the games he ran back in the summer of 1995 on the court Michael Jordan had built on that Warner Brothers studio sound-stage. This pickup play had the same purpose as those after-hours games in 1995: To get Michael Jordan back in shape. And Michael Jordan's game back in shape.

"It just happened," Artest continued. "It's what they call incidental contact. He ran into an elbow."

Elbows are rarely incidental in basketball. Not that there are players who don't incidentally use their elbows in an offensive posture. Isiah Thomas once ran into a Bill Cartwright elbow during a Bulls-Pistons game—or the elbow ran into Isiah—which made him angry enough to momentarily turn a basketball game into a Celebrity Death Match. This particular elbow Artest is talking about landed in Michael Jordan's ribs, snapping two of them like twigs.

"It was the first time I ever played against him," Artest added. "It was like, he's my idol, but then we get on the court and it was like, you know, business."

It would be fair to say that when Ron Artest's incidental elbow landed in Michael's ribs that his business plan to remake the Washington Wizards hit a breaking point. It would also be fair to say this one stray elbow alerted Michael that he was now living every day and every game at the breaking point. He had been coming to this pickup basketball venue for the past five months or so, a lavish workout multiplex known as Hoops the Gym in downtown Chicago, about a half-court shot from the United Center. At first Michael wanted to lose the jelly roll, as he called it, around his midsection that began developing when he turned the basketball court at his Highland Park estate into a cigar bar a couple of years ago. At first, he ran with the local talent and called in some business acquaintances who had kicked around college basketball for a couple years. But as he stewed while watching his Wizards muster all of twelve victories by the time the MCI Center was set to host the NBA All-Star Weekend 2001, Michael was making just enough jump shots to hatch the latest Plan to Save the Franchise.

A year ago when he was introduced as Washington's new director of hoops ops, he immediately stated he was not coming back as a player. And three years ago, he was 99.9 percent certain he didn't need to play anymore. Since then, he had achieved one of the foremost goals he set for himself in retirement: to get a pot belly. But he could no longer stomach the hijinx on the court that made Celebrity Lookalikes—the arena activity in which a picture of a famous person like Ron Howard or Bill Clinton is flashed on the Jumbotron scoreboard and a shot of a fan with a remote resemblance is put up alongside—the high point of every Wizards game at MCI Center and made Michael's general managing appear even more comical. Those who would ultimately dog Jordan about putting a team on the floor during the 2001–2002 season that included Courtney Alexander, Tyrone Nesby, Popeye Jones and Hubert Davis as part of its playing rotation were fortunate not to see the Wizards of the previous season. The 2000–2001 edition included two players named Michael Smith, and the way Washington failed to score even ninety points nine times during the first month made it all seem like a bad episode of *Newhart*. So with his team cratering and his general managing rep taking the hit, Michael Jordan read the situation as another in which the 24-second clock had ticked away and everybody was looking at him to make the move. Coming back to play for the Wizards now, he thought, was merely the next step in the process he had invented and lived by all his basketball life. Try to get your teammates involved. Let the game come to you. Set them up to make the big shots. And when they can't, you have to "cover their asses," as he once called his role playing alongside Scottie and Horace. Yes, he could take the next six months to prepare himself for a return to playing status, six months to put himself through a physical and mental obstacle course that would tell Michael if he could hold up for one more encore in the NBA. His preparations would include secret workouts and closed-door scrimmages he hoped would attract some of the old gang from the Warner Bros. lot. He knew rumors of a comeback would eventually leak out, planned for it even, so that all those who might scoff at or dismiss this effort could provide the fuel to push Michael through the six- and seven-hour-per-day regimens he anticipated needing to get ready.

When he started, Michael didn't know what he knows now: that working to get back would be so hard, harder, as it turned out, than trading Juwan Howard. Michael knew he didn't need to recapture maximum elevation to make the Wizards a winner. Get the jumper to semiautomatic, retool the fadeaway in the post to compensate for lost hang time and his mere presence would do the rest. What he didn't plan for, however—what he really couldn't plan for because he never experienced it—was the way a stray elbow to his ribs or a knee-on-knee bump could be so devastating, so debilitating. Artest's shot to Michael's ribs sidelined Jordan during four crucial weeks of prep time and was another sign to the current Bull that the former Bull might not fully regain his Bull stuff.

"Guys were playing good against him so he was talking mess because he had to show them who's the best, who's the greatest," Artest explained. "And he was winning sometimes. But back in the days, he would have won every game. But you know, he's getting older."

Fadeaways and dunks and victories in pickup games and cracks in his foundation meant nothing to Michael. When he started this mission in February of 2001, he knew the next six months would be about losing twenty-five pounds and finding his backpedal. When Michael was at his absolute best, he would fadeaway, listen to the ball swish and begin backpedaling toward his basket, elbows rising to his ears, head bobbing side to side, gum working into a lather, diabolical smile cracking—the NBA's version of the moonwalk. If it was a memorable night, he might even nod to Magic Johnson or Oprah Winfrey sitting courtside. So during this sixth-month crash course,

Michael would be looking for really only one sign that could tell him he was ready to come back.

"Sure, he was limping at first," said George Koehler, one of the few people to see the workouts from start to finish. "He didn't just come down off Mount Olympus. But when he started feeling better, he'd hit that turnaround jumper and get that little backpedal, that cocky spring. Limping less and backpedaling more."

2

THE SUPERMARKET TABLOID WATCH ON MICHAEL'S REPRISE BEGAN IN MID-March when *Sports Illustrated*'s Rick Reilly reported that a source "very close to Jordan said he is 'ninety percent committed' to making a comeback next season with the Washington Wizards." Though Michael will let the will-he-or-won't-he drag out like some bad reality TV series, those in the know can admit that he has already made up his mind. Apparently, he is not worried about the jockarazzi faction of the media again invading his privacy, seeking out his close friends and confidants for comment. Apparently, he is not concerned that his temptation might upstage an impending NBA playoff season that promises more drama than *Survivor* for the first time since that jump shot in Salt Lake City. What he dreads is no reaction, days in the Chicago summer when even though the Cubs and White Sox were so bad that they could have used Michael Jordan in left field, just two reporters are staking out Hoops the Gym to break a new comeback rumor. He might have been more worried about this than anybody ever knew, reportedly having one member of his entourage leave a voice mail for a Chicago sportswriter in early June, 2001, with the message, "Hoops the Gym. Tomorrow. Noon."

The so-called sources are reacting as if Michael was already back. Standing in the middle of his own man-against-time encore, Mario Lemieux bypassed any ifs and buts regarding Jordan. They first conversed about this in September of 1999 when they walked the Brookline Country Club golf course in Massachusetts watching the Ryder Cup matches. In leading his Pittsburgh Penguins to the brink of the Stanley Cup Finals, Lemieux addressed a minor media gaggle one morning before the Eastern Conference Finals in New Jersey by saying he had indeed discussed with Michael some ideas for getting back into shape and measuring playing time and that Jordan had called looking for some tips on how Mario managed the chaos surrounding the comeback.

Phil Jackson said he believed Michael was working out with the only purpose being a full intent to return to playing. Word coming from one of Michael's new celebrity friends/golfing buddies was less specific. Tiger Woods reportedly just winked and smiled when asked about Jordan's return. Michael's agent, David Falk, provided a similar confirmation by vehemently denying there was any truth to this story. As one columnist wrote about this, "If Falk says it's a beautiful day, I'm leaving home with an umbrella." As for any suspense, well, Michael's boss seemed to put that to an end less than a month following the Reilly rumors. "The odds are he's going to come back," said Wizards owner Abe Pollin.

If Michael needed confirmation that his comeback would maintain his national icon status, the way rumors of his reprise were greatly exaggerated must have been fortifying. Reports of every comeback development seemed to roll like the crawl across the bottom of the television screen that comes with watching CNN: . . . Jordan says he is not wavering from his initial position: "If I had to answer today, I'm 99.9 percent sure I won't play again." . . . Jordan says his jump shot has regained its form and that his legs have to catch up . . . Former Bulls center Bill Wennington runs pickup games with Mike, tells *Chicago Sun-Times* that Michael is not his old self . . . Surest sign of return yet: Jordan says his refrigerator is covered with published reports saying he can't or shouldn't return . . . Jordan seen hooping it up at Scottsdale, Arizona health club; employee tells *Sports Illustrated* Michael looks like he's twenty-five-years old . . . Charles Barkley will join Jordan in playing for the Wizards . . . Increased security ordered for NBA's Boston Summer League; Wizards spokesman says it's conceivable Michael could begin his comeback there . . .

When his six-hours-per-day workouts—sometimes more, sometimes less—ended, Michael would hang around Hoops the Gym smiling, laughing, very much content but very much considering the pros and cons his comeback had generated. At first, the training was not as much about getting his legs—he knew that would come with time—as it was getting past the doubts. For the 2001–2002 season, the NBA Rules Committee made a change to allow zone defense, vacating the man-to-man-only policy that had been in effect since the early 1970s. When he last played, the rules allowed that Michael would have to deal with one, two or three defenders only when he had the ball. A rules change would allow defenses to double him without the ball, perhaps exploiting the loss of mobility that naturally comes when you hit thirty-eight years old. He didn't worry so much about the repeated comments making the rounds like the one that former Lakers adversary and current New Jersey Nets coach Byron Scott submitted. "Some guys have to get other vices in their life to take the place of this life," Scott analyzed. "This is a drug. Some guys find it very, very tough to give it up." Michael had no problem with that. It was a drug, a vice and the thought of never, ever getting to experience that moment of rising over Bryon Russell to hit the ultimate game-winner no doubt burned inside Michael, pushing him to keep on limping. What ultimately pushed him was continued talk of how even if the old Jordan reappeared, the best he could hope for was carrying his sorry bunch of Wizards to little more than being a first-round playoff sacrifice and that he couldn't handle losing in the playoffs. To this Michael replied with more affirmation that these six-hour days were not about losing the jelly roll.

"Who says I'd lose?" he shot back.

Certainly not Allen Iverson, Vince Carter, Ray Allen, Paul Pierce, Baron Davis or any of the other players who might have to deal with Michael Jordan in the playoffs. Milwaukee, Toronto, Charlotte and every other team didn't have what Jordan had, what he was going to bring to the Wizards—the single greatest obsession with winning and anything it takes to do so in the history of sports.

And that's exactly what worried David Stern. The NBA commissioner knew the theater of Michael Jordan would boost the league's sagging television ratings and be a bargaining chip in negotiating the new network contract, which Stern would have to do during the 2001–2002 season. But Stern also knew the NBA had to get past the Michael Jordan Era. When Michael made his first comeback, the league had maybe Grant Hill and a too-young-and-selfish Shaquille O'Neal to put on its marquee. But now, Shaq had matured and Vince, Kobe and Iverson were legitimate pop icons. The league had already begun transitioning away from Michael's star power, and Stern worried about how a Jordan return could stunt that growth. Such talk became more frequent. Some of the league's young stars started to express resentment that Jordan's comeback was upstaging the 2001 playoffs. Deputy Commissioner Russ Granik said that with television ratings for those playoffs nose-diving from a decline the previous year, there was a definite impression that Jordan was coming back to save the league.

The NBA propaganda machine was already revving up to create a subplot of the comeback pitting Michael against the rising stars. But clearly there were those in and around the NBA office thinking that a Third Coming would make him bigger than the game. Some officials privately wondered if as a player/president of basketball operations whether Jordan could stand back during a free-throw attempt and whisper to a soon-to-be-free-agent from the opposing team an offer to come fly with him. Though nobody wanted to put his name to this conjecture, a report did surface detailing Michael's opportunity to set up his own version of the vaunted Triangle: His return would force him to divest his ownership interest, but he still wielded the decision-making power. Falk controlled many of the top players, enough of a concern that he supposedly had to fend off accusations of steering clients away from the post-champion Bulls at Michael's request. And on the court Jordan would show how he could play the best setup man since Magic. For sure, some were doubting this was merely an itch Michael had to scratch.

3

BEFORE THE RIB STICKING, THOSE WHO WERE RUNNING WITH MICHAEL described his game as untouchable. His legs had spring. The shot had a laserlike efficiency. Whatever degrees he had lost on his vertical jump, he added to his peripheral vision and his passes now had a certain Magic-al element. Following a month off to let his ribs baste and another two weeks to work his annual summer basketball camps, it was back to Hoops the Gym and game on again. In one of those games on this particular afternoon in August of 2001, Michael's team was trailing, nine to eight, when he worked over Antoine Walker for the tying hoop. Now, it's next basket wins. Walker, who grew up a few blocks from this gym idolizing Michael, lets Michael know what is waiting a few months from now. He brandishes a series of fakes and knowing Jordan's ego will call off any help defense so this can be a vintage one-on-one. Walker has three inches more in height and thirteen years less in legs on Jordan and uses every bit of that edge to power over Michael for the game-winning dunk.

"We just went back and forth," Walker explained of these pickup games that made up what became known as Camp Comeback. "I would score on him. He would score on me. I'd try to stop him. What we did, we had a competition saying who can win the most games. So every day one of us would say, 'I got five wins. I got four wins.' So we just made it like that and made it real competitive." Michael is now a month away from publicly putting all the speculation to rest, but as Marcus Fizer, another of the Comeback campers, related several weeks after the fact, "Before he ever announced it, we all knew." And like so many others, Fizer knew this because why else would Jordan be here dueling with Walker, working to rebuild the most important part of his game? As Walker crouched and stared at Michael in his pouncing-tiger stance, the former Jordan apprentice turned sparring partner saw the sweat dripping off the bald dome, the gum snapping, the competitive edge returning like it had just come out of a nearby phone booth.

Except for the cracked ribs, the plan had unfolded almost exactly as Michael conceived it that winter of 2001, maybe even before then. Looking back, the course of events leading to Michael's return seems almost too random. Take it from Fizer and Walker and the others on the inside who said they knew all along. Of all of Jordan's talents, George Koehler frequently points out that people tend to overlook how smart Michael is. "Brilliant," George corrects. Although he can name every state capital, Michael's is not the brilliance of book smarts. And it's more than his renowned basketball IQ. Jordan just may have been conniving enough to orchestrate each step of this return. He knew he would need four, maybe five months to get the game back on his fingertips. In the meantime, he would rid the Wizards of their losing culture. After finally trading Howard, he waived the forever disgruntled Strickland. In May he wiped out the mistake of hiring Leonard Hamilton as coach by replacing him with Doug Collins. If Michael was going to play again, he had to have a coach who knew how he could fit into the remake, who would understand how to build around Jordan, who wouldn't mind playing the subservient role when Michael asked, yet was strong enough to keep a young bunch disciplined. Hadn't Collins done that previously with Jordan? With Doug coaching him from 1986–89, Jordan won his first playoff series, hit the Shot—the first one—against Cleveland and made his first conference finals. After Chicago fired him following the 1989 season, Collins pulled off the kind of job Michael was currently looking for when he built a fifty-win team and a playoff qualifier around Grant Hill in Detroit in 1997.

After seeing the mess that Hamilton created, Jordan made only one telephone call to find a new coach. And Collins, who had forged a critically acclaimed career as the lead analyst for NBC's NBA tele-casts, related that there was only one call that would bring him back to coaching. Collins had a kinship to Jordan not many people bothered to consider. Before seven knee surgeries defeated him, Collins was Jordan, perhaps the most competitive player of his era and one who had lived the pressure Michael felt every night. In the 1972 Olympic gold medal basketball game against the Soviet Union, it was Collins who hit what many have called the two most pressure-packed free throws in the history of the sport to give the United States a one-point lead with three seconds left and set up that controversial ending that allowed the Russians to steal the victory. Jordan's heart will prob-ably always belong to Phil Jackson, but Collins understood him best.

Coaching irritation relieved, personnel situation healing, back spasms gone and cracked ribs mended, Michael's crash course back to the NBA continued with Camp Comeback. Michael set this up for the last two weeks of August and first week of September to do more than check his physical state. He knew the success of the comeback would be a test of his mettle, his legendary will, the one that led to his "competition problem." And his comeback problem. During Camp Comeback, Michael repeatedly evoked the story of the 1991 U.S. Open, when thirty-nine-year old Jimmy Connors fashioned an inex-plicable run to the semifinals, a run that included back-to-back, five-set victories. This is what Michael hoped to regain, this is what he was going to give to his Wizards. The edge that makes Tiger Woods so tough on the back nine on the final day of the Masters or Roger Clemens able to blow fastballs past hitters at thirty-nine years old or Jerry Rice faster in the NFL playoffs than defensive backs ten years younger needed Antoine Walker and a roster of other NBAers to be banged into shape. Hence, Michael put together Camp Comeback, an invitation-only series of pickup games that would generate NBA-caliber intensity. And challenges.

Michael had sent word-of-mouth invitations to Vince and Kobe and Iverson to come as well as Tracy McGrady, Chris Webber, Gary Payton, Tim Duncan, Ray Allen and Kevin Garnett. In the end, the big names in camp turned out to be Walker, Michael Finley, fellow North Carolina maestro Jerry Stackhouse, who by now apparently had learned his loyalty, Hardaways Penny and Tim, and Tyson Chandler, the second pick in the 2001 NBA draft. The rest of the guest list included Michael's friends in the league, like Oakley, and players with ties to Chicago or the Bulls. As for the missing persons, some speculated that the young stars were making a statement on Jordan's comeback by not showing. Another thought submitted that they might not be too anxious to help Michael get ready. Jordan made his own statement about the comeback when he looked at the missing persons report and told the *Chicago Sun-Times*, "They are certainly invited to come and play if they love the game of basketball as much as I do."

Camp Comeback commenced with fifteen players engaging in pickup sessions that reached three hours on some days. This was enough time to run about ten pickup games, the kind where each basket counts as one point, no free throws, first team to ten wins and the winners stay on the court. Jordan's only rule insisted that the doors remained locked to all but the players and security guards and nobody was allowed to relate any of the specifics about what went on inside.

To provide an audible perspective on what transpired, listen to Artest, who six months afterward broke the cone of silence by saying, "I hadn't really played in a lot of games like that." This from a man who had been in the NBA for two years, albeit two years with the post-Mike Bulls. In his third season, Artest became known as one of the league's tougher defenders, a craft he said he learned at Camp Comeback from trying to lock down Jordan and watching Michael defend others. "I was doing what he was doing," Artest elaborated. "Same thing he was doing to other people, I was doing to him." While Walker said Jordan was "in a groove right now like never before," it was never quite that good. In one game, Fizer, a former fourth overall pick in the draft who averaged 9.5 points per game for the lowly Bulls in his rookie season of 2000–01, said he dunked over

Jordan for a game-winning point, adding that Michael's attempt to slap the ball from his hands felt like nothing more than a tap on the wrist and did nothing more to stop him.

If every game was going to become a High Noon, Michael figured that would only be like every night of the Comeback Tour. Artest could see Jordan getting ready for that aspect of the return. "He'd shoot the ball, and before it would go in, he'd say, 'Game over,'" Artest remembered. "Somebody was playing good against him, he'd be talking mess. We're still talking mess about those games." Make no mistake, part of regaining that competitive edge was talking the good game, the weapon that made Michael an intimidator as much as a dominator. The fire, the touch, the confidence had all returned, but Michael still needed to send up one more sign to tell the group he was really back. Every one of these sessions was pretty much the same. Michael played a lot at point guard to show some of the fancy passing that he hoped would be a productive part of the Wizards' improvement. By the third or fourth game, he might not have enough on the accelerator to catch Penny Hardaway rising over him for a game-winning jumper, but he would return the favor in the next game. And then would come that one game when Michael felt it. His team would go up 7-4 or 8-4 and he would find Penny hugging his hip as Michael posted up on him. A couple of pushes knocks Penny off his center of gravity. Michael spins, falls away, hits and there is the sign: He backpedals away. As Rick Telander wrote in *ESPN Magazine* after being one of the few outsiders allowed to witness one of these moments at Camp Comeback, "Suddenly, there's hope."

For Tim Grover, Jordan's longtime personal training master, the bounce in MJ's game was the latest Michael Miracle. Grover said he never expected Jordan to return from the broken ribs, calling the four missed weeks crucial and pointing out there was still so much to do in so little time. Michael's unprecedented will to push and push and push—himself, teammates, the Jazz—threatened, however, to become his downfall. Trying to make up for the lost time sanded

Michael to the breaking point again, and this time his left knee began a cry to stop, making the sound of loose change rattling. One week into Camp Comeback, Jordan dragged a noticeable limp around the court. He called it tendonitis, an irritant like walking around with a pebble in your shoe. He would eventually realize that tendonitis goes and comes back again like a mosquito buzzing your ear at twilight, leaving temporary relief but false comfort well beyond Camp. At the same time his knee creaked, he responded to a question from *Chicago Sun-Times* columnist Jay Mariotti asking Michael to rank his game on a scale of one to ten, with ten being NBA Most Valuable Player caliber, by saying, "Six." He upgraded that to a seven a week later. Two weeks into this boot camp he clears up what minuscule doubt remains by saying, "I'm still out here playing, aren't I?" He has prepped his game like cramming for a final exam, but as Camp Comeback gives way to the Comeback Tour, Michael says he's still waiting for the light to go on.

4

SUBLIMINALLY SPEAKING, CAMP COMEBACK MIGHT ALSO HAVE PREPARED JOR-dan for Wizards training camp in ways he never fathomed. Though very few people actually got inside Hoops the Gym for an in-depth look, word spread that Michael was having days when he'd lose all the games he played. One report even had Jordan losing ten straight to a team of Finley, the Hardaways, Charles Oakley and future Wizard Bobby Simmons. Although Michael never confirmed or denied taking such a beating, asking only who said that, whispers around the gym joked that losing in big numbers here would only help Michael prepare for life with his new teammates. Actually, Michael was getting practice at something he was never very good at with the Bulls and something he would need once he returned to the court with Washington. Supposedly, Jordan was showing patience with his teammates, patience to help a player like Jamal Crawford, a twenty-one-year-old point guard with the Bulls, work on some basic skills.

According to one report, Jordan and Crawford teamed together for a serious winning streak one summer day, a confirmation to Michael that his leading by example really could have an impact on younger players. Crawford thought so, too, telling *Sports Illustrated*, "Even when he was playing, his shirt was always tucked in perfectly. I came into the gym one time at 6:30 in the morning and he was already there. The thing he kept telling me was just to be simple. Be basic."

When the Wizards arrived in Wilmington, North Carolina for training camp on October 2—eight months or so after he started down this path—the more patient, mentorial incarnation of Michael showed up as well. Though Michael never said so, some speculated that he felt Wizards owner Abe Pollin had limited his basketball operations authority, and only now, on the training camp court, was Jordan taking full charge of the team. Mostly, he did this by example. Training camp usually includes two-a-day practices, and Doug Collins had designed this one so Michael would only have to endure one workout per day. Apparently, it was never too soon to begin preserving Jordan's knees and legs for the long run of the regular season and the playoffs, as the plan called for right now.

But from the first day, Michael ran in both practices. He took time out to pull players aside, making subtle points on the most basic of fundamentals. He was excessively hard on rookie Kwame Brown, Michael's handpicked first selection in the 2001 draft. Jordan was going to build Kwame in his own image. When the rookie challenged Jordan in a one-on-one and raised the old man's fire, Jordan finished the game by destroying Brown, reportedly calling him a faggot and a pussy and trying to let the rookie know that he was missing a toughness that is the foundation of talent and trash talk in the NBA. This was the beginning of a season-long pledging, the maturation Michael thought his protégé missed by not going to college, where at places like Carolina they make plebes carry the video recorder on the road and handle the upperclassmen's baggage. If there was any doubt among the Wizards, they knew now Jordan's return was serious business.

The part of Michael's previous NBA life that also returned with the first day of training camp was the one he so gladly left behind with his last retirement. The first day of training camp drew a media mass of three hundred reporters holding pads, microphones and cameras to Wilmington. Because practice was kept behind closed doors for all but twenty minutes per day, some reporters tried interviewing maintenance people called in to clean the court during practice to get an update on Jordan. The house at 4647 Gordon Street in Wilmington received "Lifestyles of the Rich and Famous" attention with the current owners coming out on the front lawn to tell the story of how they bought the residence from James and Deloris Jordan. Wes Unseld seemed to finally be authorized to speak for Jordan when he came out after the first practice and revealed to the media, "Like everyone else, Michael sweated." For his first training camp media feeding, Jordan stood behind a makeshift barrier of several folding chairs to answer questions. If he accomplished nothing else in this return, Michael appeared determined to limit his availability to the press and here he started a pattern of waiting up to forty minutes after he was done practicing or playing to grant five to ten minutes of questions and answers.

Training camp went on like this for a week before the Wizards would break to play their first preseason game in Detroit. Michael's teammates raved about his passing. Kwame said he didn't have much time to notice Jordan because he was too worried about getting yelled at. But by the end of the week Michael was spending more and more of practice sitting on the sidelines with ice wrapped around his knees. Collins confessed his concern to assistant Johnny Bach and admitted the hardest part of this training would be getting Michael to realize he was not the McNugget-eating twenty-five year old anymore. In his own military vernacular, Bach, the ex-marine, said that the key to getting Michael through the season would be protecting him against his competitive urges. But that light never went on, and after one week, that approach was apparently failing. The first week of training camp left the feeling that the coming season would never ease up on Michael, that the season would be much like every afternoon of Camp Comeback, when he had to fight through cycles of what one reporter describes as bad days and better days.

Nine days after training camp began, Washington played its first preseason game against the Pistons. The world, at least, had these eight preseason games to measure whether Michael Jordan was again going to be the marquee name in the NBA. Not surprisingly, it didn't take even one game to find out. Collins and Jordan figured Michael's knees could use a few nights off, so they decided he wouldn't play this game at Detroit or one two nights later at Miami. Then, Russ Granik, whose deputy commissioner role was becoming more and more a job of being David Stern's bad cop, called to lobby Michael to reconsider. The Pistons has sold more than twenty thousand tickets to this game after drawing just twenty-nine hundred in their preseason opener. Granik insisted Michael play, that the fans needed this night, that America needed this night just one month removed from the disaster of September 11. President Bush was to make a speech that night about the attacks in Afghanistan that had begun a little more than a week ago, a speech that would be televised to the fans at the Palace of Auburn Hills during this game.

Pregame had never been like this for Michael. It had always been a regimen, detailed to the four hours before the game when he would eat his steak-and-eggs and the process of putting on his North Carolina shorts underneath his uniform pants. But in the moments before tipoff, Jordan now exhibits a nervousness he has rarely shown. He is not consumed with his performance tonight. There will be plenty of time to come and drop fifty on somebody. For the first time ever, he will not wear a Bulls uniform in an NBA game, not counting the hideous conference togs players were forced to wear in the All-Star Game ten years ago. He can't quite bring himself to dress out. He wiggles into the pants, but when he pulls on the jersey he can sense the night of passage. As one media observer submits after this game: He's still Michael Jordan, just not *the* Michael Jordan.

When he stepped onto the court, he was greeted by the theme song from the 1970s television show *Welcome Back, Kotter* and

Michael pretty much played like a child of the 70s and at the pace of a thirty-eight-year-old man. He started the game by snuffing Ben Wallace's layup attempt with a block from behind. He missed his first shot, a three-point attempt, then hit four of the next seven. In his point-guard role, he was called for palming the ball—a rookie call which he said he deserved because right now he's a rookie—and in the most telling moment of the night, he grabbed an alley-oop pass from Courtney Alexander and instead of announcing his presence with the authority of some Airobatic slam, he softly laid the ball in the basket. *Welcome Back, Welcome Back, Welcome Back.*

"Maybe in two weeks it will be different," Jordan said afterward more about the alley-oop than the rest of his game. It is already different. President Bush gets a heartier round of applause than Michael on this night. The last time that happened, Nixon was in office. And in expounding on the low-altitude alley-oop, Michael asserts not to expect the tomahawk jam or any touching of the top of the backboard. "It might be a more gentle dunk," he says. Among the reviews afterward come a couple more revealing observations. The media mass has grown from two outside Hoops the Gym in August to more than three hundred in Detroit. And how much of his former game Michael actually retrieves might never be known as long as he continues to play with the Bad News Bears of the NBA, as the Wizards have been called on this night.

Still, the preseason provides more of a guide to the Comeback Tour than anybody really recognizes at this point. On nights when his critics or his opponents or both have thrown down a challenge and if his knees are up to it, Michael will be that Michael Jordan. Two nights later in Miami, he cut his playing time from seventeen to twelve minutes, but it was a vintage in-your-face twelve minutes. Preying on Heat novices Rodney Buford and Ricky Davis, Michael hit six of his first seven shots on a variety of mid-range pull-up jumpers, shots off the dribble and fadeaways. He scored eighteen points on seven-for-eleven shooting and was on the runway to his first dunk when Miami's Sam Mack grabbed Michael as he took off.

The Wizards' first win with Jordan is a twenty-point rout and in the end Michael is answering the question—or the challenge—by saying, "I wouldn't have come back if I didn't feel I was capable of playing like I played in the first quarter." Miami coach Pat Riley seconds Michael's emotion after seeing the Jordan backpedal again and pays proper homage by noting that when the Heat sees the Wizards for real on November 30, "we will double-team Michael."

Jordan may have lost a step, but he had not lost the Air for the dramatic. Washington came home for its fourth preseason game, its only one at the MCI Center. New Jersey was in town, working on its own plan to break out of the same quagmire that had trapped the Wizards the past few years. The last time the Nets had any success was in 1998, when Michael and the Bulls swept them out of the first round of the playoffs. Ironically, tonight the Nets, who will become the most illustrious comeback story of this season when they make the NBA Finals, get the first look at Jordan circa 1998. He scores forty-one points, including sixteen during a breathtaking six-minute stretch of the third quarter. Seven points into this scoring soliloquy, Michael nets a spectacular nineteen-foot fallaway from the corner as New Jersey rookie Richard Jefferson knocks Jordan into a backward somersault. He finishes the frenzy by hitting a pair of three-point shots and before that he blows past Jefferson for the moment the world had been waiting to see. His first dunk left the rim rocking and the crowd doing likewise over the possibilities of what might be for Washington this season. If only this night didn't have so much to bring everything down. With Michael soaring and scoring, the Wizards outplayed New Jersey by a 82-57 count. The fifteen minutes without him in the game enabled the Nets to win 102-95. Do the math. With Michael on the bench, the Wizards were outscored 45-17. The Wizards were on the verge of becoming the Bulls circa 1987, when even Michael's repeated forty- and fifty-point nights couldn't guarantee victory.

To execute the plan that spawned the Comeback Tour, Jordan will have to recapture the most important component of his previous incarnation. Coming through when the team most desperately needed him, delivering some of those Michael Miracles could be special sauce for Washington. If the team can get him to those fourth-quarter moments, he can supply the rescue operations and fulfill his goal of showing them how to win. They would need many more nights like October 23, a return match with the Nets in Greenville, South Carolina. Michael struggled to hit ten of twenty-three shots in the game, but with the Nets threatening to send Washington to its fifth defeat in six games Jordan pushed the Wizards' lead to 94-90 by hitting an eighteen-foot jumper with two minutes, forty-two seconds left. Thirty-four seconds later he scored over Jason Kidd and with fifty-three seconds to play, Michael hit one last shot that secured the 105-92 victory.

The Wizards, however, had just played their fourth game in six nights. Two nights later, Michael would find himself mano-a-mano with Vince Carter in Toronto. Jordan would eventually score 135 points in 158 minutes played of the preseason, but the question now was how long he could hold up under that kind of duress. Clearly, it wasn't the years at this point, but the mileage. Michael's parts were already breaking down. As Vince made this battle personal by scoring thirty-one points—eighteen in the first quarter—while forcing his counterpart into five-for-seventeen shooting, Michael found himself squaring off one-on-one with reality. If the Wizards could somehow find a way to avoid breaking down without having to rely on Michael so heavily, if he could keep his knees from breaking down, there would be hope. But when Michael spent the morning of the opening-night game against the Knicks in Madison Square Garden wincing, his knees wrapped in ice, leading to the postgame lamenting of how he did not come through when his teammates delivered him to the verge of victory, well, suddenly, maybe there wasn't so much hope.

A SHOT IN THE DARK

1

THEY HAVE COME TO CALLING HIM FAIR JORDAN AND THE WASHINGTON Wheezer. And with good reason. What's for sure is that nearly one month into the season, nobody calls Michael Jordan the greatest player in the game anymore. They are still coming from as far as one hundred miles away and paying seven hundred and fifty dollars to sit courtside for one last glimpse. But they see him bending over a lot, hanging on to the bottom of his shorts for support, as if rare air now refers to the battle Michael faces each night to catch his breath. At the outset of a game in Cleveland less than a month into the season, Jordan leaps for an alley-oop pass from Richard Hamilton and generates just enough hang time to bounce the ball off the bottom of the rim. His game has come to rely on fooling a defender into going for the yo-yo fake, and he is struggling to get his shooting within the same area code as his career-long personal standard of fifty percent. He has even used the words "no confidence" and "confused" when talking about his play through the first month of real games.

Now, with the Wizards sleepwalking through an eight-game losing streak, the question is no longer why, but whether Michael Jordan still can. This skid is about twice as long as any Michael has lived through since he lost his hair, so pitiful that in a few days Doug Collins will joke, "if we go undefeated the rest of the season we can match the 72-10 Bulls." One of the musings about his performance becoming more and more frequent concludes that he is still Michael Jordan, just not *that* Michael Jordan. The losing, the lack of altitude in his game and the sudden uncertainty of the comeback triple teams Michael when he holds the ball with fifty-six seconds to play in this Thanksgiving weekend game against Boston at the MCI Center. The Wizards have all but blown a fifteen-point fourth-quarter lead, have scored one basket in the past five minutes and forty-two seconds and are hanging on to a three-point lead. Michael hovers over his dribble at the top of the key, tongue wagging in what used to be the universal sign that he was winding up to the fourth or fifth gear—you know, the last one—that made his out-of-control will so unstoppable in these situations.

Right about now, Michael Jordan would also be feeling extra drive from remembering the night three weeks ago when the Celtics' Paul Pierce blocked Michael's shot in the last minute to steal a victory from Washington. "That" Michael Jordan would, anyway. He steps quickly into his move, knowing that his aching left knee has one, maybe two pushes, and shot puts a one-legged sixteen footer. "All leather," Pierce will eventually boast to his teammates, the pickup talk for a blocked shot that leaves the blocking hand vibrating with the sting of a spanking. He finishes ass-whipping Michael with a three-point shot that ties the game with fifty seconds to play. At this moment, the Michael Jordan of *ESPN Classic* surely will rise, *that* Michael Jordan, who knows the precious quirk time and age can't touch is the obstinance that will ignite this comeback or send it crashing and burning. Misses by Hamilton and Pierce allow the drama to rewind to an appropriate pitch, and once again Michael has the ball with twenty-two seconds to play and the look of a younger man, if not the legs. He squares up against Pierce, shaking his head like a father warning his child not to climb to the next level of the jungle gym. Not this time, Paul. If only all the eight-for-eighteen nights and fourth-quarter fades weren't weighing Michael down. When the clock hits five, he backs Pierce into the lane, fumbles the ball then rushes a fadeaway that bangs hard off the back rim. In the last minute of overtime, Michael misses another jump shot then turns the ball over with the Wizards leading by two points. Eventually, Washington needs Christian Laettner—the anti-Jordan if there ever was one—to hit the difference maker with eight seconds left. Hamilton then makes the heroic defensive play of the 88-84 victory, and music blares from the Wizards' locker room afterward like David Stern is coming in to award some trophies.

As Michael dresses in an adjacent room hiding from the media inquisition, he knows he cannot hide the truth. He played forty-five of a possible fifty minutes and he feels the pain. "Especially toward the end of the game," he explains. "I mean I just didn't have the legs, the lift. You know, at the end of the game when everyone stopped to look to me to carry the load." He will take maybe forty minutes to get dressed and wait before meeting the press because he hears the whispers coming from the other room. Some are even coming from his teammates. The tread marks of his stranglehold on the game are now so faded. Even the simple drive to the basket, the blow-by some name on a uniform now gets stalled by somebody named Quincy Lewis. The punch line to all these questions was whether going to the hole for Michael has become like hitting the Class AA curveball back in Birmingham in '94.

Perhaps he can stomach the numbers of futility: five-for-twenty-six shooting one night; a game without attempting a single free throw another; two made three-point shots in sixteen attempts and a whole lot more that don't even come close. But he probably can't swallow them without choking on his pride. Nearly a month ago, he said we would be seeing things similar to what we're used to soon, but soon has come and gone. The public is used to hearing confidence and humility from Michael, but now he is slipping into excuses, comfort-zone rationalizations like, "I can't find the rhythm," or "I need to get my teammates to be a threat," or "I'm trying to move the ball ahead of the double team." What really hurts, though, is that because of the way fans have lined up outside the team bus or trolled the team hotel on the road looking for his autograph, the memorable moments now come in the parking lot rather than on the court. The comeback has turned into a barnstorming exhibition tour. And the whispers are calling Michael's team the Washington Generals. In his previous go-rounds, opposing players blocked Michael's shot, complained about how he got all the calls, scored on him and occasionally even dunked over him. But they never mocked him, not without fear anyway. And except for rare moments like the second game of the season when Michael's presence forced Atlanta center Nazr Mohammed to pump fake away the twenty-four seconds of the shot clock with Michael hovering over his layup attempt, Jordan is inspiring little fear. Even guys named Quincy Lewis are driving past Mike for career highs like the twenty points Lewis put up two weeks into the comeback.

Doug Collins knows where this is heading. Pretty much saw it back in 1988 when the Pistons unleashed those Jordan Rules and Michael played right into their hands, figuring he could beat that triangle defense all by himself. The same ego has overcome Jordan again. He figures he can beat this current barrier by continuing to move, continuing to shoot, continuing to look for that beeline left to the baseline jumper or that spin-out-of-the-post stepback jack that all opponents now know is coming and makes his teammates seem like supers in an opera. But age is as stubborn as Dennis Rodman, more so, and the harder he tries, the more Michael resorts to his quest-quest-quest-until-conquer mentality. As he falls into a thirty-for-eighty-two shooting black hole five, six, seven games in, he shoots more. After a loss to Golden State, he admits shooting on nearly every possession of the third quarter as if this is only a matter of re-calibrating his radar. Collins knows Michael must back off, that the forty minutes and more he is playing each night to recondition his game is wearing on him like an engine racing one hundred miles per hour with no oil. He will snap before he hits fifth gear, and pregame rituals of wearing ice on his knees and electrical stimulation on his wrist to ease tendonitis in both joints confirm that age has become as troubling as Paul Pierce.

Pierce represents the generation gap between this coming and the first two. Pierce's defensive machismo might have previously earned him a place in an elite fraternity. Joe Dumars, Rolando Blackman, Jeff Malone, John Starks and Kevin Johnson on their best nights, these are the brothers of the royal order of Jordan Stoppers, as Michael always called them. But in 2001, there are just too many to think that Jordan stopping denotes elite status anymore. Al Harrington, Antawn Jamison, Bob Sura, Matt Harpring, Jon Barry, Desmond Mason—some players who were in nursery school when Michael dropped his first fifty on the NBA; others who are just names on uniforms—have proven to be stoppers already this season.

What's more, the league apparently has developed some stop signs for Michael, a new set of Jordan Rules. According to a report in the *Washington Post*, two scouts have game plans for Michael that spotlight attack points to exploit his weaknesses. Make him work to get the ball so he will tire late in the game. Play "bigs," as centers and tall forwards are known, on him to exploit the dwindling vertical leap and the lack of confidence and quickness in driving to the basket. Finally, don't go for the shot fake; stay on the ground until he jumps. In other words, have no fear. That these reports evoke nothing from the Jordan Rules of the last decade, nothing about double-teaming Michael, or triple-teaming him, can be construed as a blow to his manhood.

Jordan, of course, can spin-doctor this into acceptance. Magic Johnson reminded Michael that his conditioning might not return until two or three months into the comeback, so he conjectures that when his legs come back so too will his shot. Or he hopes. And with a crying need to keep the Wizards from slipping back into their chronic losing psyche, Michael and Doug admit that they can't button down the playing time when they have a chance to win. And they have been in all but one game through the first month. Buried under Michael's toe-stubs, however, is a growing feeling that the mission is failing. The world wants Jordan to dunk and cover and be the fourth-quarter miracle worker again. So does his ego. The long-term goal of the comeback is tutoring the Wizards with the paint-by-Jordan method, but for most of these games the teammates have been extras, standing around and watching, not sure where to move or what to do. Or too scared to. Hamilton, Alexander, Nesby, even the rookie Brown take turns being moved in and out of the starting lineup, having blown chances in the public's perception to take advantage of Jordan's gravy train. Only Laettner has realized a consistent contribution, which back in the locker room translates to Michael not trusting the rest of the Wiz kids.

Johnny Bach says not to worry, not yet. He is here to help Collins and Jordan Yoda this team into becoming warriors. His forty-nine years as an assistant and head coach have taught Bach that no team becomes a good team until after its tenth loss. Still, Bach submits that early on Michael might have "intimidated his teammates with his competitive spirit," and that the locker room is "devoid of the trust that makes you feel like somebody will always pick up your man if you get picked off." Michael has felt it, too, wondering early in the season if his teammates still view him only as the boss who negotiated their contracts. He says, "I trust them as long as they feel the passion and dedication." But others aren't so sure.

After the Wizards win their first game in Atlanta when point guard Chris Whitney hits a clinching shot, Hamilton frets, "There are other guys in this locker room that can play, too." Former coach Gar Heard tells *The Washington Post* what many have been whispering about Michael's presence: It is stunting the growth of players like Hamilton and Alexander, who follows up his Rookie of the Month play the previous April by averaging five points per game in November. In his own words, Alexander observes, "Until we get on the same page, it's going to be tough." When Popeye Jones, the veteran voice of reason in the Wizards' locker room, concludes, "Nobody says it's going to be easy," he knows there is a lot more to overcome right now than Paul Pierce.

2

WHAT MICHAEL JORDAN LOVES ABOUT THE NBA, LOVES ABOUT HIS LIFE PROBably, is that another game is always coming, like it's blackjack and all he ever needs is to say "Hit me." Two nights after his opening-act failure at Madison Square Garden, Michael and the Wizards take Atlanta. He has walked into a time warp here. Michael's last trip to town drew a record crowd of more than sixty-two thousand to the Georgia Dome on March 27, 1998. The Atlanta Hawks have since moved to their new arena and tonight another record crowd has gathered. Michael has drawn more groupies than Shaq and Kobe on their last visit here, and the street value for the lowest-priced ticket reportedly is seventy dollars. They have come to see the vintage Michael Jordan and tonight he nearly plays like one of those Ultimate Jordan DVDs you can rent at Blockbuster. Less than six minutes into the first quarter, Michael is playing to wipe out the Garden failure, pounding his dribble as if he's winding himself up like the rubber band on one of those toy Styrofoam airplanes. He raises the ball high, squeezing it to look like a Nerf ball, then swoops in for a throw-down dunk. He makes five of his first six shots and scores eleven points in the first quarter. Phillips Arena is buzzing with people who crow about only having had to pay seventy bucks to see this. SportsCenter is salivating. The comeback trail will fix on these moments: quarters, parts of quarters, single plays when Michael kindles just enough belief that he can return to those thrilling days that otherwise will feel like so long ago. It will be like a weekend hacker's round of golf in which one good shot keeps you coming back for another hole. And another. And another.

This second night of the season finds Michael Bullish on his game. He adds to the eleven-point first quarter by finishing the first half with nineteen, then, as if he were back in Chicago playing the Pistons in the Eastern Conference Finals, bursts into a locker room tirade at halftime, blasting his teammates about not feeding off his passion and trailing by four points. "I want to win so bad," he explains, "that at times I'm going to say something so the guys understand what this is all about . . . and they're going to have to lay it on the line every minute."

The Wizards recover, and with less than a minute to play are protecting a four-point lead. Michael goes baseline, loading up for the shot to ice the game, the one he missed two nights ago in the Garden. The Atlanta defense collapses on him, so Michael snaps a pass to Whitney, who swishes the three-point shot that by his reckoning feels as good as the one John Paxson hit in the 1993 Finals or the one Steve Kerr hit to win the 1997 championship. Whitney has sixteen points in this game and Richard Hamilton has a Pippenesque twenty-two to support the thirty-one Michael collected against the four different defenders Atlanta tried on him. This is a microcosm of what he had planned as president of basketball operations and as player/president, and the temptation is to think that what took him eight years in Chicago can begin to take shape in just two games in Washington. Whitney and Hamilton are being called Jordanaires, the supporting cast and the other monikers used to praise Michael's co-stars. Jordan even lets it slip that, "Whitney is my John Paxson, my Steve Kerr." As the media horde waits for the word to be allowed in to talk to Michael, a security guard apparently recognizes the time warp. He ironically announces, "Bulls' locker room is open."

The kudos coming out after the game sound familiar. Hawks guard Jason Terry admits, "We didn't know how to play him. He dictated our defense." Michael even falls into the vacuum, asserting, "I'm coming. I'm dunking. I'm starting to finish around the basket." Reality bytes then follow and Michael suddenly remembers he missed fourteen of his last twenty-two shots. His game is still at the point where one more shot could put him back in the rough. "I got a little tired in the fourth quarter," he admits. This is not the only chorus that repeats tonight. Knee problems—pain to be exact—are returning as the pimple on the Third Coming. The fluid in his left knee that kept him out of practice in the days leading up to the season opener in New York has been reduced prior to the Atlanta uprising with medication prescribed by Mike's old medicine man, Chicago Bulls team doctor John Hefferon. Jordan adds that on a scale of one to ten, the Atlanta game was a seven. One small step for his confidence, to be sure. One giant leap of faith, well, that would have to come with more than a dunk.

Three games into the season couldn't be enough for Michael to make such a big leap. Two nights after taking Atlanta, the Wizards brace for their home opener. The atmosphere is thick with excitement marked by the presence of what wasn't here last year. Yes, scalpers roam the streets outside the MCI Center asking five hundred dollars for a ticket. Cadillacs and Mercedes and BMWs cruise this revitalized section of downtown D.C., men in sport coats and cashmere sweaters looking for somebody who has two tickets for sale. Last year, this neighborhood buzzed only when the NHL's Capitals played, but as *The Washington Post* reports tonight the confluence spills into such establishments as the District Chophouse, like the scalpers, another sign of the economic boon that has followed Mr. Jordan to Washington. NBC has also come to televise a Washington game for the first time in five years. The last time the network of the NBA broadcast a game the Wizards played was April 27, 1997, when a certain Chicago Bulls guard hung fifty-five points on the Wiz in Game Two of an opening-round playoff series. Tonight, however, against defending Eastern Conference champion Philadelphia, albeit without Allen Iverson, a Michael Jordan nobody had ever seen before shows a star-studded crowd the possibilities.

During a fifteen-minute crescendo of the second half, the Wizards move like the Joffrey and outscore the Sixers, 44-10. Hamilton nets eleven points, Christian Laettner, Chris Whitney, Courtney Alexander and Tyrone Nesby combine for most of the rest when the Wizards play what some who have witnessed all of the bad hoops the past several years call their best basketball in a decade. Jordan finishes the game with more assists (nine) than baskets (seven), playing the role he envisioned for the comeback. The points man was now the point man; the soloist had become the orchestrator, and Collins and Jordan share a moment over this, recalling 1987 when Doug moved Michael to play point guard for a month and he nearly averaged a triple double. If the Wizards can get that Michael Jordan to show up, they admit they will be more respondent to an MJ leading them than the one who has been Bullying them since he came to town. Hamilton puts a positive spin on what has led to a lopsided victory, commenting after his twenty-nine point performance, "One thing I've learned is to feed off Michael. Get to an open spot and he'll find you."

If only the opening-night glitters lasted more than a day. After the 90-76 victory against Philadelphia, the Wizards boarded a flight to Detroit to play the Pistons the next day. Agony could really attack Michael on nights like these. Out of the shower, he played Q&A with the media for a few minutes before George Koehler led him to catch the team bus to the airport. Somewhere along the way, those knees that had just played thirty-eight minutes per game three times in the past five nights began to harden. Joints unlocked only with ice packs and pregame treatment of deep-heating ultrasound were unsure how they would respond in what Michael may have dreaded most in this encore: playing games on back-to-back days. Lemieux told Michael this would be the most agonizing part, and Super Mario intermittently opted to sit out the second half of some of his comeback back-to-backs. Michael had only this one to deal with in the first month, but there were seventeen more ahead on the schedule. If they all went like this one in Detroit, Michael might be hearing that Washington Wheezer line coming from those who had taken out a second mortgage to scalp tickets for one last shot at him.

For when the Pistons rolled up a twenty-something lead in the second quarter, fans at the Palace of Auburn Hills began showering Michael with heckling. They called him old, among other not-exactly-made-for-prime-time modifiers. For old time's sake, Michael

digested the punch lines and at one point in the second quarter dag-
gered an eighteen-foot jump shot over Jon Barry, then found the fan
who had been cracking on him loudest and gave him, "Not bad for an
old man," that left an entire section of fans laughing. Michael walked
away believing he has had the last laugh, but also threatened that
nights like these will become the pockmarks on the comeback. He
used to shut up these fans like the playoff night in Cleveland in 1993
when he hit another series-winning jumpshot then immediately
pointed a finger at a fan in the front row of Richfield Coliseum who
kept telling Michael to put his jumpshot in a place that would be
anatomically impossible.

He can play point guard, point forward and mentor, but what
about court jester? "It's been quite a while since I took some heckling," Jordan noted to the media postgame, "and if I do my job I can
shut them out. Tonight, we didn't do our jobs, so we had to sit there
and listen to it." He made just eight of eighteen shots and now had
hit just twenty-two of his last sixty-three field goal attempts. The
Wizards fell behind by as much as thirty-four points in the third
quarter and Michael watched the last nineteen minutes and fifty-one
seconds from the bench with his knees wrapped in ice. "I'm afraid
there could be nights like this," Michael said after the 100-78 loss to
Detroit. "If we have ten or twelve, you're going to see a frustrated
athlete out there."

Frustration began bubbling like acid indigestion within Michael
at this point. On some nights he believed he could still win games by
himself. But not every night, so early in the season Hamilton, Whitney, Alexander, Nesby—pretty much everybody but Laettner, Popeye and Jahidi White—felt they had no choice but to stand around
and watch him try. After all, they had grown up seeing him do it on
so many Sunday afternoons in May. The more they watched, the
more frustrated Michael became when they weren't there to handle
his passes and hit the open shots when he did let them play. The loss
to Detroit began to amplify the conflict Jordan faced trying to break
the Wizards of their losing affliction. He worked himself free for fif-

teen second-quarter points, but the other Washington players scored just four, which added up to the twenty-four point deficiency at half-time. So while everybody wanted Michael to be Michael—including Michael—the desire or the need to do so meant compounding frustration. If he wanted to be *that* Michael Jordan, could he still? And could that leave his teammates standing around burning because as Hamilton said, "Nobody wants to be no Jordanaire." If the Wizards needed Jordanesque rescuing, would he have enough in his tanks to keep them from going under in the fourth quarter? What Michael was about to find out was that either way, he was currently in a no-win situation.

Three nights after losing to Detroit, the comeback tour played Boston and no way was Michael not going to try to be that Michael. After the preseason meeting between the two teams, Paul Pierce adopted his role as the villain. After that fourteen-point Celtics victory, Jordan said he couldn't wait for a real shot at Pierce to see if he was really an Air Apparent. Antoine Walker said Michael talked all summer about getting a shot at Pierce and that he thought Pierce matched the one Jordan skill nobody else had so far: Heart. If inspiration like this came with every game, Michael would have been that MVP Michael. In the first half, he hit six of twelve shots and scored sixteen points. Pierce fired back with twelve, but when the Celtics took a 48-42 halftime lead Doug Collins asked Michael to shut down the Boston hotshot in the second half. The story is now legend about how Michael scored sixteen more of his season-high thirty-two points in the second half while holding Pierce to two, how Michael strutted his new variety of pull-up jump shots in Pierce's face and how Pierce blocked two of Michael's shots late in the fourth quarter to stunt a Wizards comeback. As Pierce became Jordan's personal Boston strangler, there was no doubt that he had the heart to match Michael.

And Michael had heartburn. Even though the Wizards made an 11-0 fourth-quarter run to get back in the game, Jordan chastised afterward that, "the difference is knowing how to execute in the closing minutes and this team isn't connected yet in the fourth quarter." It all came back at Michael in the end with such media wizards as Bob Ryan of *The Boston Globe* pointing out that this version of Jordan had three shots blocked in one night, whereas the previous two versions might go a month without having that many blocked. Even though Jordan statistically obliterated Pierce, the fact that somebody had the last laugh on him made Michael wonder how long these growing pains would last.

Antacid seemed to come, however, two nights later when the Golden State Warriors played Washington. Golden State was one of the few teams in the NBA suffering through a worse drought than the Wizards. When the Dallas Mavericks made the 2001 NBA playoffs, Golden State stepped to the front as the franchise that had gone more seasons than any other NBA team without making the playoffs. A victory here would not only be expected but absolutely necessary if the Wizards were to learn a critical part of the Jordan/Collins plan about being tough on your home court. With four consecutive home games to follow, the Wizards needed to get phat on Golden State.

But the 109-100 loss to the Warriors left him feeling more and more like it was Michael and the Wiz kids than the genesis of a team. After falling behind by seven points at halftime, Jordan admitted that in the third quarter he was loading up and firing on almost every possession to get himself and/or the team going. He made six of eleven shots and scored twelve points in the third that mercifully ended with Golden State leading by fifteen. Maybe Michael burned a bit afterward when realizing that Antawn Jamison, Bob Sura and a point guard almost as old as he was—Mookie Blaylock—combined to hold Jordan to seven-for-nineteen shooting in the other three quarters. Or when Blaylock submitted afterward that, "Michael can't carry a team the way he used to." But his frustration bubbled over after the game. "I think we're playing as twelve individuals," he charged. "I don't know if they are trying to impress me, or management, or if it's a contract situation. But it's not a collective effort. Collective effort means team defense. Offense is not counting on one guy to score. I don't see a collective effort." If the rest of the Wizards collectively felt that way, they weren't saying. Or they were afraid to. All this came after just three consecutive losses. What would it take to make Michael blow his top completely?

3

HE MISSED THE FIRST SHOT OF THE GAME, A MIDRANGE JUMPER. TWO MIN-utes later, he snatched an alley-oop pass and left the finish short. He missed his next jump shot. And then a three-pointer clanged off the rim loud enough to sound the end of recess. After a seven-minute breather, he missed another couple of jump shots, then another, then another. He tried the head fake, the head-and-shoulder fake, the head-and-shoulder-and-eyebrow fake and for the first half of this game against Seattle, Michael Jordan had an 0-for-8 shooting line to bear and a second-year Seattle Supersonic named Desmond Mason grinning, calling his childhood idol "just another basketball player." Michael finished the half, standing at halfcourt, grabbing the bottom of his shorts, equal parts flabbergasted and exasperated. Following the halftime recess, he was stuck at a zero balance, a third quarter of six more missed jump shots and not a single move that indicated a desire to go to the basket. Finally, seven minutes, forty-six seconds into the third quarter—more than thirty-one minutes into the game—Michael Jordan tipped in the layup that Wizards center Jahidi White missed. At the time Seattle led 64-47. By the end of the game, Michael missed seven more shots, including three layups—one that Gary Payton blocked from behind—was called for a technical foul with nineteen seconds left and finally lost it. A five-for-twenty-six shooting performance left Jordan standing grabbing the bottom of his shorts, doubled over, laughing. Yes, laughing.

And he wasn't the only one. The Sonics' Brent Barry saw the humor in Michael's ineptitude and dared him to take a fifteen-foot jump shot in the second quarter. Jordan would normally net it and shoot Barry the this-is-your-worst-nightmare grin. But the MCI Center crowd joined Barry by mocking Jordan with a lengthy standing ovation when he tipped in the Jahidi miss for his first hoop of the game. It was a night for throwing punch lines. Nobody dared point this out to Michael, but his thirty-eight percent shooting for the season was worse than the current Chicago Bulls team. The *Seattle Post-Intelligencer* reported on of a couple of Jordan fans, former Chicagoans who had made the trip from Pittsburgh to see Michael and paid more for their seats ($175 per ticket) than they did for the airfare ($100). One of those fans then called Jordan's game "like stale beer. No hops." Another shot making the rounds ribbed that Michael looked like he was playing in slow motion. So far in 2001 he had been mocked in as many games as he had won.

Of all the punch lines, the ones about the magic disappearing and Michael passing the autumn of his career never came up. Losing four games in a row—the first time in eleven seasons he experienced such futility—and five of the first seven wasn't as big a concern as what was happening to Michael's team. Hamilton had hit just eleven of twenty-six shots in the past two games. Kwame Brown started the previous two games and scored just five points against Seattle. Judging by the box score, the best player against the Sonics was shooting guard Bobby Simmons, a Camp Comeback alum who hit five of six and scored thirteen points. Alexander was beginning to feel like one of those punching-bag clowns—taking a shot, getting knocked down, popping up to another punch in the gut and hitting the deck again— with the way he had been in the starting lineup, then out, then in, then out again in the first two weeks. Against Seattle, the Wizards tried a first team of Jordan, Brown, Laettner, Whitney and Nesby, then in the next game the starting lineup included Laettner at center, Brown, Whitney and Simmons with Jordan. Collins eventually admitted that he could have used another month of training camp to see who could play, who was worthy. And the biggest hurdle seemed to be that the Wizards, like the fans from Pittsburgh, were all waiting for Michael to bust a move, several actually, and regain some of the Flair Jordan. The longer they would have to wait, the more they would share the sentiment Michael sent up about his five-for-twenty-six fermenting against Seattle. "You get confused," Michael said. "You start pressing, and that's no way to get out of a slump."

Not that this was, three nights later against Milwaukee: Playing against Jesus for the first time, Michael put on a little Superman. The Bucks' Ray Allen had been cast as one of the Air Apparents for his 1999 venture to Hollywood playing the lead role of Jesus Shuttlesworth in the movie *He Got Game*, a flick nearly as critically acclaimed as *Space Jam*. This game was Allen's first close-up with Michael, and Jordan did what Jordan always does. Or used to do. He went to the basket. He scored the first hoop of the game on a layup and finished a pair of other drives in the first four minutes. For an encore, Michael made five of his eight shots in the third quarter when he scored sixteen points.

Old habits, however, die hard, and if Michael carried the team like this he would take the Wizards right back to the lottery. But could they carry him? So with the score tied at twenty-nine heading into the second quarter, Jordan stepped back. He went five minutes and forty-one seconds without touching the ball. And by the time it passed his way again, the Wiz kids were well on their way to a 58-41 halftime step back in time. Michael's third-quarter heroics combined with the other old pros—Popeye and Laettner—and adding another thirteen points cut a twenty-one point third-quarter deficit to zero early in the fourth. Michael knew it couldn't go on like this. He missed three key shots and turned the ball over in the fourth, when Milwaukee used a 7-0 scoring run to hand Washington its fifth straight loss, 107-98.

If they were scoring in Hollywood, Allen gets the nod primarily because, like having Denzel Washington as his co-star in *He Got Game*, Glenn Robinson, Sam Cassell and Michael Redd made the Wizards seem like Bugs, Daffy and too many *Space Jam* characters, too intimidated to get Jordan the ball. Though Michael hit twelve of his twenty-four shots to make the fifty-percent shooting mark for the first time all season, Allen filed the preview of coming attractions when he said after the game, "Clearly, without him on the floor, the Wizards didn't have a chance."

With him, too, maybe.

The first month of the comeback, as it turns out, has Michael going one-on-one with his legend and his legacy. That double team hounds him when the Utah Jazz come to Washington on a Friday night, two days after the loss to the Bucks. The pregame talk, of course, is all about the last time Jordan played the Jazz, not that anybody needs to be reminded about that one last shot. Michael meets the naysaying about all the missed shots lately threatening to change the course of history by saying, "You can't take that shot away. You can't take away what happened. It's a memorable shot." Then, he falls back into a defiance he hasn't shown since attacking the Jordan Rules, adding, "I will always remember that shot but that shot itself did not make Michael Jordan." He obviously wants to demonstrate as much, picking up almost where he left off against Utah. He warms up by hitting four of eight shots, forcing Utah into a defensive switch that casts Bryon Russell once again defending Jordan. Michael immediately lines up Russell, drains a fifteen footer over him without any need for a pushoff and backpedals away, asking Russell, "Did you miss me?"

Michael went on to do the time warp again, scoring twenty-four points in the first half on the way to tying the league high of forty-four this far in the 2001 season. Utah's Karl Malone and John Stockton turned back the clock as well, with thirty points from the thirty-eight-year-old Mailman and seventeen assists from his thirty-nine, soon-to-be-forty-year-old sidekick. Doug Collins immediately observed that the Jazz looked like they were playing the 1998 Bulls, except that Utah's twenty-year-old Russian rookie Andrei Kirilenko blocked Michael's last shot at rescuing what became the sixth consecutive loss. Jordan looked over the shrapnel of the game in which he topped the forty-point plateau for the 202nd time, noticed that his seventeen field goals (in thirty-three attempts) were more than the rest of his teammates combined and sighed, "Hopefully, we're not going to have too many more nights like this." If this pattern persists, however, Michael might ultimately have to face the idea that the Wizards might not have many more nights this good. The isolation on the court of Michael trying to break down the myriad of stoppers is nothing compared to the isolation breaking down the locker room.

4

AND NOW, THE SPIT HAS HIT THE FAN. A SEVEN-GAME LOSING STREAK HAS turned the Wizards from Michael and the Jordanaires 2002 to Michael versus the Jordanaires. The most recent dissension in the ranks has come from locker room sage Popeye Jones, who tells the *Washington Post* the morning after the loss to Utah, "Maybe he has to have a little more confidence in us. Sometimes, superstars like that have to have confidence in the players that they can make big plays down the stretch." The morning of the next game—the last of the five-game homestand, against Charlotte—the mood has swung so black that Christian Laettner calls a players-only meeting in the Wizards' locker room. A renowned clubhouse cancer like Laettner taking such action is like Madonna calling a meeting of the Conservative Coalition. The Wiz kids say they need some male bonding, that they need Michael to be more like one of them and not so much the general manager. Or the general. Center Etan Thomas puts his finger on the problem by commenting that Michael doesn't force the idea of being boss, "but the idea is still there because he is." Jordan has tried the group thing, inviting such teammates as point guard Tyronn Lue into his famous card games. And he has picked on Courtney Alexander and Tyrone Nesby in the pregame locker room public, offering them some of his custom Nike gear because maybe that will help them make a shot or play better defense. From

Michael, these are his terms of endearment. He knows the meeting allowed his players, rather teammates, to forgive the imperfections that are usually allowed in an all-for-one locker room, but his statements afterward only confirm the us-against-themness undermining the comeback:

"I'm more disappointed than frustrated," he begins. "I think if we could understand the fundamentals, understand what the coach is talking about and execute that in the games . . . We made some improvements since day one, but we're not nearly where we should be. Change is happening through this organization, but unfortunately, it's through a manner of losing. We don't want to get to where we start pointing fingers and that could happen."

It happens. The Wizards immediately go into their throw-it-to-Michael-and-go-for-the-rebounding-position offense at the outset of the Charlotte game. If Jordan is hitting, this is a good thing, and he has been, going twenty-nine for fifty-seven the past two games. He nets a couple of jump shots and even a dunk in the first quarter against the Hornets, then catches fire in the second to finish the first half with eighteen points on eight-for-sixteen shooting. But when Michael takes just two shots in the third quarter, a two-point halftime lead becomes a seven-point deficit that winds up being the final margin of defeat. With his thirty points on thirteen-for-twenty-three shooting, Jordan has all but one of the baskets the Washington starters score on this night. How much longer Michael can put up with this isn't clear, but Doug Collins has had enough. He has given practically everybody on the roster a chance to start but they all have produced the same results. In the fourth quarter, Collins stops talking to his players on the bench, because as he observes by reading the lack of passion at work against the Hornets, "It's almost like they don't want to play."

This is the difference Michael has made: Hamilton, who averaged eighteen points per game last season, is closer to his rookie numbers of nine points per game the season before. The Wizards' 2-8 record is exactly the same as after ten games a year ago. Collins is worrying about how many of his players are already saying, "Another season down the drain." Popeye implores his teammates to look themselves in the mirror and respond to Collins and Jordan. But the revolt is mounting. And so are the injuries. Michael has averaged forty minutes per game through the losing streak and he shows the wear and tear before a Thanksgiving night game in Indiana. The ice wrapped around him could cool a couple of kegs. The electrodes stuck to his wrist combat the tendonitis that's trying to do to his body what the Pistons and Knicks used to. Collins has warned Jordan that if he doesn't give in to cutting down on his minutes played, there is no way he will last an entire eighty-two game season. The wear and tear also shows on this night, when the ninth consecutive loss comes not so much because Jordan makes just eight of twenty-six shots but because he throws the ball away three times to launch a 10-0 scoring run by the Pacers that earns them the victory.

The triumph two nights later against Boston stops the losing streak but not the woe that makes Michael feel like Despair Jordan. For some reason, he is the only one in the locker room worried about the way the Wiz kids have pumped up the volume on music and the mess talk celebrating the one win in the past nine games. Michael pontificates that, "Sometimes you've got to go through these stretches just to understand what it all means." But he is not sure the Wizards do. If this were a veteran team, he'd probably have thrown a temper tantrum in the locker room by now. But maybe the team needs a good, swift kick in the garbage can.

Problem is, Michael's not sure where to direct his anger. Three days after the Boston victory, the Wizards play their worst game of the season to date. In the 94-75 loss to Cleveland, the most telling number is the thirty-one minutes Jordan played because the game was so far out of reach so early. He scores just eighteen points and for the first time in one hundred and sixty-two games he fails to shoot a single free throw. More mocking comes when a Cleveland media man writes that he looks like a fat Elvis on the floor after taking a lob pass from Hamilton and alley-ooping a rim shot—a bottom-of-the-rim shot. More personal agony comes when an anonymous Cavaliers guard, Ricky Davis, crows about this being the night he dunked on Michael Jordan. Davis, another guy named Jones (Jumane) and Lamond Murray have been added to the list of Jordan stoppers and Michael feels like he has been left holding the ball. The tantrum, the finger-pointing, the pain in various extremities spill out when Jordan screams postgame, "I just think we stink." He accuses his teammates of not covering his back, expecting him to cover theirs and concludes, "It's something I'm not going to live too much with."

Sitting next to Michael on the flight that night, Collins said he could sense the pain filling Jordan. His team was losing, losing worse than he ever had. He had fluid drained to reduce the swelling in his ailing knee and it hurt so much he couldn't practice the past ten days. His one last shot is on the verge of becoming the one Pierce blocked, and somewhere in the back of the bus somebody must be thinking: He stinks. The question he is asking himself is not why or whether he can, but how? He can't be the Michael Jordan of 1998. He doesn't want to be. And now, just one month into it, he is facing the defining moment for this Third Coming.

COMING OF AGE

1

7

WHOA, MICHAEL JORDAN SAID WHAT?

The Wizards' locker room sounded like happy hour at the Hard Rock. The victory on this almost-winter Sunday afternoon at Air Canada Centre glowed with historic ramifications, but not just because Washington recovered from a nineteen-point deficit to defeat the Toronto Raptors. And not just because the Wizards had won their sixth consecutive game or because Washington's newly anointed defensive Wiz had just slapped Vince Carter around like a CBAer. The wonder of this day unfolded beyond the public domain, behind the curtain, within that inner sanctum of a basketball team known as the showers. Under baptismal pomp and circumstance, Michael Jordan stood with his teammates and conveyed soft, never-before-heard, and quite honestly never expected, words of recognition that finally washed away the stink of the season's first month.

"Isn't it great?" Doug Collins revealed about the sermon Michael had just presented to his teammates. Nothing more. Nothing more needed. After toweling off and splashing on some of that cologne with his picture on the box, Michael Jordan amplified his message meant to compliment his mates for finally getting it, for finally figuring out what he had been talking about, yelling about, whining about these past few weeks. "Winning is an attitude," he re-emphasized, "and if you step into every game with the attitude, you have a chance to win." Michael talked about this coming of age for the Wizards like the proud father who had just seen his son climb to the top of the jungle gym for the first time. They hadn't stepped like this before. At the end of the first quarter/start of the second they rebounded from a 33-14 hole to outscore the Raptors 20-3. For all but six points of this rebirth, Michael Jordan watched from the bench, and as the hot water soothed his aching back he told the Wiz kids to savor the sweetness of the comeback because only after a victory like this is when you can truly "go home and have a great night."

For Rip Hamilton being more Vince than Vince, outscoring his Raptor counterpart sixteen to four over the final three quarters. For Kwame finally growing some manhood and playing like a six-foot-eleven kid with ten rebounds. For Chris Whitney hitting the "bare-ass" threes, as Collins called the big shots in the fourth quarter, that Michael opened for him. For the sixth consecutive victory that finally washed off the "stink" of Cleveland right here in these showers, Michael let out his approval in a way only he could, with one resounding I-told-you-so.

"I can deliver a soliloquy," Collins continued, "but one word like that from Michael means everything." More words like that were slowly starting to come from Michael since he sent up the S-word three weeks ago in Cleveland at the end of a 3-10 disaster to start the season. He took this moment in the shower—where, like the back of the team charter, players reveal sides of themselves to each other that they never show the public—to accentuate what had been a defining moment of his comeback. December was the month when Michael Jordan stopped referring to himself as the greatest player in the game, and this victory convinced Michael that if he couldn't be that guy every night he could accept new standards to measure his worth.

After Michael dribbled the ball off his foot for a turnover that set up a three-point shot by Carter in the first quarter, the Wizards began growing up. The next nine minutes and twenty-one seconds produced some of the gutsiest and hopeful basketball the franchise had seen since 1978. For nine minutes and twenty-one seconds, the Wizards became the team Jordan hoped they could by sometime in 2003 when he would kick off the Air Jordans, break out the Armanis and return to his perch atop the franchise. Richard Hamilton played the part of Michael, starting the run with a layup and adding a short jump shot. Kwame Brown showed the potential to wear the franchise tag in the future with a pair of high-rising fast-break dunks, two steals and nine of the twenty points. Emerging sparkplug Brendan Haywood, the seven-footer Michael pilfered in a draft-day trade with Orlando, jump-started the flurry by stealing an inbounds pass after a Hamilton layup and dunking in what Collins called the play that turned around the game. Then came Mr. Jordan, switching to his preconceived position of mentor and demonstrating the nuances of winning.

His four points, three steals and two assists in the closing minutes of the half had little to do with interpreting Michael's renaissance. What Jordan gave this team might only have been seen in the shower. Some call it character. Some call it heart. Michael always called it his will, an altered state he could go into that screamed, "Follow me" and enabled him to make the plays that, plain and simple, needed making. Over the years, Michael would say about this character, this heart: The great ones have it. One of those great ones, the triple crown–winning race horse Secretariat had it like nobody ever knew. When the big red colt—the Michael Jordan of race horses—died, legend had it that an autopsy showed his heart was larger than the size of a normal thoroughbred. Some experts argued that they would find the same anatomical edge in Michael. On this afternoon, he showed it during a flash of the third quarter by scoring eight quick points, setting up Hamilton for eight and completing not exactly a transformation of his game but more like a reinvention. On an afternoon when Vince wanted so much to show he could be that Michael Jordan, Michael held him to 0-for-the-second half of shooting. Vince had twenty-three points at halftime when the Raptors led by six and twenty-three at the end of the game when the Wizards danced into the showers with a 93-88 victory, the words that really set up this defining victory still echoing:

Whoa, Larry Brown said what?

"You guys are idiots," the Philadelphia 76ers coach shouted to the local media in the same tone he might use to send his son, L.J., to bed without supper. Brown still smarted from his team's 94-87 loss to Washington on a last-week-of-November night in 2001, the second time the Wiz had taken out the defending Eastern Conference champions in the past month. The day of the game, the *Philadelphia Daily News* greeted Michael Jordan's arrival by plastering a full-length photo of him on its front page with the charge, "Here Comes Nothin'." Brown began his postgame tirade by making sure everybody knew that rumors of Jordan's demise had been greatly exaggerated.

"Here's a guy who hasn't played in three years, and I hear you guys calling him a punk and saying he shouldn't come back. He completely controlled the game tonight. The guy hasn't played in three years and to come into this league and because the team hasn't won, you put the finger right on him. He's not gonna dunk and be highlight film, but he controlled the whole game."

Long before Michael hit Toronto, Brown saw it coming, maybe heard it, when Jordan launched his "We stink" tirade in Cleveland. One night after the stinker, Brown witnessed the reinvention of Michael Jordan and how he could now assert his control, alter the course of the game like a flash of light. Every night, the Wizards were going to run into a player geeked up like Allen Iverson was here, bent on turning the game into a one-on-one with Michael. Jordan wouldn't try to match Iverson's twenty-seven first-half points. He couldn't. But a four-and-a-half-minute run of the second quarter previewed not so much a reverberation of his past life but a rekindling of how the drama might unfold on any given night during the next two months. Michael started with a pair of free throws, then made a move he hadn't had the legs for all season, blowing past Matt Harpring for a one-handed, extended scoop off the glass. After two more free throws, a sixteen-foot jumper and another two more free throws, the one shot came that always intensified his belief that there would never be any limit to his game: a fadeaway from thirteen feet as the shot clock hit zero. A seventeen-footer finished off the run of fourteen consecutive Washington points from Jordan that not only offset Iverson but left Michael realizing that his calling for this team would be to save his legs for crunch time. When Philly reverted to the Jordan-stopping strategy of 1998 in the third quarter, Brown said Michael "stayed one step ahead of us by continually moving the ball ahead of the double team." This merely sprung Rip Hamilton to exploit what Collins called the best midrange jump shot in the game for thirteen third-quarter points, in which the Wizards outscored the Sixers 25-16 and asserted the upper hand. In the fourth quarter, Washington needed a little more defense from Michael, and his steal of an Iverson pass with one minute, twelve seconds to play ended in a Hamilton runaway dunk for the last of his Jordanesque twenty-eight points that accentuated the victory.

Doug Collins admitted after the game that he was baffled, even asking his coaches if this was the same team that stunk up the joint in Cleveland the night before. As for whether the Wizards' turnaround was a response to Jordan's scolding, Collins said, "I hope so."

Apparently one word from Michael can mean everything.

2

MATT HARPRING FIGURED TO TAKE HIS PLACE ALONGSIDE CRAIG EHLO OR Hersey Hawkins, or at least LaBradford Smith. Harpring, Philadelphia's hardscrabble forward, figured to be the victim of another Michael Jordan drive-by. But on this night, he is being stubborn about playing the crash dummy. In the first quarter, Harpring makes moves that leave Jordan a statue of his former self, a drive for a layup which will afford the young gun a few laughs after the game. By the second quarter, Michael completes his nightly ritual of shaking the stiffness out of his legs and lines up Harpring for an up-close look at the new Jordan. Isolated on the left side of the basket, Michael holds the ball in front of Harpring's face, reducing him to the little brother trying to get the ball away from the older brother, exploiting his size advantage to keep it just out of reach. Then, like a boxer, Michael jabs with the ball toward the basket, thrusting his right leg and hips at Harpring in rocking-chair motion. Once, twice, three times and Harpring finally bites, taking a swing at the ball. In an abracadabra motion, Michael ducks under Harpring and buries a thirteen-foot jump shot. Harpring has just seen the new model Jordan up-and-under over which the young wannabe will shake his head after the game and confirm in more lookahead than looking-back posture, "it wasn't the same Michael out there tonight."

He knows. They all know. Harpring, the third-year pro from Georgia Tech, and his entire generation know Michael Jordan. They studied him for years. They know the moves he imprinted on the game, tried to replicate them and eventually put their own spin on each one. The NBA game of the new millennium evolved from what Michael created. The one-on-one isolations that compounded into the league allowing zone defense again in 2001 originated with the way Michael could line up a defender, hold the ball out with one hand, yo-yo it and take off to the basket. This isolationist theory left the shot clock ticking like a time bomb and teammates edging toward Michael step-by-step to bail out a helpless defender. When this became a way of life in the NBA, it led to repeated calls of illegal defense mucking up the game, so the rule makers thought allowing zone defense would clear up the clear-out Michael used for so many years to prey on Dumars, Starks, Reggie Miller, Clyde Drexler, et al. Later in life, he even honed this with the one-handed shot fake, a move to toy with a defender like tricking the family dog by hiding the stick behind your back instead of throwing it to fetch.

Michael was the first one, too, to perfect the Airobatics to leap

Doug Collins would try to get Jordan to rest more during games, but it was hard at times for Michael to watch the way his teammates played without him on the floor. JOE GIGLI

Jordan said the prolonged ovation when he returned to the United Center on January 19, 2002, almost brought a tear to his eye. CHICAGO TRIBUNE

One thing that didn't change from the First or Second Coming was the fans who would line up just to get a chance to see Michael walk on to the court. JOE GIGLI

The nights of soaring and scoring were not as plentiful in 2001–2002 as they were in 1998 when Michael easily glided around New Jersey's Sam Cassell en flight to a layup. THE RECORD (BERGEN COUNTY, NJ), MEL EVANS, STAFF PHOTOGRAPHER

In perhaps his most courageous performance ever, Jordan needed Scottie Pippen's help to get to the bench after overcoming food poisoning to score thirty-eight points in Game Five of the 1997 NBA Finals. *CHICAGO TRIBUNE*

For Jordan and Pippen, the best part of every season seemed to be the gathering in Chicago's Grant Park with hundreds of thousands of fans to celebrate another Bulls championship. *CHICAGO TRIBUNE*

At the beginning of the comeback, Phil Jackson—who had been there for the best of Michael through six championships—said he wasn't sure if we would see what we're accustomed to with Michael Jordan this time around. *CHICAGO TRIBUNE*

Jordan said part of his goal in the comeback was to be more of a setup man, a leader of the fastbreak more than a finisher. JOE GIGLI

Jason Kidd and many of the league's other stars tried to turn their confrontations with Jordan into "High Noon." And in the Third Coming, Jordan didn't win them all. JOE GIGLI

During the Third Coming, many defenders figured out that getting physical with Michael actually became a way to slow him down. JOE GIGLI

But on one of those few nights when the knees were feeling good, Jordan could make the fake to his left . . . JOE GIGLI

. . . and come back with the stampeding dribble right to get around even the league's best defenders, like New Jersey's Jason Kidd, and rise for a jump shot. JOE GIGLI

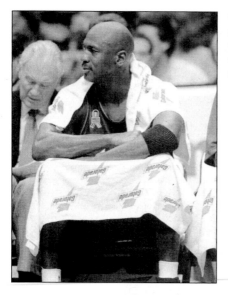

Washington assistant coach Johnny Bach, seated behind Michael, wondered if Jordan would ever regain the "predator" mode Bach saw as an assistant with the Bulls in the early 1990s. JOE GIGLI

Of all his Wizards team-mates, Popeye Jones, seated on Michael's left, became Jordan's closest friend and confidant. JOE GIGLI

Some nights just didn't go as Jordan planned, like this one against New Jersey in January. The Wizards lost by forty-three points, and Michael sat out the entire second half. JOE GIGLI

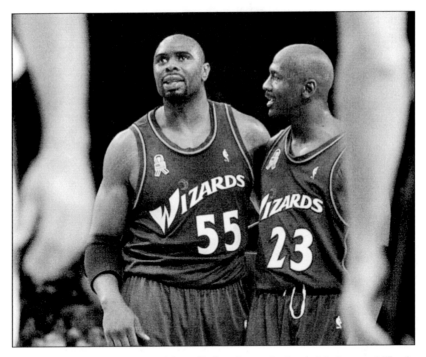

Time was running out on opening night at Madison Square Garden, but Jordan urged Wizards center Jahidi White that there was still time for one more run. THE RECORD (BERGEN COUNTY, NJ) BETH BALBIERZ, STAFF PHOTOGRAPHER

The universal sign for being tired in the NBA is clinging to the shorts, and Jordan assumed this position more than he probably wanted to during the comeback. THE RECORD (BERGEN COUNTY, NJ) BETH BALBIERZ, STAFF PHOTOGRAPHER

Even on bad knees, Michael's post-up move to set up the turnaround fadeaway jumper was still one of the best in the NBA. *THE RECORD* (BERGEN COUNTY, NJ) BETH BALBIERZ, STAFF PHOTOGRAPHER

He had more than one last shot in him: Wizards guard Chris Whitney mobs Jordan after his jumper with 3.2 seconds left proved to be the winning shot in a defeat of the New York Knicks at Madison Square Garden in December. *THE RECORD* (BERGEN COUNTY, NJ), MEL EVANS, STAFF PHOTOGRAPHER

into the defense, force them to grab him and somehow get off a shot attempt that would land him on the foul line for two free throws, two easy points on a play in which most of his predecessors would be content to just duck and cover the ball. Additionally, the deterioration in fundamentals—passing, ball handling, jump-shooting, boxing out on rebounds—coaches like Larry Brown relentlessly preached can be traced to Jordan as well. Though not a player or coach would have trouble tapping Michael as the most fundamentally sound player east of Larry Bird, his propensity to dunk and score created the new millennium player who would rather soar and score than box out or set back picks, thinking fifty-point nights had become the measure of greatness more than victories, championships, last-second shots and *ESPN Classic* best-game marathons.

Apparently, Harpring could see this was not the same Michael, not just the guy shooting for the thirty points and seven assists he rang up in the 94-87 victory. The fourteen consecutive points he scored and the up-and-under moves he used to trick the 2001 version of Craig Ehlo unveiled Michael's realization that in this comeback, "I didn't want to relive my career all over again. I can't."

The true reinvention of Michael took root on this November night in Philadelphia. Finally, the Wiz kids were gaining an understanding. Hamilton had realized that playing with Michael Jordan meant not being afraid to take a shot and miss it and have to deal with the wrath of the boss. Laettner and Popeye had been telling the rest of the players that if they just hustled, kept moving, Michael would find a way to share the ball and that all it would take is making one good play, one fundamentally sound play, to earn his trust. It had almost been like a pledging for the Wiz, and so far Rip, Popeye, Laettner, Jahidi and Whitney had endured the initiation. They found the way to play with Michael Jordan—this Michael Jordan. And now, the NBA was going to have to deal with this Jordan, Jordan the defender, Jordan the passing fancy, the fake-out artist with the sucker punch, the ultimate thinker, the best player of the game in two- or four-minute flashes and, as the evolution/aging process continued, the one who would find just enough stubbornness to overcome a knee flaring up like an alarm clock every morning and save himself to at least regain his rep as the best closer in the game. Still.

3

ONE OF THE CHILDREN OF THE MILLENNIUM, OF COURSE, IS VINCE CARTER. Vince wants to be Michael more than Michael does, and before their first-ever regular season meeting, one of Carter's teammates is talking about what he sees in Jordan now that others seem to have been missing. Hakeem Olajuwon, in his first year with Toronto after seventeen seasons and two championships in Houston, saw all the Jordan moves develop long before they became the stuff of study tapes. By mid-December, Hakeem has seen one quality in Michael that wasn't there all those years ago, one that he wishes Vince would pay attention to most. "Michael knows the quality of a leader, that generally it's not just the individual's accomplishment, it's also the team's accomplishment. That should be the motivation there for Vince." Hakeem says he has noticed Michael's reluctance to carry the team, that physically he is not capable of playing the forty-eight minutes and scoring the fifty points to do so. What Hakeem said he has noticed is Michael picking on the inexperience of the league, passing when they expect him to shoot, scoring when they back off on the double teams, drawing fouls when they try to play him with one defender. "He can shoot and he can drive, but he's not just bringing one aspect," Hakeem details. "Guys around him have that confidence they can win, which means a lot. I can't find a weakness in his game."

As he continues his dissertation on the new Michael Jordan, Hakeem finally comes to the one trait he believes has made all the difference in this re-reincarnation. "I think Michael's mental will has made all the difference in the world. He will not compromise. That kind of desire is very unusual. I think it can make up for what you don't have physically. When you get older, you don't feel like you lose anything. Maybe you can't jump as high, but you don't need to jump as high. You don't feel like you lose anything unless you have a major injury. Because of this desire, you know you're getting older but you don't feel that."

The further they progressed into the season, the more the film of Wizards games would show Michael siding up to Chris Whitney or Tyrone Nesby or Tyronn Lue, pointing and explaining and maybe slapping one of them lightly on the side of the head for emphasis. This, of course, was how Jordan had always been warm and fuzzy with his teammates, and the ones he chastised, condescended to, slapped to see if the light was on were the ones he liked best. This was what they would have to learn about playing with Jordan, for if you asked Michael, his most influential attribute now was his ability to impart wisdom. His teammates got to hear him tell the secrets of domination. Opponents would come at Jordan with more foot speed, more hops and quicker reflexes, and Michael would look at them and as NBC television analyst Steve Jones observed "say, 'I'm gonna sucker you. I'm going to out-think you and I'm gonna come out of this smelling like a rose.'"

This was Michael's intent right from opening night. If everything ran in sync then basketball would be like a poker game, Jordan knowing exactly what the other guys held in their hands, forcing them to play in deference or fear or both. Knicks coach Jeff Van Gundy admitted after his team survived Michael in the season opener that he completely changed his defensive philosophy, opting to double-team Michael close to the basket or at the free-throw line or even eighteen feet out on the wing. Van Gundy hated to do this because it freed other players for open shots, especially the back-breaking three-pointer. And that's exactly what happened in that game until the last few minutes, when the Knicks decided they could no longer give up the open shots. And then by his own design this gotcha-sucker game plan would leave Michael fresh to go one-on-one to win the game down the stretch.

Michael was always at his most dangerous when thinking was the premium. If you think about it, instincts are a by-product of experience and power of the mind. How else do you know that raising the ball high in your right hand as you take off from the free-throw line will draw three Lakers defenders and leave you the opening to switch the ball to the left for the scoop layup? Michael's mind always moved faster than time, it seemed.

Popeye said he always thought of himself as a head-of-the-class student of the game, something Collins confirmed by observing one day that he thought Jones would be a renowned coach in the NBA. But Popeye learned that his knowledge was B-minus compared to Michael's when Jordan would call him over to watch a pregame tape of that night's opponent, "and show me things I had never noticed before." Some of Jordan's happiest times came when slapping around media members with pregame, off-the-record brain teasing or matching wits with Jerry Krause about why Elgin Baylor or Wes Unseld could never have succeeded in Michael's era. And in this return, he would be at his most visionary by using his head more than his legs to help the Wizards realize winning ways, a process that became the bedrock of Washington's December winning streak.

Physically, the 2001 edition Michael Jordan had two distinct ambitions. One would be to remind the NBA why he was an eleven-time selection to the league's all-defensive team. In the open court, he no longer could be a match for even somebody named Ricky Davis or Quincy Lewis flying in for a dunk. But in key situations, he would get opponents to understand why they called it crunch time. On opening night, he alternately forced Knicks gunners Latrell Sprewell and Allan Houston to become passers, lamenting, "when I went to one, the other got hot," then continuing, "I'm not afraid to go out there against the hot guys, something Doug is going to ask me to do, to create momentum from a defensive standpoint. I'm going to jump on the hot guy and relish the opportunity." Paul Pierce learned about Michael's defensive prowess when, after he went off for those fourteen first-half points in early November, Jordan locked him down and held him scoreless in the second half. And once he got the feel for Vince Carter's rhythm, Michael notched another scoreless second-half defensive stand.

The reinvented Michael would also live for moments like in the victories against Philadelphia and Toronto. Amid all the early season talk about Michael getting his legs back and shaking the rust off his jump shot, Judd Buechler discerned that the older Michael could be the old Michael during flashes of the game. Then, after watching Michael play his fourth game in five nights on a caving knee against his Orlando Magic, Buechler said his former teammate could be the guy he played with in Chicago, "for spurts that dwindle because of fatigue." If Collins could make good on his plan to get Michael eight minutes of rest each half—four at the end of one quarter and four at the beginning of the next—he could generate enough hot flashes to be the closer in the fourth quarter or turn the momentum in the second quarter, as he did by scoring those fourteen consecutive points against Philadelphia. Similarly, Michael could produce short scoring bursts on fresh legs, like the eight he scored at the start of the third quarter against Toronto to help turn a six-point deficit into a six-point lead. A secret weapon was also developing when the Wizards would come out of a timeout with the ball: Get a freshened-up Michael to flash for an open jump shot as he did twice against the Raptors.

The reincarnation or resurrection or reinvention or whatever of Michael Jordan actually happened while nobody was looking, or looking for something else. Expectations wanted him to be his former self every night, not just in flashes. But the flash fires were more than okay with Michael, who reconciled the expectations by admitting, "That was my past life." The first month of the comeback which was weighed down by the expectations of so many, from Courtney Alexander to Bryon Rusell to Heidi Klum, whose opening-night observation of, "Michael Jordan always comes through in the end, doesn't he?" underlined the urgency to put his past behind.

4

JOHNNY BACH FLASHES BACK TO 1986, HIS FIRST YEAR AS AN ASSISTANT coach with the Chicago Bulls. Jerry Krause and Jerry Reinsdorf were in their second season running the Bulls when they asked Doug Collins to take over as head coach and build some kind of system around growing superstar Michael Jordan. Within three seasons, the Bulls were in the Eastern Conference Finals and a few growing pains away from becoming champions. Bach can see those ups and downs fresh in his mind, Michael reluctant to share the ball with Brad Sellers or Pete Myers or Darren Daye and at first rookies Scottie Pippen and Horace Grant. Charles Oakley was about the only player who found a place in Michael's inner circle—on and off the court. As Bach explained, Michael went through a process of finding out deep down in a crisis who could play and, "developing the emotional wrap for what he expected and who he trusts. It took years in Chicago."

As Bach works the hallways of Philadelphia's First Union Center, greeting the usual gaggle of friends he sees in every NBA venue—the residue of forty-nine years in coaching—he realizes the Wizards are trying to do in months what the Bulls did in years. "It just isn't working out well," he says indicating that the trust has been little more than cosmetic. Bach, however, has a warning about what to watch for, an almost psychic reading on what will happen to the Wizards a couple hours from now. "You reach that moment of truth in any game where you're coming on and you keep coming on to win the game or come from behind. And at the moment of truth when games are going to swing one way or the other or when something has to get done, the team has to be painfully and manifestly destined to come together at that point."

Translated from Bach's marine-speak, the Wizards are in crisis mode, and Michael's "We stink" cover-my-back plea is his way of finding out once and for all who he can trust. The turnaround in the team about to take place will come only partly from the transformation or reinvention of Michael's game. Even after Washington defeats Philadelphia, there seems to be such little trust in the Wiz kids that rumors again bubble up about Charles Barkley bringing his three hundred-pound ego to join the Wizards because reportedly he is pissed that Michael has been left hanging so much by a group of anonymous teammates, who supposedly are pouting about Michael shooting so much and how his presence has been detrimental to their development. Like Charles these days, the rumor is just talk. But it is also a trigger point and the message is not lost on the venerable Popeye, who admits, "We need to catch up to him and figure out how we can help. We're all frustrated. Nobody is helping anybody do anything. There's a love and a passion we're trying to teach and the young guys here don't have it."

The player who keeps coming up in the where-are-they-now of the first month is Richard Hamilton. He is known as "Rip," for the way his laserlike jump shots ripple the nets. He might as well have been R-I-P in November 2001. Hamilton can relate to what Scottie Pippen felt on many nights, the questions always coming at him after a loss about why he wasn't there to give Michael more support. November has made his head throb like Pippen's had that Sunday afternoon in Detroit in 1990, when a migraine left him on the bench and left Michael hanging in Game Seven of the Eastern Conference Finals, the only one-and-done game Jordan ever lost in the NBA playoffs. As if the light went on in Philadelphia, Rip and Michael and Doug realize what's been missing. Hamilton doesn't need to be Scottie, he needs to be Michael. The Jordanesque third quarter Rip puts up against the Sixers submits the concept that in all this *Michael* must play Scottie to Hamilton, and numbers like Jordan's seven assists will become a barometer of success for the Wizards.

From Pip to Rip, Michael has gone from having one running mate who eventually flushed the bond of six championships because nobody allowed him to be Jordan to a partner who seemed to forget how much Jordan he had since upstaging Duke with an MVP performance in the 1999 NCAA Tournament title game. Michael wanted Rip to want to be as good as Michael wanted him to be and realize more nights like Tuesday, December 11 in Memphis, a 91-81 defeat of the Grizzlies that is the third entry in their December to remember. Hamilton hit eight of his twelve first-half shots as Washington rolled up a seventeen-point lead. He finished with thirty points, hitting fifteen of twenty-four shots at the start of a stretch that ended with Rip being named the NBA's Player of the Week. Jordan says his nine assists make this a day of reckoning. "I'm complementing him," Michael announces as if this is the final piece of the reinvention. "That's how we're going to build this team for the future. This is my focus, to make sure those guys understand how to play. That's one of the reasons I came back, and they're starting to understand that."

Michael's attempt to make Hamilton a Jordan clone might not come to fruition for years after December 2001. Jordan says he will know if he can see Rip passing on the knowledge to other players in a sort of Jedi lineage. Hamilton apparently has no problem playing the diva, either. At the end of his Player of the Week week, Hamilton entertains the notion that his twenty-seven points against Toronto came as a result of him finally learning to play with Michael. Apparently Rip has learned how to play the defiant diva from Jordan, responding that, "I think Michael is learning how to play with me."

At this point, Collins conjectures that if Michael and Rip could combine for fifty points per game, the Wizards will have a shot to win any game. They are becoming that formidable of a tandem. Consider that after the first month of the season, the highest scoring tandem in the NBA was Shaq and Kobe, putting up an average of more than fifty-two points a night. Paul Pierce and Antoine Walker are combining for 51.8 points per game and Dirk Nowitzki and Michael Finley of Dallas have manufactured 43.8 points per game. Michael and Rip were next on the NBA list at 43.6. In their last season together Michael and Pip combined for 47.8 points per game and in the Bulls 72-10 season of 1996, they struck for 49.8 points per game. Rip says the newfound success comes because Michael wasn't shooting as much, and in fact the twenty-eight or so shots per game he was hoisting in November is now down to twenty-one. Michael says it's because Rip—and others—aren't standing around as much. Not exactly a feud of Shaq-Kobe proportions from the spring of 2000, when Bryant was so despondent over having to play second chair that he called Michael daily to beg for a trade that would bring him back east, but both points of view explain what is happening to the Wizards.

When Michael found he could join the supporting cast, other Wiz kids flourished, too. Brendan Haywood became the presence in the middle that Doug Collins said would be the interior foundation of the Wizard's future. Michael celebrated Haywood's contributions by saying he was a better player than Kwame Brown, Jordan's own choice to be the future of the franchise. Brown played himself out of Michael's dog house enough to contribute spurts of points and rebounds, and Jordan's other repeatedly scrutinized offseason acquisition, Tyronn Lue, put some run-and-gun and defensive quickness into the Wizards. Two significant differences began showing up in the Washington box scores as a result. Jordan actually reduced his playing time to less than thirty-five minutes per game, and the Wizards' defense tightened its hold on opponents to an average of eighty-five points per game allowed. Michael summed up the transformation in these words:

"At first, guys were afraid to play with me. But now, it's working."

Remarkably, the building process Johnny Bach witnessed over the course of three years in Chicago happened in less than a month in Washington. Or a *Reader's Digest* version did, considering the time Michael had left. Like clockwork, one month after Michael missed the three-point shot in Madison Square Garden, Jordan and the Wizards started doing everything he dreamed of back on January 5 when he started thinking about this encore. On the last night of November, a Friday in Miami, Michael cut his shots down to twenty and made ten—his first five of the game and four of seven in the fourth quarter, when the Wizards overcame a thirteen-point deficit. Michael explained this deferment by saying he forced the double team, then passed off to Hamilton, Chris Whitney and Hubert Davis, who combined for twenty of the Wizards twenty-three third-quarter points. Michael then scored six in the 12-2, fourth-quarter run to seal the victory.

Jordan feels the start of something, now calling this win progress as opposed to saying the other night in Philly that the Wizards, "hadn't really accomplished anything yet." He will ride the team mercilessly if he has to make the Wiz kids understand how much they will need to endure—the price they will have to pay, is how he phrases it—to rinse away the loser signet. Pushing too hard, though—that will be the ledge Michael tightropes all season.

Perhaps the Wizards can keep from clenching but Jordan is about to go over the edge. For the past month, Michael's off days consisted of him riding an exercise bike at courtside, watching his teammates practice. The left knee he hyperextended in training camp has not been able to absorb the daily grind. He couldn't practice on it, and now he couldn't play on it. He tried, going thirty-three minutes against Orlando but hitting just six of nineteen shots in a long-anticipated, but never consummated matchup with Tracy McGrady. Afterward, Michael succumbed to the pain in his knee, revealing that he was flying to Chicago the next day for a consultation with Dr. John Hefferon, who could read Jordan's aches and pains better than anybody. If Hefferon suggested Michael miss a game or two or perhaps more, then he would consider the option. As it turned out, Michael passed on playing when a telling December road trip began in San Antonio where thirty-four thousand fans had bought tickets to see him. The consensus figured Michael was starting to crash and burn and even he put fuel on that fire by saying, "My body is sending me messages."

In effect, however, maybe he was sitting one out and starting over. Collins submitted that Michael's absence led to a bonding that turned the Wiz kids from frat brothers to brothers in arms. He said that it forced his guys to depend more on each other and helped the team understand what was missing without Michael. Nothing to do with scoring, Collins said, but "our best defensive player, our best low-post player, the guy who creates shots for other guys." Could this be the crisis that formed their emotional wrap?

Michael's return two nights later in Houston began a sixteen-day run that played out like Collins had just explained, just like they planned. Rip took the lead role in the third quarter, hit a pair of jumpers at the start of the fourth quarter to top off his game-high twenty-six points then handed over to Michael. In scoring ten fourth-quarter points, Michael hit four of his first six shots to turn a 60-58 Wizards lead after three to 74-67 with four minutes to play. Rocket science dictated that now was the time to start running extra defenders at Jordan, and he squeezed passes to Lue and Popeye for two crucial jump shots in the final minute that preserved the victory. For Collins, the most memorable aspect of the night was that down the stretch he kept reminding his players, "Don't just stand around and watch Michael try to finish the game off." And they didn't.

Each subsequent game seemed to present some epiphinal moment for the Wizards. Two nights after Houston, Washington finished its Texas three-step road trip in Dallas and through three quarters Jordan had made all of three shots, including a follow-up slam off his own missed free throw and an *ESPN Classic* back-to-the-basket flip over seven-foot-six Mavericks center Shawn Bradley. But the Wizards proved again they can stand on their own and held a fifteen-point lead at halftime because Brendan Haywood, the gangly rookie who could have passed for a young Bill Cartwright, had already scored sixteen in his breakout nineteen-point game. The Mavericks of course wiped out the lead in the fourth quarter, and with the score tied at 80 at the four-minute mark Jordan willed a growth spurt, saying during a timeout, "We're going to win this game, and whoever doesn't want to be out there can sub themselves out." Even if his physical skills were deteriorating, Michael's will appeared to be more powerful than ever. The Wizards would have to learn that the gift he still had, even at thirty-eight years old, was making bold statements about winning and manufacturing melodrama to make it so—fifteen fourth-quarter points in this case.

The next week not only served to extend the Wizards' winning streak to five games— the longest since a certain president of basketball operations started prepping his comeback—but also to cement Jordan's reinvention. While Rip connected on thirty-nine of sixty-seven shots and averaged twenty-nine points per game to knock off Memphis, Miami and the New York Knicks, Jordan was averaging better than seven assists and less than thirty-four minutes per game. Another awakening came when the Wizards held off the Heat for an 82-80 victory in which they had to survive a potential game-winning three-point shot at the final buzzer. With 11.3 seconds left in the game, Michael said he brought the team together and implored, "We are on a string. That means we are going to have to cover each other's tails." Finally, he was saying this to his teammates rather than about them, something Popeye knew he was trying to do since training camp. Hamilton confirmed the importance of such an occurrence when he asserted after the Wizards beat Atlanta to push the win streak to seven, "The difference is that we don't have any guys bad-mouthing each other."

Part of the lore surrounding Michael Jordan was that nightly feeling of coming to the arena and wondering whether he would come up with something nobody had ever seen before or might see again, something that might send statisticians searching through the record books to put it into context. By the time the Wizards win streak hit six with the victory in Toronto, the pages in that record book were becoming more and more ruffled. When Washington recovered from a nineteen-point deficit to win, the Wizards had registered the largest comeback ever by an opponent in Toronto. The 103-76 pasting of Atlanta was the Wizards' largest margin of victory since a twenty-eight point shellacking of Toronto in January nearly two years ago. At 12-12 six weeks into the Third Coming, Washington hadn't forged a record this successful this far into the season since the playoff year of 1997, and the seven-game win streak was the franchise's longest since 1996. The feeling that Michael might come up with something nobody might ever see again returned as well. In the second quarter of the victory against Atlanta he regained that shooting-gallery look in his eyes, going off for eighteen points by making nine consecutive shots.

Throughout this life-altering run, Michael hoped his competitive addiction was rubbing off on the Wiz kids. This would be their staying power, and no matter what happened he couldn't return to the executive offices until he knew they didn't have to hide in the showers. The first glimpse that his guys, as he was now calling them, could let it all hang out came when the win streak suddenly was in jeopardy in Orlando on December 21. Eight minutes into the first quarter, Rip felt a twinge in his right groin that reverberated like a broken guitar string. After Hamilton hobbled to the locker room for the night with a strain that would bench him for six weeks, Michael foundered to three-for-sixteen shooting. Michael even said he felt "panic trying to pick up Hamilton's load." But the will, the heart, whatever part of the anatomy, then coursed through Popeye Jones, Hubert Davis and Tyronn Lue. Davis scored nineteen points, Jones added thirteen and Lue cashed in three of Michael's five fourth-quarter assists to blow out the Magic, 93-75.

That the Wizards tied the franchise record of nine consecutive victories at Madison Square Garden when Michael hit a game-clinching eighteen-foot jumper with 3.2 seconds to play provided an indication that the December to remember was more a liftoff than a one-hit wonder. Coming back from a ten-point deficit to beat the Knicks provided an indication of how the Wizards had grown some will, some heart, some whatever Michael said could only be seen—and heard—in the showers. A franchise-best winning streak, ascension in the Eastern Conference standings and the complete reversal of fortune for the team built around the reinvention of Michael Jordan spread the feeling that maybe there were a few more Miracles in him.

THE THIRD COMING

8

1

MAGIC JOHNSON WIGGLED INTO THE FLUORESCENT GOLD WARM-UPS, THE ones with the midnight blue trim known universally as Lakers. He spread out on the locker room floor and bent the through forehead-to-kneecap contortions used universally to stretch legs in preparation to run the fast break. Sweat seeped out of Magic's head stubble as he twisted his upper body from side to side. A mass of media gathered around him, and Magic provided commentary in the hard-copy way that used to make Kareem cringe because tipoff was too close to be so loose. "Gonna have some fun tonight," he promised with enough energy to momentarily wonder if Magic was about to make *his* Third Coming to the NBA.

The sweat, the crosscourt smile, the game face, the exuberance came flowing out of Earvin Johnson as he anticipated his part in NBA All-Star Weekend 2002 in Philadelphia. Magic led the Lakers entry in the three-ball event, a four-team three-on-three tournament with each squad comprised of an NBA legend, a current NBA player, a current WNBA player and a celebrity from the entertainment world. L.A. point guard Derek Fisher, WNBA queen bee Lisa Leslie and R&B singer/Hollywood Hoops League reigning MVP Bryan McKnight joined Magic's team in a competition that also included comedian Jamie Foxx, homeboy Justin Timberlake playing for the Sixers team wearing a winter hat and Britney Spears as the head cheerleader. Magic wanted no part of the made-for-television court-jester role in this competition and even spent parts of the game complaining to the officials, "Don't you know I get that call?" And "Thank you," with that big-eyed game face when he finally did. The way his blood boiled and his hook shot swished and the no-look pass made a cameo did not catch Magic off guard. Just a few minutes ago on the locker room floor, Magic had explained how this was the same every-shot-is-going-in arrogance—the one that made you feel twenty-three years old every time you stepped on the court even at forty-three—grabbing a hold of his friend, Michael Jordan, the past few months.

"It's just inside here," Magic said, pointing alternately to his heart and his head. "You can't describe it in words. Michael has always been the strongest player that's ever played in terms of just mentally. The hardest part is you got to know what you've lost and then be satisfied and be happy with the rest of your game. I know I'm twenty, or fifty, steps slower but I'm still effective because I *know* I'm twenty, fifty steps slower. A lot of guys lose something, and they're like, ooh, my whole game is gone. Michael just uses his head."

Nobody can relate to what's going through Michael Jordan's head more than Magic. At least that's what Magic says. He knows this from the bond he and Michael forged as teammates for the 1992 United States Olympic basketball team, the original Dream Team. Magic and Michael stayed up until six o'clock in the morning almost every day, playing cards and talking about how they were brothers caught in the arms of NBA expectations and celebrity impositions. "Last time I beat him in anything were those card games," Magic says. He also knows what Michael was missing, what has been driving him this last year and what has made him recapture his thirtysome-things the past two months. Magic says he too gets that leading-the-fast break, fans-rising-out-of-their-seats feeling every year, right when the NBA playoffs begin. "That's when I miss it. My hands start sweating, and I'm like intense. Same thing I did as a player. I have a rule at my office, you cannot mess with me during the playoffs.

When we lose, I can't go to dinner. I got to go home. I'm grouchy. I'm moody."

The past seventy-five days in the life of Michael Jordan have hit much of the basketball world like one of Magic's no-look passes. You suspected it was coming but you never knew when, and what Michael and the Wiz kids accomplished is as scintillating as Worthy or Kareem flushing the no-look and igniting all of L.A. into a gold-and-purple haze. The Wizards have gone from a team that by assistant coach Brian James' reckoning at the beginning of the season would have been "lucky to win twenty games" to the greatest revival in sports with a 26-12 record during this time, and Michael has re-established himself by Magic's reckoning as a Most Valuable Player. Magic, too, is stunned by all of this. "Where I have been surprised is his level of consistency. I thought his legs would go. It's crazy. Where other guys have a quit point, he doesn't have that quit point. Hopefully, these young guys who think it's their league will grab some pointers from him, because he's come back strong and none of them could do what he's doing right now."

Magic, of course, has backed off his words from the first week of the season when he went on national television and said he had begged Michael not to do this. Michael more or less force-fed Magic and all his other doubters their words of skepticism with ten days in December of rollercoaster, can't-bear-to-watch/in-your-face moments that just might become the most memorable parts of the Third Coming. A game-winning shot at the Garden followed by the he's-too-old performances many observers hoped they would never have to see followed by back-to-back scoring arias of early 1990s vintage marked ten days—maybe the only ten days of this whole ordeal—when Michael Jordan was the game again. The Third Coming had already confirmed that those final thirty-seven seconds of the 1998 NBA Finals would forever be the climax, the final chapter of Jordan's career. But these last ten days of 2001 became the sequel, the addendum, the up-and-down-and-up-again resiliency of his thirtysomething days, and nights, that will always make Michael feel the comeback didn't crash and burn at a whim, that his ego didn't write checks his body couldn't cash.

When Michael Jordan rebounded from a career-worst night of scoring six points at Indiana on December 27 by blasting off for fifty-one points on December 29 against Charlotte and forty-five more against New Jersey on New Years' Eve, he recreated the how-in-the-world buzz that is so much a part of his legend. How was not that inexplicable to Mike. He reasoned that this was the way he had been playing last July before he broke his ribs. The source of it, though, goes right to Jordan's ego. Forget scoring, steals, assists and all-NBA selections. Michael always wanted to lead the league in can-you-top-this and doing-what-nobody-else-has-before, and the last ten days of 2001 meant so much because he had for the moment what he always wanted—the last word, the last laugh.

The explanations and analogies for this rebirth flowed from all points. Doug Collins said whereas Michael used to be a sports car, he was now a luxury car. Indeed, even after 2001 struck midnight, Jordan had all of twelve dunks to show. Some of his moves had come back, but Michael felt he had recaptured some of his youth by flaunting the one attribute he would always hold over every other player. "He's showing that in basketball an old head can beat a young pair of legs," said his other good friend, Charles Oakley. During those last ten days of December, Michael made his point of proving to the world that this Third Coming was not all in his head.

2

HE PERCHED AT THE TOP OF THE KEY JUST BEHIND THE THREE-POINT LINE and snapped off a shot, the flick of his wrist so exaggerated it nearly echoed through the still-empty Garden. If he had hit from this same spot two months ago, with nineteen seconds to play on opening night, how would that have changed the course of history? Tonight, he wasn't taking any chances if that shot came up again, so almost two hours before this game against the Knicks, Michael Jordan worked through shooting practice like a golf pro on the driving range trying to fine-tune his swing. Michael had pretty much foresaken these pregame workouts back in the mid-1980s when his fame made it too difficult to come out and shoot in peace. Except on a day when tipoff came shortly after brunch, Michael would never venture to the court prior to the official team warm-up twenty minutes or so before game time. But here he was, shooting himself into a glistening sweat, working from one corner around to the other as if he was playing "Around-the-World" with Larry Jordan on the dirt court Pops built out back in Wilmington. A three-for-sixteen shooting performance like he put up last night in Orlando wasn't going to happen again. And it wasn't going to happen in the Garden.

If Michael picked any place to stage another uprising, it would have to be Madison Square Garden. As he splashed practice jumpers on this night before night-before-Christmas Eve, he might have been thinking back to November 8, 1984, his first game here as a pro. Seven games into his NBA career, Jordan commanded the Garden in a one-on-one with the league's reigning scoring soliloquist, Bernard King. Michael hit for thirty-three points, King one-upped him for thirty-four and the Knicks escaped with a five-point victory. In his next visit, Michael dropped forty-two on the Knicks, eight better than King and from that night on, MJ seemed to officially name this palace, "Madison Square Garden, One Of My Favorite Places To Play."

His Garden scrapbook has multiple volumes, each page adding more drama than the last. His first fifty-pointer, opening night of the 1986–87 season and the first night for Doug Collins as an NBA head coach, when Jordan scored the game's last ten points, rates second to the fifty-five he dropped five games after coming out of retirement in 1995. During the 1987–88 season, Jordan showed New York his will by coming back from a sixteen-point night in a December visit to score thirty-eight and forty-seven in return visits. When the All-Star Game came to New York in the NBA's 50th anniversary season, Michael crashed the party with fourteen points, eleven rebounds and eleven assists, the first triple-double—as topping ten in all three statistical categories is known—in the history of the league's midseason show. In March of 1997, Michael left New Yorkers with the "Con Air" game, a thirty-six point slap after Knicks coach Jeff Van Gundy popped off about Jordan being a con artist on the court for befriending players only as a means to lure them into a false sense of security. For an encore that season, Michael scored twenty of the final twenty-four points of a 105-103 Bulls victory. Maybe because he was born one borough away in Brooklyn or maybe because Rory Sparrow and Gerald Wilkins and John Starks and Spike Lee played some of his most renowned protagonists, Jordan was preordained to make this the most captivating theater off Broadway. The Garden might have been the only venue in the world to bid a more enthralling adieu to Jordan in 1998 than Utah's Delta Center. Days before his last appearance there on March 8, Michael recalled Juanita cleaning out a closet at home. Underneath years and years of snow boots, magazines and videotapes of the Mighty Morphin Power Rangers, she found a box of Air Jordans, the original ones from 1984 with the hideous collage of red and black and more red that David Stern supposedly banned Michael from wearing. He laced them up for this farewell performance, ignored the blisters and went off for forty-two points.

And now, the libretto for another Garden party seems cast. Michael can imagine how a franchise record–tying ninth straight win will bring a critic-eating grin to his face and remind those in and around the Wizards' locker room whose life this is, anyway. And if they are going to do this, Michael must white knight it because Rip has been sent back to his phone booth with a groin tear from the night before that has left him immobile. As Michael bull's-eyes pregame shots, Hamilton sits on the bench, watching, missing the action and sensing, "With Michael here, every game is more special. With Michael on the court, you never know when something is going to happen that you remember forever."

The first quarter, however, threatened to make this a more forgettable night than the Halloween horror two months ago. The Wizards needed a Jordan layup and another driving scoop from Tyronn Lue to crawl back from a onetime sixteen-point first-quarter Knicks lead to within 40-37 at halftime. Bad seemed headed for worse in the fourth quarter when Jordan missed a jump shot then threw the ball away on consecutive possessions to fuel a run that put the Knicks ahead, 80-70, with a tick less than seven minutes to play. At that point, Michael locked down his defense on Latrell Sprewell, who finished his three-for-sixteen shooting night by going 0-for-the-fourth-quarter, including a miss that left the score tied at 83 with 24.4 seconds to play. Still, another heroic night at the Garden seemed to be as likely as John Starks coming back to play the stooge when Michael had but seven fourth-quarter points and missed a pair of jump shots in the final minute.

Yet with nineteen seconds to play, Michael Jordan held the ball high over his head, looking straight into perhaps the defining moment of the Third Coming. If he misses this shot, the Jordan quotient dwindles to less than zero and the importance of Michael Jordan in the NBA hierarchy falls somewhere below a Cleveland-Golden State game in mid-January. Maybe it already had because the Knicks haven't even moved to double-team him here, perhaps thinking he is no more than Quincy Lewis. Michael resorts to his best asset, now. Sprewell is going to be expecting the dribble, drive and head-fake combination, but Michael plays the mind game, taking one power dribble to his right and with 3.2 seconds showing on the clock elevates to shoot without hesitation. The only other person in Madison Square Garden who expected the shot to rattle in like it did was the man who had seen so many of these here before. According to a *New York Times* report, Knicks television announcer Marv Albert provided a psychic reading just as Jordan was setting up, telling his broadcast partner Walt Frazier and a tri-state audience: "Let's not close the book on him yet."

Another legend seemed to be born out of this moment, a Miracle on Ice feeling swirling around the Garden when Jordan danced toward center court and into the celebratory arms of Popeye Jones, who led the Wizards to form a this-is-what-we've-been-waiting-for circle of life around Michael. Dissection of the replay vilified Sprewell for not even jumping to defend Jordan and castigated Allan Houston's after-the-fact attempt to lend a double team. Postgame accounts described the shot as a fifteen-foot swish and a nineteen-foot flush, and years from now it will no doubt gain as much distance as legend. This became another feat that put Spike Lee's name back in the newspaper, the face of disheartenment over another Michael Miracle and a shot that set off an *Entertainment Tonight* need for courtside celebrities ready to wax on about Jordan again being Captain Marvel.

One front-row face flashed a you-can't-touch-this smile on Michael's behalf, this one belonging to Ron Harper, Jordan's back-courtmate for the second run of Bulls championships. Harper chastised the Knicks for not double-teaming Jordan, asking, "C'mon, they don't know that by now?" And while nobody else wanted to admit it, Harper ventured that the shot shouldn't have come as a surprise because "this is still the same old guy." He brought back that same old feeling, the one that made even teammates want to stand in line to get Michael to autograph a shoe or a sweatband, any paraphernalia to mark the historical significance. Wizards center Brendan Haywood interpreted what this Third Coming had been for most of America by turning giddy afterward, saying in his best hero-worship, "You've seen it and heard it all your life. But to be right there under the basket when the net splashes was unreal." Point guard Chris Whitney put into words what everybody else was probably thinking. "This," Whitney reminded, "is what he came back for."

Not that this was one of those nights when years after forty-thousand people will say they were at the Garden. And lost in the celebration was a scrap of controversy over what happened in the 3.2 seconds following the heroics. Sprewell tried for his shot at redemption but turned the ball over when he stepped out of bounds with Jordan guarding him. Michael seemed to bump or push Sprewell on the play, perhaps the surest sign of his return to legend status because the call went his way. Michael seemed to be at a loss for words afterward, explaining getting the shot off by saying, "I was able to use my quickness." No, it wasn't that kind of night, when the Jordanology posse might expect Michael to be waving an "I'm back" fax in their faces. Not yet. Michael didn't miraculously regain quickness lost to three years of cigar smoking and aging knees. But a certain feeling did return this night, an optimism Richard Hamilton surmised after watching Michael win the game:

"He makes you believe anything is possible."

3

SO THIS IS WHAT ALL THE TALKING HEADS AND COUCH VEGETABLES EXPECTED Michael Jordan's Third Coming to render: A three-day rest following the Miracle at Madison brought a ripe and ready Jordan home to North Carolina. "Wipe your feet, you're about to enter heaven," he used to tell his Bulls teammates before they stepped off the plane here. The Wizards marched on Charlotte with a chance to win a franchise record tenth consecutive game, and the accompanying hype left a Michael-mattered-again trail. The state's second most famous MJ, the female one, Olympic sprinter Marion Jones, was here to see if the real MJ had finally come back. The Hornets were fast on their way to becoming the NBA's black eye, a city refusing to give its owner a new arena and casting its vote on the past election day to pack up the team and move it to New Orleans. Once again Michael Jordan had changed the course of an entire franchise. If Hornets owner George Shinn had made Michael his partner back in 1999, the buzz that has filled the Charlotte Coliseum for this game might be a nightly ritual. Instead, the 23,779 who have scalped their way in are more than three times what Charlotte has been drawing this season.

But what's most important is that all the trimmings are here to continue the third coming-out party. When Michael steps to the foul line to attempt his first free throw less than eight minutes into the game, the fans behind the basket he is shooting at rise to their feet. In a state where folks believe that although they didn't invent the game, they taught society that life is a metaphor for basketball and not the other way around, this situation would normally call for screaming and sign-waving and anything to distract the shooter into missing the free throw. But now they rise to shower Jordan with cheers. He has given them as vintage a first quarter as he is capable of these days, eleven points on four-for-seven shooting, an effort consistent with the 31.7 points per game he has averaged in games here his entire career. You have to believe Michael wants nothing more than to bestow on what he believes is the basketball capital of the world one more shot of him, for it is places like these—the Garden, North Carolina, Detroit, Chicago—where he most wants to stamp this return.

Accordingly, the game builds with a chance for him to swoop in to the rescue. The Wizards fight back from a nine-point deficit with 2:45 left in the game using a Jordan layup and three-point shot to cut the lead to 95-91. The crowd is bubbling so loudly when Michael hits the three-pointer with 23.9 seconds to play that any second now it seems Gary Glitter's comeback anthem—"Rock 'N Roll Part II"—will crank up, the Luv-a-Bulls will dance at center court and the fans will be echoing that universal chorus for ain't no stopping us right on cue. That "Hey" apparently jolts Charlotte's Baron Davis into missing a pair of free throws, and now the game is in Michael's hands with 12.3 seconds to play.

What all the talking heads and couch vegetables claimed—and feared—in this comeback was that Jordan would come to a moment like this and pull a Willie Mays. The lasting image of Mays, the great New York/San Francisco Giants centerfielder, is of an old man in a Mets uniform, dropping an easy fly ball to short center field at the end of his career. The children of the seventies don't really know this Hall of Famer running to deep centerfield of New York's Polo Grounds in 1954, making the over-the-shoulder catch on Vic Wertz's deep drive that earned him that Say-Hey Kid distinction. Mays left the Giants to return to New York and finish his career in the never-really-right Mets colors, and his succumbing to that fly ball is the gaffe the kids who never got to see him play in his prime were left with as a lasting image. With 12.3 seconds to play, Jordan suddenly has his Willie Mays moment. Pulling up on the right baseline, the ball slips out of his hands. Squirts, actually, like a hot potato, like an old man handling a hot potato. The Hornets' Lee Nailon recovers the fumble and heads off to the free throws that will seal the embarrassment and a 99-93 victory.

More than a game seems to have slipped through Michael's hands. The Wizards' win streak ends at nine, one short of breaking a forty-one-year-old franchise record that could have put Jordan's name in the Washington record book where he wanted it most: the page documenting winning. His eleven fourth-quarter points could have been a sign of yet another Michael Miracle. Instead he is left with a line of taking twenty-eight shots to score twenty-eight points. There is a pain seeping through the Wizards' locker room after all this. In his appraisal of how the Wiz kids have learned their winning ways, Celtics sage Red Auerbach explained to the *Washington Post* that the impact of Michael has been, "He instills confidence and makes them play defense." For the first time in ten games, though, the Wizards failed to hold a lead they took into the fourth quarter when the defense gave in and allowed a 22-7 Charlotte scoring run. Chris Whitney seems to lay down a monumental statement when he says, "The feeling in here is very different. We're surprised to lose. It's not like we're supposed to lose." That would be all well and fine, and the team might even laugh when Collins jokes, "Did you think we were going to run the table?" But Michael is irritated and angry because he knows what went wrong and afterward he spits out an observation as hard to stomach as the loss. "I," he said, "was the big culprit."

You don't want to mess with Michael Jordan when he's pissed off like this. Back in 1994 when he began his attempt to play professional baseball, Michael was going through hitting instruction at the Illinois Institute of Technology gymnasium, across the street from Chicago's Comiskey Park, when a couple of students tested Jordan's ire. Supposedly, they goaded Michael by saying they didn't believe he could take off from the free-throw line and dunk as he had in those All-Star weekend slam dunk contests eight years ago. Or they didn't think he could do it now at thirty-one years old. After several minutes of repeatedly charging, "You don't think I can do it," and these kids goading him by saying no, Michael banished them to go find a basketball. Moments later, Jordan was smoldering, walking off his runway and completing the space jam, showing the don't-ever-think-I-can't obsession that might never allow him to put down the ball.

He was smoldering again, twenty-four hours after going Willie Mays on the Hornets. His six points against the Pacers in a twenty-seven point loss marked the first time in 866 NBA games that he failed to hit double figures in scoring. March 22, 1986, when he had eight points against Cleveland ironically was the last full game he played without scoring at least ten points. He was also the culprit, so to speak, when the game got out of hand in the first quarter for allowing the man he was guarding, Jalen Rose, to ring up fifteen points. The defiant Michael reared his head after sitting out the final seventeen minutes of this game. "I know where I was in terms of that," Jordan said of his scoring deficiency. "That's not important to me. If I felt it was an issue, I would have returned (to play)." He cut the analysis short, adding that what he needed now was "a good practice" before the rematch with Charlotte two nights later.

4

TO TRULY HARKEN THE THIRD COMING NOW, MICHAEL WOULD NEED TO DO something over the top, as *Chicago Sun-Times* columnist and long-time Jordanologist Jay Mariotti observed. In his previous acts, Michael was always best personified by degree of difficulty, or as those who knew him best described it, degree of vindication and validation. Just when you thought he was human, he would elevate beyond all expectations. In the 1991 NBA Finals, he missed the would-be game-winning shot in Game One against the Lakers, then recovered in Game Two with that I-told-you-so change-of-hands, floating, up-and-under *ESPN Classic* highlight. The next year, Pat Riley and the New York Knicks supposedly had found a way to contain Michael in the second round of the playoffs by using a more rough-and-tumble version of the Pistons' Jordan Rules. Then, in his greatest Game Seven ever, Michael reaped revenge from the start, scoring fifteen of his forty-two points in the first quarter and crescendoing with that spinorama move past Gerald Wilkins, around Charles Oakley and over the top of Patrick Ewing for a slam, which he decided was one of the best eight moves of his career. In the 1993 NBA Finals, he listened to all the talk about Kevin Johnson slowing him down in the triple-overtime Game Three loss then came back with that drive for fifty-five points to nail down Game Four and for all purposes the third consecutive title. Now, in the wake of his most recent back-to-back human errors, Michael was hearing the echoes of Pat Riley and Kevin Johnson from Isiah Thomas, presently the innocent bystander as the Indiana coach, who noted after Michael's career-low deep six that "He's not the Jordan of age twenty-five." So with Charlotte coming to Washington, the pregame look on his face demanded a basketball to prep for a 2001 version of taking off from the foul line.

Michael's history on nights like these had been to take on a prize fighter's fury. Like on that March night in 1993 when he prepped his vengeance on LaBradford Smith for scoring thirty-seven points against Michael the night before. He sat at his locker, rocking back and forth, expressions becoming less and less PG-rated, loading up the venom that would send him on a Tasmanian Devil tear to thirty-six in the first half and forty-seven total for the game. An hour or so before this December 29 game against the Hornets at the MCI Center, however, Doug Collins said he noticed a more playful Michael Jordan, like nothing he had seen before. Or seen recently. And though Collins submitted that Michael's pride had been hurting— once the sure-fire sign that a Jordan never-before-done-that moment was coming—for the first time nobody knew for certain if his legs could keep up with his ego.

Less than three minutes into the first quarter, though, the Third Coming was in full swirl. Michael rained jumpers from the outset, hitting from all points, and made his first four shots. He drove for layups, he tipped in missed shots and he had the fadeaway on automatic pilot. The same variety of Hornets who forced Jordan into missing seventeen of twenty-eight shots in the game three nights ago became prey to the yo-yo fake, spin, up-and-under move. Michael scored the Wizards' first thirteen points in less than six minutes and had twenty-four of their twenty-nine during a first quarter when he was tougher to keep up with than the Tasmanian Devil. Tonto had become the Lone Ranger again at the four-minute mark of the opening period when Michael jitterbugged around stringy forward Jamaal Magliore, found hang time from those thrilling days of yesteryear, went over the top for a fourteen-foot jumper off the glass and drew a foul that led to a three-point play and a 25-19 lead. Seeing the move played back after the game, Michael realized the resurrection, saying "It's been a long time since someone said I was hanging in the air."

Michael went on to explain that he had the defense guessing and that "it was one of those nights." It was another one of those nights when Jordan rewrote part of the record book, another one of those nights to believe he still had that ability on any given night to show something nobody had ever seen before. Nobody had ever seen a Washington player score twenty-four points in one quarter since Bernard King did that eleven years earlier. Michael followed up his ten-for-fourteen shooting in the first quarter by making five of eight in six minutes of the second period. His thirty-four first-half points broke the franchise record of thirty-three, which Jeff Malone scored in one half against Phoenix in 1988. Michael scored eleven more points in the third quarter when the Wizards blew open the game, and he only needed those first three quarters to notch his forty-fifth point and break the MCI Center single-game scoring record he had set with forty-four against Utah in November. By the fourth quarter, the Air began leaking out when a 107-90 Washington victory was all but assured. Jordan added six more points early in the fourth quarter to finish with twenty-one-for-thirty-eight shooting, the twenty-one made shots being another team record. He also added one more never-been-done-before, his fifty-one points being the most a thirty-eight-year-old had ever scored in an NBA game, five more than when Kareem became the old standard in 1984.

The wake of Michael's whirlwind always left the main characters to put these fifty-point arias into words. Scottie Pippen and Horace Grant struggled repeatedly with this, often pouting with commentary about how many shots Michael would take. One time, Karl Malone refused to even discuss the subject. After this one—the thirty-fourth game of scoring fifty or more in Jordan's career and his first since Game Three of a 1997 playoff series against Washington—Hornets forward P.J. Brown said "Michael went back in time tonight." But for Charlotte coach Paul Silas, this was not a journey through the way-back machine for Jordan, rather an exhibit of how Michael had found a way to be the dominator once again. Silas likened Jordan's method to the only other athlete ever to rise so again and again.

"He is almost like Ali," Silas began, "when Ali used to fade back and you couldn't hit him with the jab. Mike is the same way, fading back on his shot. There is no way to get to it. It's almost impossible to stop him."

Michael, of course, flashed a low-wattage smirk and went into his I-told-you-so rhetoric after the game when even he relented that this could be the Third Coming. "After scoring six points, I'm pretty sure you guys were saying how old I was. I'm sure everybody was contemplating whether I could score big numbers again. And I certainly wanted to make a statement offensively. Tonight, I'm pretty sure people are going to say I can still play the game." Then, he tried to explain why this happened, why now. "I always felt like if I got into a good rhythm, I could score big numbers again. If I worried about my individual accolades, I'm sure each and every day I could come out and be more aggressive offensively and shoot it enough to meet those needs."

Wizards guard Chris Whitney turned a little Pippen or Grant when trying to answer the latest why about Michael Jordan. "What am I, Miss Cleo?" Whitney, who seemed to think only a renowned psychic would have seen this coming, told the *Washington Post*. "It just happens. No one knows how he does it. He just does it." Still, a revelation for the Wiz kids has come out of Jordan's record-setting night. Hubert Davis, one of Michael's offseason acquisitions, who brought experienced outside shooting prowess and the Dean Smith way of life to the Wizards, is one of the grown-ups here who recognized, "He, more than anybody else, knows you can get comfortable losing. He didn't want us to do that. We all just fell in line." If Michael can become the guy who stops the losing, perhaps with a little personal vindication for motivation, and he is only required to play that role every so often, then he can be the guy covering their backs and even drop these fiftysomethings every so often.

Suffice to say, then, Michael is feeling it now. A night like this could lead to a steak dinner, maybe a few drinks and end with taking a few pots off Reggie Miller or Ron Harper or even Magic in several hands of I-told-you-so cards. But Michael is feeling it like he never has before, so his next move is getting up early the morning after to begin working out at 8:30 A.M. He hadn't been lifting weights much this season to give his knees, back, wrist and other aches a break. But on this Sunday, he met the dawn with a burst of energy and went through an hour and a half of muscle-building, power-building, ego-building training sessions he had resumed just three days ago. No other point of the season so far had felt so right, so comfortable and Michael now looked at the world through I-believe-I-can-fly-colored glasses. The statistical geeks were busy researching for data documenting how Michael followed up his fiftysomethings in the past. Yes, there was the run in 1987 when he laid fifty-three on Indiana, fifty on Milwaukee and sixty-one on Atlanta in back-to-back-to-back games. The last time he had followed a fifty with a fortysomething was November of 1992 when a forty-point assault on Phoenix came two nights after dropping fifty-four on the Lakers. If he could get over the top of that, he could lend this third coming out a true legacy.

So much for going over the top, or so it seemed at first. Michael tried at the start of Washington's annual New Year's Eve game. But New Jersey's Kenyon Martin blocked Jordan's first shot hard enough to take the Air out. Martin swatted another Jordan offering and also stripped the ball twice from Michael in the first quarter, and suddenly the highlight of this New Year's Eve 2001 threatened to become the postgame concert featuring Sinbad. Or maybe, just maybe, the coming out party needed a little lore, something to spice up the legend, and here it came. Martin let it slip out that his back was starting to hurt in the second quarter just enough to slow his step slightly. This, of course, is like showing Michael your hand at the poker table, and he took off on a tear, during which New Jersey coach Byron Scott said Jordan looked like an assassin.

He closed out the first half by driving for a jumper over Keith Van Horn, drawing a foul and completing a three-point play, blowing past Martin for a layup, hitting another jumper and then taking Jason Kidd one-on-one for a hoop and foul. Four straight shots and ten consecutive Washington points turned a second-quarter deficit into a three-point halftime lead. The start of the third quarter was nothing anybody had seen before, at least not in about fifteen years. Jordan circumvented the Nets' defense for four straight layups. He mixed in a jumper and two free throws to finish off a soliloquy of twenty-two consecutive Washington points. These were not the Cleveland Cavaliers getting the back of Jordan's hand but the New Jersey Nets, with the best record in the Eastern Conference and Kidd finally playing the MVP-caliber ball Michael told him he was capable of five years ago. The last time Michael went off like this was on that sixty-one point night against Atlanta when he scored an NBA record twenty-three consecutive points. Jordan called his third quarter an "unstoppable roll" and finished it with forty-two points. He had forty-five when with about three minutes remaining in the game and with the Wiz well on their way to a twenty-two point victory, Doug Collins gave Michael the rest of the night off.

He skipped the I-told-you-so speak after this game, save for noting that the Nets and most teams for that matter had been trying to defend him one-on-one and "that's probably going to have to change." This was Michael Jordan's way of saying, "I'm Back." No fax required, this time, but an effusive Jordan, reassuring that both he and his knee felt better than it had all season, that more of this could be coming, that another fifty was not beyond the realm of possibility. Outside the Wizards' locker room, Collins tried to explain what had happened the last two games, the last ten days. "Before, he used to just beat you with sheer will, skill, energy," he began. "Now, he slices you just like a surgeon. And he's got a clock in his head. I've always said the older you get, the easier the game comes to you."

Michael was finally showing as much. One theory for his recent coming of age indicated the he had been spending more time lately watching game tape of himself and noticed a flaw in his jump shot, that he wasn't pushing off with both feet and as a result wasn't getting enough lift. His theory was that his legs were coming back and added, "If I can keep that tendonitis away, I'm pretty sure you can see this type of game again."

As 2001 rang out, Michael hit the NBA with an auld lange zing. He did what he said he wanted to do—and could do—back on January 5 when he started this. The Wiz kids were eleven games better than a year ago at this time, their 17-14 record holding steady at a playoff-pushing sixth in the Eastern Conference. As he sat on the floor in Philly, Magic might have been stretching it a bit when he said, "If Michael needs a point guard for twenty, twenty-five minutes, I can break it down and dish it to him." Yet as the new year set in, Michael was again the talk of the league, the best I-told-you-so he could ever have wanted.

Now, he set out to get that last word he privately admitted had become part of this comeback.

9

BULL

1

MICHAEL JORDAN IS ANGRY. GUM-CHAMPING, HEART-RACING, CATATONIC-STARE furious. Ron Artest is elbowing Michael, poking him, holding him, sticking a forearm in the small of his back and a knee up his butt. Artest is defending Michael with the same schoolyard bully abandon that fragmented Jordan's ribs six months ago. He assumes he is licensed to do so, having been assigned to shut down a reincarnated Michael Jordan, who finally has given reason to believe he's everybody's target again, everybody's checkpoint after scoring ninety-six points in his past two games. But Michael has had enough of this spit, or so it seems. He doesn't want to be standing here six months from now, explaining how this was the way he was playing before that January 4 night when the Chicago Bulls came to the MCI Center for the first-ever Jordan confrontation with the franchise he feels owes him everything. And oh how he was playing against the terri-Bulls, a second quarter to perpetuate the Third Coming with nineteen points that showed off the entire Jordan repertoire, circa 2002: Eighteen-foot fadeaways; sixteen-foot turnarounds; driving, stop-on-a-dime jumpers off one leg; and a blow-by reverse layup for old time's sake. He made seven of ten shots, first sending Artest to the bench with foul trouble and then abusing a rookie named Trenton Hassell, whose commitment to what seems to be the company line yesterday only infuriated Michael by calling him "just another player."

In the third quarter, Michael hits his fifth shot in a row, a stop-and-pop jumper over Artest to give the Wizards a 64-41 stranglehold, and the Bulls toughman hits the fan. When a shooter gets as hot as Jordan has now, the defense typically resorts to a tactic known as denying him the ball. One defender will shadow every move to keep his offensive counterpart from finding an opening to receive a pass. This is tantamount to shadow-boxing with a real opponent; you don't get any closer slow-dancing with somebody.

On most nights for the past eighteen years, there hasn't been one man capable of denying Jordan the ball. But Artest is playing like a combination of a National Football League cornerback using the bump-and-run and Stone Cold Steve Austin in Wrestlemania. Michael is caught in denial, and if he does get the ball, it's with four seconds or less on the twenty-four second clock and he has to force up what Phil Jackson coined the "bail-out" shot, often a twisting, off-balance, catch-and-release or spin-and-fadeaway maneuver Jordan seemed to make part of his standard game. Only he can't make bail now, and the lead has dwindled to nine when Michael launches an air ball with five minutes left in the fourth quarter. He tries to beat the hand-to-hand combat by driving on Artest but gets called for an offensive foul. The Bulls are within six points now when Michael tries the stop-and-pop and gets it shoved back in his face. He shoots a catatonic stare at two officials, not quite believing Artest does not get sent to prison, let alone called for the foul. At the same time, Ron Mercer picks up the rejected ball and darts off to a layup that can whittle the lead to four points with fifteen seconds left. But as Mercer goes hard to the glass, a savior seems to come down from the heavens of the past. Taking off from a full sprint, Michael Jordan ascends to pin Mercer's shot against the backboard with two hands. Picture a scene out of a Van Damme or Jackie Chan movie with Michael's rage-combusting spring. His elbow is about a foot above the rim, and the largest crowd so far this season at MCI Center lets out a where-did-that-come-from howl.

"I was pissed," Michael said nearly an hour after playing thirty-eight minutes, scoring twenty-nine points and skying to previously unseen and inexplicable defensive heights in this 89-83 revenge on the current nerds of the NBA.

His latest uprising came from "one of those situations when anger gave me a little bit more energy to go up." What Michael is pissed about isn't exactly certain. Artest is a possibility, what with his constant slapping and hacking making Michael feel like a pinball. Michael, though, never really minded physical play unless it was Bill Laimbeer or John Starks taking a cheap shot. Yet he might be a little scared of breaking something else or he might still be irritated about the rib sticking in July that has taken until about a week ago to fully get over. He might be frantic over what the world will find out in a couple of days, that Juanita Jordan has filed a petition to divorce Michael and end their marriage after twelve years because he will never become a stay-at-home dad or because of rumored infidelity or because she is tired of being the second priority. Or he might be at a boiling point because all throughout the week leading up to the game against the Bulls he has had to answer why he is not running basketball operations in Chicago, why this Third Coming didn't necessitate the number 23 jersey being lowered from the rafters of the United Center, why he "turned" on the city he gave a worldwide identity. In two weeks, he will return to Chicago to play the Bulls, play the United Center for the first time as the enemy and damn if that breakup of his Bulls in 1998 that came because Michael had had enough of Jerrys Krause and Reinsdorf still isn't pissing him off.

Not that Michael is hiding his true feelings about the Jerrys, Krause in particular. Not that he ever did. Michael was one of the original creators of the nickname "Crumbs" used on Krause because supposedly he could be found time and again with donut residue on his clothes. Michael also never got over Krause's comments on the day before training camp opened for Jordan's last season, the one about organizations winning championships, not players. "Players are parts of organizations," Krause went on to point out. He later tried to back off of what he had said, but Jordan didn't buy it, retorting with his thoughts about how organizations help. "They make it possible for us to get to the games. They treat our injuries, too," Michael said with some of that in-your-face wit he uses when pissed off. Two days before the game against the Bulls, Michael apparently was still bent on Jerry-picking. On the way back from practice, he heard a reporter submit a question about the impact his former teammate, Bill Cartwright, was having as the new Bulls head coach. Without stopping or even being asked, Michael called out, "That's the best thing the Bulls did. Now they've just got to get rid of Jerry (Krause) and replace him with John Paxson."

Michael is probably pissed off because Krause just doesn't get it. Perhaps he could have looked up at a sign a fan seated behind Krause at the MCI Center on this night was flaunting: WITH HIM: SIX TITLES . . . WITHOUT HIM: 51-193. In four seasons without Jordan, the Bulls had combined to win fewer games than Michael had won in any of seven different individual seasons playing in Chicago, and they have lost just about as many as Michael did in his last nine full seasons there. If Michael had heard Krause describe this meeting in a pregame chat as, "just one in eighty-two," he might not have been so polite with his commentary. As it was, he made two penetrating observations. When asked about the progression of the franchise compared to the Bulls, he said, "If we have to step on other people to move up, then that's what we have to do." As for looking back on the breakup, he reiterated, "They chose to go a different direction. I chose not to go that direction." In other words, enough of the bull. If Michael was pissed off, it's because he always gets that way when going one-on-one with his most hated rivals—Isiah, the Knicks, Pat Riley and Jerrys Krause and Reinsdorf. Life had most definitely become him against Chicago, a race to see who could rebuild their franchise first, and even though this wasn't the only reason for the Third Coming, it would certainly be one of the rewards.

2

ALL THIS ACRIMONY AND ANIMOSITY, AND WHERE DOES IT LEAVE MICHAEL
Jordan to get ready to face his past for the first time? In bed. The first
week of January in Washington brings weather definitive of the cold
and flu season, and Michael has come down with a sinus infection or
a bad case of the sniffles, depending on whose diagnosis you believe.
If only the Elias Sports Bureau—the official stat hounds of pro
sports—had kept track of how many points Michael averaged playing
with a cold or flulike symptoms or coming off an injury. Probably be
forty-plus. Ironically, on this historic night in Washington, what
Krause remembers most, or what he chooses to recall most prominently, is the way Michael played hurt. When asked to tell his
favorite Jordan story, he delivers one of his standard Crumbs cakes, a
classic yarn about a night in Phoenix in 1986 when Michael came off
a forty-three point throwdown with an infected big toe that looked as
pink as a newborn pig. Krause remembers the Bulls team doctor
opening up the wound to let the infection air out and "puss squirting
everywhere. Doctor told him he was out for two weeks and to fly
home. He said, 'Take me to Dallas. I won't cause a problem. I won't
raise hell.' Doug thought, what can it hurt. So we take him and he
goes out and scores like fifty-three the next night. I never thought
he's going to walk. After that, I'm saying this guy can do anything."

Actually, Michael scored forty-three and it was in San Antonio.
And this was the best Krause could do on this night? Maybe Krause
thought that the shot against Cleveland and the three-point feeding
frenzy against Portland and the thirty-eight with food poisoning and
the final thirty-seven seconds against Utah had less to do with winning six championships than his organizational philosophies. Think
of how pissed off Michael would have been had he heard this Krause
dissertation an hour or so before tip-off:

"We play eighty-two games a year. He's in the league. We gotta
play against him," Krause responded to a question about the signifi-

cance of the game. "Is it special? Every one of them is special to me." He added insult to the injury talk by relating that he had taken no interest in following Jordan's recent coming out, not even through the box scores in the newspapers. "You know what box scores are good for?" Krause offered. "If you ain't got any toilet paper, you can wipe your ass with them." Krause never had any trouble playing the heavy, but what if he was speaking on behalf of the reportedly growing sentiment of Chicagoans who felt Michael betrayed them with his move to Washington? Could Krause be saying he had no plans to talk to Michael on this night, "because we're flying right out after the game," even though Charles Oakley spent considerable postgame minutes with Jordan because he too was pissed off? Krause did add that he had no animosity toward Michael, but you have to wonder about a chief executive who says about the greatest player ever, the guy who won him six championships, "I cease to worry about Michael. He would be no different than any other player I deal with." After five minutes with Krause, you had to wonder if Michael against the Bulls had become a pissing match, more than a game. Jordan isn't above this either, and the reason he is driving the Wizards so hard is because he feels every little victory, every morsel of success is something he can throw back at the Jerrys. Like winning nine games in a row or eleven of the past thirteen or showing Rip Hamilton how to become a top gun is the equivalent of a championship because the Bulls are firing the coach and becoming a longer-running punch line in town than the Cubs.

"Sure, I want to beat Chicago," Michael said before the game, standing by the my-franchise-is-better-than-your-franchise pettiness of the situation. There are those, however, who wonder if more is bothering Michael than he will admit. Even though the Jerrys have taken the hit for the breakup of the Bulls, even though Michael has been on record as saying he wanted to keep playing when he retired in 1999, comments from Krause like, "We tried to talk him out of it," have cast a shadow of doubt over Jordan. Could he be reeling over a compulsive decision that took away the remaining best years of his basketball life?

Then, there's the how-am-I-ever-going-to-explain-this predicament stirring. The way the jockarazzi tailed him, Michael wound up getting into situations in which his words were thrown back to haunt him. For the most part, he had a knack for glossing over these incidents, having to double back on his two retirement speeches that professed he had run out of challenges being prime examples. But sometimes, he had to confess, and like rationalizing the all-night gambling foray he made to Atlantic City during the 1993 playoffs or accounting for the time one of his checks wound up in possession of a convicted drug dealer, Michael is pissed now about having to justify his repeated statements that he never wanted to play outside Chicago. The pall cast here is probably digging into him, tarnishing him in a way that icons of his stature never had to face. DiMaggio, after all, never had to hit against the Yankees. Mario never had to play against the Penguins. But here was Michael having to play against the Bulls, and tonight somebody was going to pay for it.

Doug Collins sensed emotion brewing. He admitted that driving to the MCI Center for the game he felt a knot in his stomach for the first time this season. Collins has already promised "There's going to be an air in that locker room that's different from any game we've had this year." Is that air or Air? Tonight, he has seen that look of fifteen years ago when Collins would be thick into his pregame speech, look over at Michael's locker, and "he's sort of lethargic. But what Michael always seems to do is he finds something to piss him off. I was kidding today, that we've got him sick, we've got some pizza being flown in from Salt Lake and before we go out, I've got Jeff Van Gundy calling him. So I'm pulling out all the stops tonight for motivation." All kidding aside, the air or the aura has told Collins that knowing Michael as well as anybody does, he wants to do something special against the Bulls, not something as incidental as a game-winning shot but a relentless hammering to show Kwame and Rip and the other Wiz kids how domination is the residue of resolve as much as ability.

Nobody has to tell Bill Cartwright about the look on Jordan's face right now. "We've seen it before," the Bulls coach for all of the past twelve days relates. "Regardless of whether he's thirty-eight or whatever, he's not a normal athlete. He's going to be a problem."

While all the pissing and moaning is filling the pregame, Michael sits in the steam room and sauna trying to open his sinuses and lungs, trying to find a breath of fresh Air. If this were Hollywood—and of course many nights it seemed like it with Jordan—Michael would be emerging out of the sweat box, steam rising behind him like he had just burst from some kind of time machine. Or something like that, for after a first quarter of hitting just one of five shots, Jordan played a second quarter straight out of yesteryear. And last year, if you think back to the Jersey game five nights earlier.

After sitting down for the first one minute, thirty-two seconds to catch his breath, Michael showed the Bulls what they had been missing. He quickly buried a jumper from the foul line when the Bulls figured they'd forgo the double-team option in favor of a zone, perhaps to create a last line of defense that had everybody ganging up on Michael, Pistons style. That, however, led to an illegal defense whistle and a Jordan free throw, followed by Michael's eighteen-foot fadeaway. He had not moved like this since, well, last year certainly but maybe not even last year. No dribbling, hesitating, yo-yo faking; just straight catch-and-shoot and any second now he was about to blow on the fingertips of his right hand like a gunfighter winning a shootout, or more appropriate, a man on a roll at the craps table. A sixteen-foot turnaround made it seven straight from Jordan, and only a Popeye Jones tip-in of a Michael miss slipped in between what would have been eleven straight points as Jordan dropped four more free throws. Trenton Hassell found out Michael was not just another player when he hit another jump shot over the Chicago rookie, then burned him by taking a give-and-go pass from Brendan Haywood to drop a reverse layup off a page out of the North Carolina playbook and leave Hassell turning back and forth from right to left in a which-way-did-he go posture. One last twenty-one–footer seemed to accentuate one of the most satisfying scoring solos of Michael's career. With 3.6 seconds left in the half, Collins subbed in Bobby Simmons for Jordan, and he sauntered off the court slowly, perhaps to rub it in to the only person in the MCI crowd of 20,674 not standing and cheering.

If he indeed had thoughts about beating the Bulls all by himself, Jordan nearly did so in the second quarter. He finished with nineteen for the quarter. The Bulls finished with nineteen in the quarter. He shot 70 percent from the field in those twelve minutes. The Bulls shot 38.1 percent. Michael even exacted a little personal revenge on Artest. With about five-and-half minutes remaining in the quarter, Michael had scored thirteen points already. He came into the game needing fifteen to hit thirty thousand for his career, a plateau only Kareem, Wilt and Karl Malone had previously reached. Of those thirty thousand, 29,277 had come with the Bulls. But when Artest fouled Michael at the 5:28 mark, he dropped the two free throws to complete an ironic Around the World. Ironically, the first point of his pro career had come more than seventeen years earlier against Washington. Though Michael scored just four more of his twenty-nine after halftime and only two after hitting a stop-and-pop over Artest early in the third quarter, he maintained perspective on what was important on this evening.

"Thirty thousand points is a lot and that was more or less the highlight of the game," he said of the Wizards' twelfth win in their past fourteen games. "And any time you can beat your former team, it's a plus, too."

Beating his former team, which had only one piece remaining from the championship years—Krause—was both the reason and the reward tonight. Collins wondered when was the last time he had seen a game take so much out of Jordan, that he was "dead on his feet" in the fourth quarter and that his incensed block on Mercer at the end came only because Michael found some of that Mystic Pizza laying around or some otherworldly force to add to the almost inexplicable rap sheet of Jordan's never-did-befores. Actually, Collins conjectured that Michael had "no idea where that block came from."

But Michael did.

"I had enough frustration, if that's what you want to call it, that I went for it." The anger, the animosity, the acrimony just continued to build. He would have to face it again at a greater volume in two weeks, and now he was beginning to wonder just how much more of this Bull he could take.

3

MICHAEL NEVER LET HIS ANGER BOIL OVER OUTSIDE THE LINES. HE MIGHT holler at officials or snap at teammates for mental lapses. Aside from the occasional trashing of a garbage can in the locker room at half-time or the reported tantrums at practice, Michael's public eruptions consisted of raising his voice an octave when he disagreed with a question or comment from the media mass. Only once, when a Chicago television reporter questioned whether Jordan's junket to Atlantic City in between Games One and Two of the 1993 Eastern Conference Finals series against the Knicks was an escalation of his gambling problem, did Michael explode. And then he merely turned and walked away like a schoolyard kid taking his ball and going home.

Following a four-day weekend in the wake of the Bulls stuff, the Wizards defeated a burgeoning young L.A. Clippers team on January 8—a developing youth movement that seemed to relish springing one another to fast-break dunks with in-your-jock defense Michael hoped his Wiz kids could be like—but in the postgame inquisition, not everybody wanted to talk about the game. The day before, the world learned that Juanita Vannoy Jordan had filed a petition in a suburban Chicago court seeking dissolution of her marriage to thirty-eight-year-old businessman M. Jeff Jordan for irreconcilable differences. The hard copy world of investigative reporting had been waiting for a moment like this to expose M. Jeff Jordan, and now the full court of press was coming like he had never known. Before the game, Michael presented the controlled response to the news, saying, "Obviously, when you have personal issues, it can drain you. Sometimes, work is an avenue to deal with it and move on. That's basically where I am right now. I come out and do my job and focus on what's been enjoyable for me, which is playing basketball, and things will work out for me in the long run." When his job was done for the night, however, the probing of just what was so irreconcilable about the differences was beginning. Out of the postgame inquisition came this question:

"What hopes do you have for reconciliation?"

"None of your business," Michael replied according to an account in *The Washington Post*. "Quite frankly, I don't want to talk about my personal life. When the time comes, you guys will hear it."

An attempt to turn this conversation back to basketball gave way to another confrontation. "Michael do you think your divorce is inevitable?"

"None of your business," he again retorted.

How long before he would reach the boiling point?

For several years now, whispers from his followers raised questions about the stability and happiness inside Michael's twelve-year marriage to former secretary Juanita Vannoy. He was smitten by her resistance to fall for his star power when they met at a Chicago restaurant in 1985, but her lone public appraisal of Michael as the guy she needed to take on more car-pooling responsibilities seemed to paint an underlying strain in their relationship. Their marriage did not consummate until after a breakup and after Juanita hit Michael with a paternity suit over the birth of their first son, Jeffrey. She reportedly served him those papers just as he was about to take the court for a game. Talk that she might have trapped him and rumors of a prenuptial agreement disintegrated when Michael responded by whisking Juanita to Vegas and improptuing through a 3:30 A.M. wedding at the Little White Chapel, during which he wore that outfit every man dreams of when getting hitched—jeans, loafers and no socks.

During their marriage, those who followed Michael's career often heard rumors about how he was seen crawling out of a limousine with one woman or another. But as he grew a family that added another son, Marcus, and a daughter, Jasmine, Michael would say after games that he had to run because he was looking forward to having dinner with his wife. The rumor talk always gave way to the conclusion that he really loved Juanita. Michael even let it slip that one of his passions was having candlelight dinners with her. Though they kept their life cloaked in privacy, Juanita seemed to be cast as the sullen one. In a 1992 interview, she was quoted as saying, "If someone didn't step up and say 'No,' there would be no time for his family." Fred Whitfield, the childhood buddy who Michael made Wizards director of player personnel, told the *New York Post* that Juanita is the supportive wife, "that's heard, but heard in private." She was a woman set in her ways, however, and every Sunday she took the kids back to her church in her parents' neighborhood on Chicago's South Side.

Apparently, Michael wasn't listening, according to the new rumors and reports making the rounds in January. Friends of Juanita intimated that this was the third time she was threatening Michael with divorce, that she had enough of waiting for basketball to end and family to finally take priority, a priority so important to her that the most non-negotiable demand she made of Michael before they ever got married was to promise never to move her out of Chicago, away from her family. If reports were true that Michael tried to smooth over his return to playing duty by placating Juanita with gifts, including a sapphire-and-diamond watch, the rumors of her coming to this dissolution because of the Third Coming were not greatly exaggerated. Michael never hesitated to say he missed the time with his family he enjoyed during retirement, and he knew how serious the situation had become. When he took a two-day leave of absence from the Wizards at the beginning of December to return to Chicago, he was supposedly there to have trusted physician Dr. Hefferon examine his deteriorating knee. But he was also there to see a supposedly fuming Juanita and he pledged to make these trips regularly to return what little sense of family life is possible when the husband and father works in another city.

Other rumors about Michael's infidelity weren't so easily confirmed, but put Jordan's life where he had worked so hard to keep it from going: the world of the tabloid. Only Michael's gambling with gangsters back in 1991 had been the source of tabloid type, but following the divorce petition becoming public domain, one of the supermarket tabloids published a headline that promised, "Exposed: Michael's secret sex life." A day after the divorce hit the streets, the supermarket tabloid of the daily newspaper industry—the *New York Post*—reported that Juanita had a private detective following Michael for four years and "spotted him in public with at least six women." Rumor mongering placed him in gentleman's clubs across the NBA, routinely hitting on dancers as if mingling with Michael, even lap-dancing for him, was no more indicting than waiting in line for his autograph.

If Michael is upset, though, because the *Chicago Sun-Times* has tabloided his private life with the front-page headline, "So who gets the house?" he isn't saying. Word from his inner circle indicates he's not going to let his marriage come down to the final thirty-seven seconds, that he knows she will give him one last shot, if only for the sake of the kids. He's probably equally pissed off about how his personal life has diverted the focus from what's happening inside the lines. The victory against the Clippers, of course, is the Wizards' thirteenth in their past fifteen games, and the rumor making the rounds in the NBA now is that if Michael can lead this team into the playoffs, he should be the league's Most Valuable Player. And he might just be pissed off about his personal life getting in the way of him enjoying his greatest I-told-you-so since he was cut from the Laney High School varsity basketball team.

Ironically, remember how a year ago anger oozed through Michael almost as vehemently? After the Wizards blew a twenty-one point lead to the Clippers in December of 2000, Jordan treated the players like a garbage can with his "loser's mentality" speech, in which he called them all a disgrace to the fans. But now Michael's mentality seemed to come full circle with *Washington Post* columnist Michael Wilbon writing about this victory that looking out on the floor he saw the young Chicago Bulls when Doug Collins was nurturing a champion in the making. Chris Whitney and Hubert Davis were sticking timely jump shots with the daggerlike precision of John Paxson and Craig Hodges. Popeye Jones was rebounding and battling with an exuberance that recalled a young Horace Grant. Michael took his turns being Michael or Scottie Pippen. At the end of the first half, he strung together four consecutive jump shots, two in the final minute. Jordan acquiesced to Davis in the third quarter, who scored fourteen of his sixteen points, and after the Wizards nearly blew a twelve-point fourth-quarter lead, Michael, Popeye and Whitney combined for ten straight to finish off the 96-88 triumph.

Michael finished with a line that had become typical of the team's thirteen-of-fifteen run of success: eighteen points, ten rebounds and eight assists. *Los Angeles Times* columnist J.A. Adande, a one-time Jordanologist from his days covering the Bulls for the *Chicago Sun-Times* in the mid-1990s, described this as "getting Jordaned," meaning Michael had forged another team that could win with whatever resources they had available. Rip has been out for six games now and his return is still weeks away, but Davis and Whitney are hitting just enough jump shots to give the Wizards—and Michael—enough confidence to keep the ball moving on offense, rather than watching it when it lands on Jordan like they had been for so much of the first few months. What's also surprising to Michael is that none of his Bulls teams ever Jordaned anybody like this. Popeye, Haywood and Jahidi White are giving the Wizards an inside story Collins argues will be the foundation of the post-Michael era. Against the Clippers, the three-headed monster up front combined for thirty-three points and twenty-two rebounds.

Nevertheless, as the season rolled into mid-January—the week leading up to the return to Chicago—it wound up stirring more rage in Jordan. Both Michael and Doug Collins called this week the toughest, most telling stretch of the season with games against Milwaukee, Minnesota, San Antonio and New Jersey—three division leaders and all four rated among the best in their conferences at the time. James Jordan believed his son's intelligence showed up most prominently at times like these when Michael would sense a need to make a statement of bravado as his way of providing leadership.

When the Bulls finally beat the Pistons in the 1991 playoffs, Jordan said before that series that he thought his team finally had grown enough courage to stand up to Detroit. Now, before the Milwaukee game Jordan told the media that the way he felt made him believe he would keep on playing beyond this season, letting his team know they were on the verge of something big, something to contend with the Milwaukees and Minnesotas of the NBA. "I can still be dominant in different ways," he explained. "I've gotten to a point where I really understand the game of basketball, but also I'm still learning. As long as I can continue to do that and challenge myself, there's always going to be a place for me playing the game of basketball." Even though this game hits close to home and truckloads of reporters have made the one-hour trip from Chicago, Michael seems to be nearly stress free. Jeffrey and Marcus have also made the trip from Chicago, and they lead their daddy off the Wizards' team bus into Milwaukee's Bradley Center. Michael even takes time to talk about his marital problems, a rare moment of letting the world inside that in the past has always indicated the situation is not quite as bad as it seems or at least that he can accept what's happening.

"For years, you hear positive things about an individual and then you see something that's questionable, and the ears perk. It's more now than ever. I didn't step into this without knowing that. I'm fully aware. I just try to operate my life the best way I can. I know I'm open for judgment by anybody. Once I'm on the basketball court, I'm in my own little world and I could care less about what you guys think or say."

But what if that little world suddenly started falling apart? If the Wizards' success of the last six weeks suddenly hit a breaking point, would Michael fall apart with it? Tim Thomas, Milwaukee's gang-buster forward, sees this game as an opportunity to gun down Jordan and he does so by hitting his first five shots. With Ray Allen still staking a claim to be the Air Apparent by stroking three-point shots, the Bucks take an eighteen-point halftime lead and take Michael out of the game. Jordan sits out the final quarter of the 105-86 loss hoping to regain his touch for a meeting with Minnesota the next night in Washington.

And he does, hitting four of his first five shots and ten of sixteen to score twenty-six first-half points. Minnesota's Kevin Garnett had called this game a duel with Jordan, and he holds up his end by answering with seventeen first-half points. In a fight to the finish, Jordan hits a couple of jump shots to bring the Wiz back from a twelve-point fourth-quarter deficit. But his thirty-five points aren't enough to offset thirty-one from Garnett and twenty-nine from Timberwolves guard Chauncey Billups. Falling short in the 108-100 loss inflames Michael, who admits afterward, "This is a game I desperately wanted to win."

But it's getting worse. Against San Antonio three days later, Michael suffers through his second-worst shooting night of the season to date, a five-for-twenty-one disaster. What Michael can't handle, though, is missing six free throws in this five-point loss. To Michael, free throws always were proof of being a player who can produce under pressure, and he is so pissed about this that before the next night's game in New Jersey he spends the entire pregame warmup practicing his foul shots. Apparently, it's all starting to get to Jordan. After the San Antonio defeat, the Wizards have their first three-game losing streak since before that telltale night in Cleveland. And after struggling through one of his worst games in long-term memory, Michael admits, "I stunk."

The New Jersey game afforded no time to recoup. Before Michael breaks a sweat, the Nets have made their first thirteen shots and are on their way to a twenty-five point lead. (Maybe they are pissed about that forty-five two weeks ago.) This game will be the low point of the season, and not just over the margin of embarrassment but because on repeated occasions in the first quarter, Jordan wound up being the one man back when the Nets seemed like they were running fast-break drills. And in these two- and three-on-one situations Michael looks immobile. He looks old. The Wizards trailed 72-33 at halftime, and Michael came out for the second half wearing ice. Sitting on the bench for two quarters, he had to listen to a crowd filled with just enough New York sarcasm, cracking alimony jokes. After the game, he has to listen to more inquisition about going back to Chicago in three days. He tries to downplay, confirming that it will probably be like a playoff game but saying that it has no other added significance because, "It's different people in those uniforms. I can understand if the players that I played with were still in those uniforms, but it's a different situation. They're not. I'm in a different uniform. I'm with a different organization. That's the way it is."

Yes, he's getting a little testy now, especially when the issue again surfaces about whether Michael, as rumored, told free agents thinking about signing with the Bulls the past few years his feelings toward management. With more money to spend than just about every team and a menu of free agents that included Antonio McDyess, Damon Stoudamire and the one the Bulls wanted most, Tom Gugliotta—not coincidentally a David Falk client like Mike—who eventually signed with Phoenix, the Bulls' big catch wound up being Brent Barry. He again denies any involvement, coyly suggesting that the Bulls didn't need his help to be portrayed as a disaster with Tim Floyd coaching them into confusion and adding that "If they did ask, I wouldn't give a comment. I wouldn't try to pollute the situation."

One last question comes from longtime Jordanologist/Jordan antagonist Lacy Banks of the *Chicago Sun-Times* who asks if Michael still harbors discontent for playing at the United Center. "That's a crock of shit," Michael responds, his voice climbing an octive. Maybe if they had called it the Jordan Center, Michael might not be so emotional, but perhaps this response reveals what to expect in Chicago on January 19. A jam-packed United Center for this Saturday matinee might even look at Michael and Krause and wonder: So, who gets the house?

4

MIKE LUFT HAS BROUGHT FOUR OF HIS FRIENDS FROM MICHIGAN STATE University to the United Center on this Saturday afternoon. He is a resident of Glenview, a Chicago suburb in the same general geographic and demographic vicinity as Michael Jordan's Highland Park home. Mike Luft is using the season tickets his father has had for Bulls games since before they ever played in the United Center. Mike Luft remembers when he was a pre-teen the feeling of coming to the old Chicago Stadium to watch Michael Jordan and, as he put it, "see something you might never see again." Luft and his college buddies are typical of the fans who have come to the United Center this afternoon. "We will boo," he insists. "I think he betrayed the city. We want him to score two points. Or fifty."

All of Chicago seems caught up in this ire. Should they boo Michael or cheer him when he returns as the enemy? Is he the enemy? Or is it the Jerrys? That is the other perplexing conflict taking place in Chicago on this day. Who is to blame for Michael Jordan returning wearing another uniform? Krause and Reinsdorf or Michael Jordan? At the end of this day, one or the other could become the most renowned scapegoat in town since Mrs. O'Leary's cow kicked over that lantern and started the Great Chicago Fire. Michael has said he doesn't expect to get booed, and he shouldn't.

After all, this is the guy who made a lot of folks in Chicago wealthy, resurrected the city's west side neighborhood long dismissed as mired in endless poverty and hosted an annual party for one million people every June by Lake Michigan to celebrate championships that created a culture, a nucleus that everybody was no more than six degrees removed from Michael Jordan. Still, at the Bulls game against Atlanta played two nights before Michael's return, the *Chicago Sun-Times* sampled fifty Bulls fans to ask what they would do. Twelve said they would boo, twenty-nine said they would cheer, nine said they would do neither and the individual responses were as varied as a Chicago election. Some fans accused him of selling out, cheating them for not being able to see him retire as a Bull and wear no other uniform. Others indicated they would cheer just because he's Michael Jordan.

One group of fans is intent on giving Michael the love, that being the twelve-and-under contingent, which has staked out the part of the United Center where Michael will make his entrance and is holding up signs with messages like, MICHAEL, MY CHRISTMAS PRESENT WAS COMING TO SEE YOU. Another faction of the crowd, however, seems to be believing everything it has read this morning. A report in the *Chicago Tribune* blamed Michael for the breakup of the Bulls dynasty. Jordan walked away, the story contended, because he was burned out on basketball, because he was frustrated with Scottie Pippen for waiting until the last championship season started to have his ankle surgically repaired and for getting into his own pissing match with Bulls management, and because he was not exactly excited about another run with a deteriorating Dennis Rodman and Luc Longley. As for the popular sentiment that Michael might have stayed had Krause been asked to ride off into the sunset like Phil Jackson did, well, propaganda indicated that Crumbs couldn't be brushed aside because he was the guy who put the pieces around Jordan to win those six titles.

Those who sided with management maybe thought differently

when hearing about what happened to Ray Clay as a result of this day. Clay is the longtime Bulls public address announcer, the man whose voice is known worldwide for his deep bass *From North Carolina, number twenty-three, Michaelllllllll Jorrrrrrdannnn* introduction. Prior to the Wizards game, Clay was asked whether he would reprise the call for Jordan's return. He did, though maybe a touch short of the echo of yesteryear. Ray Clay was relieved of his duties after the 2002 season ended, and reports indicated that Krause had him cut for the Jordan intro.

Betrayal played off against the projected pigheadedness of Krause for putting together a team that has won just fifty-three games since Jordan departed, seems to have much of Chicago seeing Michael as a photographic negative, the blue number twenty-three exposed where the white one should be. But he is caught in another battle of affection on this day. For the first time in ten years, the Chicago Bears have made the National Football League playoffs, and in a city that currently has no other winners, in a city where one Super Bowl championship generated as much conceit as six NBA titles, a Bears market is more compelling than a Bulls market. A doubleheader of greater historical impact than this city has ever known features Michael versus the Bulls in a noon matinee followed at 3:30 P.M. by the Bears' first playoff game against the Eagles. This might even top that October day in 1984 when the only other man in Chicago sports lore to enjoy a Jordanesque existence—Bears running back Walter Payton—broke Jim Brown's record to become the NFL's all-time leading rusher a couple of hours before the Cubs blew a chance to go to the World Series by losing the deciding game of the National League Championship Series to the San Diego Padres. A Jordan-Bears back-to-back is such a hot ticket that livery services are posting premium rates to ferry fans from the United Center to Soldier Field, where the Bears play, in time for kickoff. Some people reportedly have even looked into the idea of chartering a helicopter. Michael knows that there is only one game in town today, so he attempts to pacify the city once again by saying, "If I advised anybody, go to the Bears game."

Nobody, however, is giving up seats at the United Center. So it has come to the moment of truth, of honesty, of reckoning for all Chicagoans. The game will begin in about twenty minutes, and as Michael emerges from the locker room, a herd of television cameras comes backpedaling down the hall like they are trying to defend a Jordan catapult to the hoop. A security detail large enough to protect the president or maybe Madonna leads Michael around a corner and up a corridor to the court. A roar like a jet engine warming up starts, but the clamor comes to a silence when a buzzer sounds a wake-up call for the starting lineups to be introduced. Nobody can deny the power Michael still holds over this city, this building and this franchise. On the cover of their 2001–2002 media guide, the Bulls have pictured the two high school stars they selected among the top four picks in the last NBA draft. Tyson Chandler wears number two. Eddie Curry wears number three. Standing next to each other in the pose they subliminally form the number twenty-three. Or maybe not so subliminally. The Bulls will always be under the power of number twenty-three, and if there is a person pissed off at Michael for his turnabout in the building, none of them can be heard when a Wizards forward from North Carolina is introduced.

Five, maybe ten years after, some people will swear the standing ovation that greeted Michael Jordan's introduction on this day lasted five minutes. It probably should have. It easily could have. The United Center seemed to rise in a wave and the volume reached old Chicago Stadium decibels and the roar that built like a jet engine preparing for takeoff continued for one minute, eighteen seconds. Michael waved three or four times then eventually hung his head, the only explanation for this being that he was trying to hide his tears. After seventy-eight seconds, the ovation was unplugged when the house lights were doused to begin the usual ritual for the home team introductions. Who put the lights out created another battle of ill wills. Good thing Krause and Reinsdorf weren't there or they no doubt would have been blamed. One report indicated that NBC, televising the game, wanted to get on with it. Counterintelligence pointed the finger at the Bulls for pulling the plug. Maybe it was Michael's idea, for afterward he responded to a question of how emotional the introduction became by saying in a watchoo-talking-about-Willis tone, "You didn't see any tears. They cut the lights out way before you could see anything. I was getting close. Thank God they cut the lights out or we would have been sitting there still probably."

This Kleenex moment was about the only part of the day that lived up to the hype. It was hard to tell who was worse—Michael or the Bulls. Jordan nearly posted an ignominious triple-double with sixteen points, twelve rebounds and nine turnovers. Bulls defenders Ron Artest, Ron Mercer, Eddie Robinson and Fred Hoiberg each had a hand in stripping the ball from Michael on his drives to the basket. He hit seven of twenty-one shots and epitomized the sadness of the day with about seven minutes left in the fourth quarter. Michael took a lob pass from Hubert Davis and finished off what would qualify as an alley-oop only in an over-forty league. Otherwise, the game could have been a reject from an over-forty league. The Bulls scored just twenty-seven points in the first half, eleven more in the third quarter and shot a touch under twenty-five percent for the game. In a place where the fourth-quarter shouts of "Hey" used to echo through the west side of Chicago, the "YMCA" sing-along now provided the only spark of electricity. With four minutes left in the game, Chicago apparently saw a need to once-and-for-all purge itself of Michael Jordan and so a chant of "Let's Go Bears" erupted. In so many ways, this game seemed to officially declare the end of an Air-a in Chicago.

"I'm glad it's over with," Michael said, more likely referring to the game than to his place in Chicago's pop culture. He is more sad than angry after the game, at least initially. He takes back some of what he said about the acrimony coming in, commenting, "I can say whatever I want to say about the uniforms and the people that's changed in those uniforms, but Chicago is Chicago, the Bulls are the Bulls and the fans make the whole situation tough. When the crowd started that whole thing, it's tough for me to play. It's like playing against a relative in a sense. The enthusiasm and the emotion was not quite the same as I normally play."

He did get his dander up some in the postgame responding to the *Chicago Tribune* report by revealing that the Bulls did talk with him about "something very simple" with their organization but none of the opportunities that he has now. What seemed to be most infuriating for Michael on this day was the revelation that came with the game still in doubt in the fourth quarter. As Wizards point guard Chris Whitney held the ball in his hands to go to the foul line and hit ten consecutive free throws in the final fifty-seven seconds, Michael Jordan stood in a corner, trying to be a decoy of sorts. That and seven-for-twenty-one shooting and a boring 77-69 Wizards win led Jordan to this conclusion.

"I'm not the same player. As much as my competitive nature relished trying to carry a team, carry a franchise, that's really a goal I don't know if I can meet. That takes a lot for me to say that."

When the Wizards' team bus rolled west on Madison Avenue and the United Center appeared in the clearing hours before this game, Michael diverted his eyes and ordered full speed ahead to the players' entrance. The talk was, he didn't want to see the statue of himself on the eastern front of the arena. Indeed, the hardest part of this return to Chicago was that it made him understand that it wasn't about all the thirtysomethings, the couple of forty-pointers or even the fifty. He had to face it that he just wasn't that guy on the statue anymore.

10

AIR BALL

1

SOME RITE OF PASSAGE IS ABOUT TO GO DOWN, AND SAMUEL L. JACKSON
and Britney Spears and Magic and Doctor J and the *NSync guys and
Ali and Frazier—together for the first time since the Thrilla in
Manila—and Magic Johnson and that woman from *The View* and
Li'l Bow Wow and Elton John have come to Philadelphia for this
very moment. The 2002 NBA All-Star Game has broken into a full
sweat, and with about three minutes remaining in the first quarter
Michael Jordan slips behind the defense, gathers a touchdown pass
from Shareef Abdur-Raheem and is ramping up for another historic
flight. Nobody expects the take-off-from-the-foul-line assault or any
helicopter moves from a past life. A little fresh Air, though, with just
enough hang time to flash one last pose of the Nike logo does not
seem to be out of the question.

Anticipating the possibilities, Eastern Conference all-star teammate Dikembe Mutombo rises from the bench with hit-me-baby-
one-more-time exuberance, and Dominique Wilkins, seated three
rows up in Philadelphia's First Union Center, drops his popcorn,
presumably to maneuver for a better view. One signature slam here
can validate the past few months, for as Doug Collins points out, no
matter how many points Michael scores, they always want to remember the dunks. With an entire arena holding its breath, however,
Michael gets lost in space. He winds up bunny-hopping toward the

rim, looking a little like he has stubbed his toe. Perhaps he is hung up trying to meet the expectations here, for a would-be can-you-top-this jam ricochets off the back of the rim with the power of a cannon shot and recoils toward halfcourt like that bouncing ball fading out the last lyrics of one of those cartoon sing-alongs. Magic immediately jumps up, points and shoots a smile that at the same time promises you'll hear about this one and also understands what Michael was feeling a few weeks ago in Chicago: No matter how many games he wins or points he scores, expecting the Michael Jordan who can throw down the unexpected at every turn is pulp fiction.

"All right, who's going to be the first to ask?" Michael extends to the postgame inquisition. Before anybody can take a shot at him, he will make sport of what he realizes might become the signature slam of the Third Coming, at least. "I laugh at myself. If I can't laugh at myself, I can't laugh at anybody," he continues. "It was one of those situations, you got a wide-open dunk and every athlete who loves to create loves that opportunity. Been a while since I've been in that circumstance. Obviously, that told it's own story. Wheels start turning; you try to figure out, well, what will you do? At the last minute, you think just dunk and you lose concentration. As much as you want to be creative, you listen for all the signs; your mood, your body and you worry about something popping or whatever. As you get old, you don't have the same type of confidence. You got to go through a checklist. I went through the checklist, and by the time I was there to dunk the ball, I wasn't there." No, he wasn't. Isn't.

Another telling reminder to Jordan that he isn't there anymore comes in the second quarter. He has been put on ice for the rest of the half when NBC reporter Jim Gray takes a seat next to Michael on the bench and asks him to justify to the people in more than two hundred countries watching the game how in the world he could miss the dunk they had stayed up through the middle of the night in Istanbul and Manila and other such NBA hotbeds to see. But as Michael begins to rationalize, Orlando's Tracy McGrady shocks the world by finding rare air nobody in the NBA has walked in three years. Holding the ball just beyond the free-throw line, McGrady—who has gone from being one of those high-school-to-NBA flops to another one they are calling the next Jordan the past two seasons—bullets a pass off the backboard, soars to catch it, jumps over Dirk Nowitzki and windmill dunks with so much force that the basket shakes into a blur.

Michael stops in midsentence to digest what has just passed. Tomorrow morning, kids on playgrounds and ballers in high school gyms will be trying to imitate McGrady's alley-oop to himself. But thank god they're mimicking T-Mac, for they might be mocking MJ. "I don't know why everybody's tripping because Jordan missed a dunk," McGrady observed, adding himself to a bandwagon gaining more and more passengers who wonder if the time has come to let the Air out of the ball. "He's not that Jordan, where it used to be he could put his hips up to the doggone rim."

But this is why everybody is tripping: Because on playgrounds they still want to be imitating Michael Jordan's dunks and hang time and miracle moments. This is why this All-Star Game has taken on significance not felt in Philly in about two hundred years. Or since Wilt played here. Or Doc. In the three weeks leading up to the All-Star Game, Doug Collins is hearing, and saying, that Michael is playing his best basketball of the season. Cleveland coach John Lucas has retracted his statement of late November when he said, "He's Jordan but not that Jordan," now contending that Michael is the MVP of the league. The Wizards are 26-21 going into the break, fourth best in the Eastern Conference, and the Michael Jordan conundrum has bubbled into All-Star weekend. That he finished fifth in the fan voting for the game behind Vince, Shaq, Kobe and Iverson should be an indication that the public seems ready to move on from the Michael Jordan era. That Milwaukee's Ray Allen insists he is the voice of the new generation when, after being asked again and again to wax on about the first half of the Third Coming, he screams, "No more Michael Jordan questions," is an indication that the other players want to get their share. Even the biggest Jordan fan in the history of the NBA seems to want to put Michael in his place. In an all-star weekend interview with the *Philadelphia Daily News*, Commissioner David Stern remarks, "We are in the post-Jordan era yet we still have Michael. He's an All-Star but he's not the transcendent player he was."

Which would all make sense if they all could only explain or rationalize how the Jordan effect is filling arenas across the NBA more than any of the league's other attractions. The Wizards lead the league in home and road sellouts. Allen Iverson reveals in his weekend media briefing two critical points that capsulize the presence of Jordan, with or without the dunks. "The mystique don't ever go nowhere," he reminds. "You can take Michael Jordan's shoes and try to fill them, and all of us could try to put our foot in them, and they just wouldn't fit." Additionally, Iverson says when he's home playing on the toy basket with his four-year-old son, Little Deuce, that Deuce always says, "You're Allen Iverson and I'm Michael Jordan." Even though Ray Allen doesn't want to hear it anymore—and he is not alone—all the talk this weekend is about Michael Jordan, and what's becoming clear is that the more the league and the game want to move on from him, the more the league and the game just can't seem to let him go.

2

REALLY, WHAT HAS THE LEAGUE SHOWN THAT RIVALS THE THEATER OF Michael Jordan? Kobe, at twenty-three years old, has thrown down as many fifty-pointers as Michael at thirty-eight. Allen Iverson is winning Most Valuable Player awards hitting forty percent of his shots. Michael is hitting forty percent of his shots this season. Sadly, the NBA has Shaquille O'Neal muscling past guys half his size, dunking from a hop-step away and shaking down basket supports as its showpiece. Not that being six-foot-six with an arsenal of acrobatics, a laserlike jump shot and a will the size of the Grand Canyon is everyman, but it's a lot easier to be that than a seven-foot, three-hundred-and-fifty-pound Goliath. If Reggie Miller weren't throwing in thirty-five footers at the buzzer in the playoffs, would the NBA have any last-second miracles to show off?

Really, what has the league shown that rivals Michael Jordan on this January 24 night, just three weeks from his thirty-ninth birthday? Cleveland has come to the MCI Center, and there is a stink in the air. Michael remembers that last meeting in November. Before he launched into his postgame filet of his teammates on a night two months ago that now seems like another lifetime because of the Wizards' winning ways, Jordan had to stomach Cavaliers guard Ricky Davis ramming home dunks with the Cavs up by twenty, as if shaking the basket support with Shaq-like bombastity had become the NBA's measure of a man. "Those type of things don't go without being noticed," Jordan said of this rematch. "It was one of those things you didn't want to happen again, so the best way to do that was to sit him down over there so he can watch us."

Right next to LaBradford Smith, Nick Anderson and Kevin Johnson.

With one minute, twenty-three seconds left in the first half, Jordan faked his way past Davis for a layup and a foul, the fourth on Davis. The basket gave Michael twenty-two points so far and in slightly more than twelve minutes of play Davis had four more fouls than points. By the time Davis scored his first point, the midpoint of the fourth quarter had passed, and fifteen seconds later Michael hit a jump shot for the last of his forty in the 94-85 Wizards victory.

Jordan also slapped a little retribution on Cleveland forward Jumaine Jones, who had intimated his wannabe back on that November night. As Michael prepared to inbound the ball toward the end of the third quarter, Jones reportedly took one last shot at Jordan, saying, "You should wear Adidas." Silent but deadly, Michael left Nike footprints all over Jones by putting consecutive jumpers in his face. Michael might have lost a step, but apparently not a step on the hierarchy of who's got game. Following Jordan's fourth forty-or-better of the season, Davis popped off about Michael then and now. "He told me he remembered the last game," Davis told the *Cleveland Plain Dealer.* "We're going to remember this when they come back to our place (next Thursday). Everyone's scared of him. I'm not." A week later, though, Davis and Jones would take a seat right next to Craig Ehlo and Gerald Wilkins.

Collins, apparently, was right: Michael did have a clock in his head. He said that right around the All-Star break Jordan would be back on his game, and he was. In the ten games leading into the break, Michael averaged 30.7 points, 6.7 rebounds and 6.1 assists per night. He had been hitting 47 percent of his field-goal attempts. Compare those numbers to the 1998 season, when he averaged 28.7 points, 5.8 rebounds, 3.5 assists and shot 46 percent, or 1997 when he averaged 29.6 points, 5.9 rebounds and 4.3 assists and shot 48 percent. These were the ten games when Michael was probably truly healthy and back up to speed. Ten games when he was the transcendent player again. Ten games filled with the drama and promise that Michael will go into the All-Star weekend having regained that hold-your-breath hold on the game.

A game-winning shot here, a record-breaking quarter there and the anticipation effect injects Michael into occasions like his first trip to Minnesota since 1997. The ten-game crescendo to the All-Star break begins here in Minneapolis, where tickets to this January 21 game sold out three months ago in seven minutes. The 20,320 fans at the Target Center produce what Jordan has seen in every building during the Third Coming: the largest crowd of the season. Even though it's been a mere two days since his seven-for-twenty-one soiree back home, Chicago seems so far away in the second quarter when Michael finishes a flurry of hitting six consecutive shots. His twenty-two first-half points are reminiscent of his past dominance of the Timberwolves, who needed eight seasons to score that first-ever victory against Jordan's Bulls in 1997. Once again, the league has taken to measuring Michael with these kinds of transcendent milestones. What has changed, however, is the feeling around the league that they can beat Michael, and what they are having to go through to try seems to have cured attendance, television ratings and minimal exposure of their post-Jordan depression.

On this night, the T-Wolves find a flaw in Michael that never used to be there. He can't beat the triple team, especially when Kevin Garnett gets help from six-foot-ten Joe Smith and swingman Anthony Peeler to guard Jordan in the second half. Michael never used to shoot two-for-fifteen in the second half like he did in this 105-101 loss, but then they never used to guard him with a six-eleven and a six-ten guy. Have they reinvented the Jordan Rules? And supersized them? And by doing so, has the rest of the league cast Michael in the lead role? Really, who else gets the kind of attention Michael has just seen against Minnesota? Shaq and Tim Duncan, when opponents collapse waves of defenders on those mastodons in the fourth quarter, turning the play underneath the basket into a mosh pit. Jordan said he doesn't have the stuff to carry a team anymore a few days ago when the usually baritone resonance of his voice seemed muffled with humility, for it was easier to hear it from himself than his critics. Or maybe he was just revving himself up for another comeback when he followed up the thirty-five against the T-Wolves one night later by wreaking havoc against Philadelphia like nobody has all season. In the first quarter, he hits nine of fourteen shots and scores nineteen of the Wizards' twenty-three points with a variety of jump shots and layups against a variety of defenders. He adds four-of-five shooting in a short stint of the second quarter, making his twenty-eight first-half points the most any player has scored on the Sixers in one half this season. That, of course, came after he scored more points in one quarter than any player has on Philly this season. In the second half, when Larry Brown counters Michael with multiple men out of a zone defense, Jordan hits just one of eight shots, the one being a dunk, and the Sixers turn this into a 91-84 victory. The numbers—Michael's points and the final score—start to seem somewhat reminiscent of November. Tonto is missing the Lone Ranger, and Hamilton is still a week away from returning. But there is no negativity, no tension in the Washington locker room, perhaps because Michael has no wrath to take out on anybody with the way he has been playing.

What compelled the interest to keep coming back to Michael Jordan during the Third Coming played out most vibrantly during this ten-game stretch. He would get some of his game back but sputter in the fourth quarter, and then just when he seemed to be passing his prime, Michael would pull off some of that Bulls stuff. Following the shortcomings against Minnesota and Philly, the you-stink-Ricky victory over Cleveland regenerates the lore, not just for Michael's LaBradfordizing of Davis but for the sequel it has set up a week down the road. By then, Davis and Jones no doubt will have a plan to keep Michael from hitting another forty, perhaps his strongest forty of the season when he cured his second-half blues by matching his sixteen first-quarter points with sixteen second-half points on seven-for-fourteen shooting. When all the boys gather in Philadelphia in two weeks, they will talk about this night when Michael hit eighteen of his twenty-nine shots—62 percent, he will remind them—and they will talk about the next several nights as well. "My legs are starting to come back to me," Michael said after throwing in forty-one points against Phoenix in the fourth of Jordan's ten games back to the top, a 112-102 Washington win. In the process, he had become the first player in the NBA to post back-to-back forty somethings twice this season. "My legs, my moves, my first step are definitely coming back," he continued. "I've been waiting for this."

Michael never made statements like this as false bravado. He knew that his only vulnerability now was to injury, or maybe Kevin Garnett. And after a two-day weekend following Phoenix, he was waiting for an opportunity like this game against Detroit on January 29. Collins confided that the vintage Michael Jordan not only wanted the points, the wins and the bravado, but he wanted to do it spectacularly. So you can imagine that with the Wizards down ten to the Pistons in the fourth quarter, he is seeing Isaiah and Joe D. and Dennis Rodman out there blocking his way to another miracle. The Pistons, generating their first resurgence since the Dumars-Rodman-Salley Bad Boys of the late 1980s, were no match for Michael early in the fourth quarter when he stopped and popped a jump shot, bullied through for a layup and hit one more shot to tie the game. Not even two minutes of the fourth quarter had passed. Having played all of the third quarter, Jordan took a quick breather and Detroit took advantage to ratchet the lead back up to four.

Upon his return, Jordan hit a jump shot, found a last word on another of those preseason big mouths by blowing past Jon Barry for another layup and finished off a six-for-eight shooting rush to tie the score at 84 with two-and-half minutes to play. Two Jordan free throws actually gave the Wizards a lead with a minute to play before the Pistons' Clifford Robinson dropped a pair of jumpers, the second with 18.8 seconds on the clock, to regain a two-point advantage. The Wiz shot to tie the game was supposed to come to Michael after he inbounded the ball. He juked Pistons defender Michael Curry and appeared to be sprung for a back-door layup. But Curry went Dumars on Jordan, denied him the ball and pushed him back out beyond the three-point line. Michael never got the ball, Chris Whitney's shot rolled off the back rim, and despite scoring fourteen of his thirty-two points down the stretch, Jordan was left to lament, "I felt like if I could just get the ball . . ."

In the never-ending soap opera of Michael Jordan, what transpired next really only happened one other time in his career. The opening round of the 1989 playoffs had come to a moment in Game Four when Michael could have sealed a series-clinching victory with a free throw. He missed. The series went to Game Five and Jordan gave rise to his legend by hitting "the Shot" in Cleveland. Now, here he is back in Cleveland. This could only happen in Cleveland, site of "the Shot: Part II," the sixty-nine pointer and all that. Trailing by one with 1.6 seconds left, Michael does get the ball this time. History should note that the Wizards ran a play they had never tried before to get Michael open, which only helped to make it seem like Cavs stooges Ehlo and Wilkins were here under the aliases Stith and Jones. Bryant Stith and Jumaine Jones somehow swarmed Whitney on the inbounds pass. Michael set up and in less time then he had to take the Shot, put up more history. "I didn't have any doubts," he said after one last shot at the Cavs netted a 93-92 victory. Terry Pluto, the renowned *Akron Beacon Journal* columnist who had been through the other side of Jordanology for so long, chronicled the impact of this shot by writing: "Close your eyes and you'll see it. Michael Jordan at the foul line, the ball leaving his finger tips, his right hand waving at the rim . . . and the ball nestling in the net. Only in this dream Michael Jordan is 67 years old."

Adding a third decade of hitting game-winning shots has generated a buzz that will crescendo in a week with Kobe saying, "I can't say it surprises me. He's done nothing but go beyond everybody's expectations," and Paul Pierce warning, "You're going to see a better Jordan after the All-Star break. I just hope I can get that shot again in March." The victory against Cleveland has become yet another jumping-off point. Michael's game makes another full-circle turn the Sunday before the break against Indiana. No six-point disaster, no stopping Jordan, who scores seventeen of his twenty-three in the second half, takes on Jalen Rose in a nose-to-nose confrontation over getting physical and rubs the Pacers' guard's face in a twenty-point defeat. Washington's fourth consecutive win then comes when Jordan again puts second-half shackles on Vince Carter, holding him to four points in the final quarter. After the Wizards hold off Sacramento on their way to the best record in the Western Conference, a night on which Richard Hamilton announced his return from the ripped groin that kept him out seventeen games with thirty-three points, Jordan admitted that the winning mentality created among the Wizards, "is almost the equivalent of winning a championship."

Michael also admitted that the Wizards' winning twenty-three of their past thirty-four games and his being one of three players in the league averaging more than twenty-five points, five rebounds and five assists per game has surpassed what he thought he could do by the All-Star break. Now, the talk is whether Michael will consider playing beyond the two years he has reserved for this Third Coming. Now, the talk is how the Wizards are a team the Nets and the Sixers will have to reckon with in the Eastern Conference. At All-Star weekend, the talk will be all about Michael Jordan.

And some can't believe what they're hearing.

3

SUNDAY AFTERNOON, TWO HOURS OR SO BEFORE TIPOFF AT ANY ALL-STAR weekend exposes the real world of the NBA. Players who have carved out hiding places across the league to avoid the open-to-the-media locker room before every game sit around like they are in the club-house or the treehouse or the frat house this afternoon. Kobe is lounging in one corner, working over some Bubble Yum, Tim Duncan is in another corner actually smiling and Peja Stojakovic holds court with the Eastern bloc media. Even though he is hurt and will not play, Shaq is here, dressed in a three-piece gold plaid suit and matching beret that makes him look like an extra on *The Road To Perdition*. Down the hall, Paul Pierce and Antoine Walker are answering questions like the Olsen twins, Alonzo Mourning is yelling at the ballboys and even the reclusive Allen Iverson is sitting at his locker, dispensing his rap. The Eastern Conference locker room is decidedly more crowded, and a mass has circled around a corner cubicle where Michael Jordan is supposed to be headquartered for the game. Michael is the only All-Star sequestered behind closed doors, and the foreign media men and women—some two hundred and ten countries deep—are perplexed because they need some Jordan bits and bites right now to tell what they have said is the most illustrious feel-good story in a world desperately needing one.

With no Jordan in sight, though, an industrious reporter from the Brazilian equivalent of ESPN doesn't let a missing Michael get in the way of the story. He interviews the locker, getting film of the uniform, shoes and famous North Carolina shorts lying about. The amazing story is that he is doing it straight-faced, and soon several other foreign journalists join the pack to make a scene that would lead anybody just walking into the locker room to swear Michael had to be right in the middle of it all. If he is must-see TV without even being there, maybe Michael really is that much bigger than the game today.

Not that this is anything new. The Jordan Effect has been part of the NBA landscape for several years, ever since *Fortune* magazine conducted a study in 1998 that measured Michael's overall economic impact to be more than ten billion dollars, including his endorsement value, contributions to franchise and television contract worth and entertainment ventures. NBA Entertainment president Adam Silver was quoted as saying at the time that if international broadcasters were allowed to pick the forty games included in the league's satellite distribution package to foreign markets, they would all be Bulls games. "And the Bulls would be playing the Bulls," he quipped to *Fortune*. Jerry Reinsdorf paid Jordan more than thirty million dollars for each of his last two seasons yet came out way ahead when realizing his $9.2 million investment to buy the Bulls in 1985 had grown more than 1,000 percent in thirteen years. The Jordan Effect was creating similar cha-ching during the Third Coming. Although ten million fewer viewers tuned into the most recent NBA Finals than the crowd who watched the last Michael Finals, NBC upped its advertising rate for games by 14 percent and Turner Network Television upped its asking price 25 percent for its NBA telecasts during this Third Coming. The NBA had estimated that increased ratings from 3 percent to 3.4 percent were worth an extra eight thousand dollars per thirty-second commercial.

Ironically, two weeks before All-Star weekend, just as Michael was transcending the game again, the NBA announced a new television contract. The league was dropping its eleven-year association with NBC to go into business with Disney. ABC and ESPN anted up $2.4 billion to be part of a conglomerate that would put NBA games on free television, cable and a soon-to-be-conceived NBA network. AOL Time Warner added another $2.2 billion to the pot for a six-year deal that increased the television revenue stream by 25 percent over the four-year deal that expired at the end of the 2002 season. Nobody said as much, but the opportunity to have the two most recognizable brand names side by side had to be a factor in partnering Michael Jordan with Mickey Mouse. As the dollars continued to roll in, New Jersey, Charlotte, Dallas, San Antonio and Miami joined the list of teams reporting their largest crowds of the season when Michael came calling. League officials also indicated that revenues were rising everywhere and attributed a quarter to a third of the growth to increased attendance at games Jordan played. Though Stern and deputy commissioner Russ Granik did their best on the eve of the All-Star Game to downplay the Jordan Effect, clearly Michael's return rippled through the cash register like a stone being thrown into a mill pond and the NBA needed this.

The NBA players, however, did not. When asked about the Jordan Effect, Shaq commented, "I don't know. I haven't been paying attention." Some of the other co-stars weren't so polite. Although he knew he would still have to prove it by beating Michael in a down-the-stretch confrontation or playoff matchup, one that really counted, Pierce offered to be a voice of the new generation when he declared at the start of All-Star weekend, "The Michael era is just about over. I think the league is ready to take its next step. You got a lot of better athletes in this era, more guys who can play many different positions. We're trying to create our own identity." Antoine Walker wasn't trying to minimize the effect of his childhood idol turned workout partner when he observed that the best part of Jordan's return for the Wizards was that "They got the maximum games you can play on TNT, the maximum you can play on NBC and they get to play in front of sellout crowds every night."

Like Pierce and Walker, Ray Allen knows that Michael Jordan opened the door to most of their fame and fortune. Michael is still the one for the Pepsi generation: The Capital Classic all-star high school basketball game—the second most renowned of the annual spring showcases after the one McDonald's runs, and one he played in twenty-one years ago—has been renamed for Jordan. And instead of matching a team of the top national stars against a team of top D.C.-area stars like it used to, two teams of the best high school players in America will run in this game and be rewarded with two pairs of Jordan brand sneakers, including the two hundred dollar Air Jordan XVIIs that come in a silver steel carrying case with a Nike CD-ROM. Apparently, the best kids play in Jordan brand rather than Kobe or McGrady brand.

Still, as Allen sits at his table during the tell-all meeting with the media that kicks off All-Star weekend on Friday afternoon, he has grown a little fidgety. More than half of this interview hour has passed and Ray apparently has been answering the same question over and over. He finally snaps back: "I have no idea about the impact of Michael being back in the game. I couldn't tell you. Mike is still Mike, but I think everybody is grown to who they're going to be, what they're going to be. We all have our own egos and hype, too. I can't really answer questions about Michael Jordan. I don't know Michael Jordan, so I can't answer a question about something I don't know." Before he can get to the don't-let-the-door-hit-you-on-the-way-out-Mike part of his commentary, Allen flashes the no-more Michael Jordan-questions sign and stands up to leave. When he gets called out about being dressed in Nike spin-off Jordan brand Jump23 attire, for which Allen is part of the endorsement team, he responds, "It's a business thing, not a buddy thing."

Nobody, however, seems to be living with the Jordan Effect more than Allen Iverson. At home, Little Deuce, the hip-hop handle for Allen Iverson II, wants to make believe he's Michael, and at work his daddy has inherited Jordan's title from the 1980s as the guy who can lead the league in scoring but can't win a championship. Iverson attempts to become the voice of reason out of the pregame verbal pop-a-shot by reminding, "Michael is the one we all want to be like. We want to be in game situations like Michael. We want to overcome the things he's overcome." But if the Jordan Effect on the game is everybody trying to show Mike how much they can be like Mike, Michael says he doesn't want to play. Between the Friday show-and-tell and the Sunday afternoon club meeting, Michael steps up to the microphone for his one-and-only pregame press conference. He and Iverson skipped the Friday session, so they perform a duet on Saturday, a panel discussion during which Michael takes four questions for every one to Allen. Jordan quickly taps into his mind-is-willing-but-body-isn't-able schtick by giving up that his competitive juices made him want to go out and relive 1988, when he scored forty points in Chicago and won the first of this three All-Star MVP awards. But this is not personal for him. He drops the punch line that he told Kobe if he does make it personal, he is going to foul out in the first five minutes, though by Sunday afternoon Bryant says he hasn't heard that yet. And then Michael sticks it to the new generation.

"I don't have to prove anything with these young kids. It's their showcase. It's not my style of game at this point of my career. I was there once. I don't have to be there anymore. In terms of going out and trying to prove something, go one-on-one with somebody, I've been in too many Finals for that."

Applying the Jordan Effect to Jordan, maybe accounts of his desire to acquiesce here are not altogether accurate. He doesn't need to prove anything, but does he want to? Saturday of All-Star weekend included both the West and East stars practicing for the paying public. One phase of the East practice splits the team in half for a shooting drill competition. Each team must shoot three-point shots from the corner and the top of the arc, trying to make the most in one minute. The drill goes six or seven rounds, but during one Michael's side is losing by one when he comes up. He hits from the corner, races to the top and buries another shot just before the shot clock goes off. When the last shot drops, he moonwalks into the backpedal, a sign, perhaps, that Michael has a purpose here this weekend other than to boost television ratings.

4

ONE SIDE OF THE FLOOR AT THE FIRST UNION CENTER DURING ALL-STAR WEEK-end looks like a warehouse sale at Circuit City. Televisions, computer screens, extension chords and various unidentified gizmos plug in networks from thirty-five countries broadcasting live from Philly. Alpha TV in Greece, Channel 13 in Costa Rica, NTU in the Ukraine, JTV in Jordan and NBN 4 in the Philippines, among others, should see their television ratings get a boost. The game will actually be heard in forty-one languages, giving rise to the question of what Michael's missed dunk sounds like in Bahasa Malaysian, Creole or Thai. Tony Parker says this is all part of the Michael Jordan Effect. The nineteen-year-old San Antonio Spurs guard is at his first All-Star weekend, having played in the Rookie Challenge game on Saturday. Growing up in France, he first heard about Michael through some family members living in Chicago, then as he honed his own skills he would stay up through the middle of the night to watch Jordan in the NBA Finals. "You don't know how big NBA is in Europe?" Parker challenges, breaking away from speaking French to the foreign legion from his country that has come to cover this weekend. "Just as big as it is here. All because of Michael Szhjordan. When I go back, first thing they will ask me, did I meet Michael? Kind of crazy, huh? I find him on TV at night, and now he's right over there in the locker room."

After all that came to pass this weekend, maybe it would have been better if Michael had been more of an ambassador than if he played an active role in the game. His thirteen All-Star selections put him one ahead of Magic and Larry, and if he had never retired, he'd probably be one short of Kareem's record of nineteen. He didn't need to take a shot or score a point to remain the third-leading scorer in the history of the game. Kobe can try all he wants, play this game like it's an NBA Finals, but really is he going to top the forty Michael scored in 1988, the most anybody has put up in one of these exhibitions in the past forty years? And you wonder if Mike's heart is really in it when he says he wants to play maybe twelve or fifteen minutes, just enough to break a sweat.

Oh, there is a brief stretch of the first quarter when Michael played like the guy kids were still trying to imitate on the playground. Walker deferred to Jordan on a fast break that began a first-quarter run in which Michael hit three straight and scored six of nine Eastern Conference points. The peak of this was a High Noon moment when Jordan motioned Garnett to defend, accelerated around him and skied over Duncan to throw down a one-handed, swinging-on-the-rim slam. Another driving layup had Garnett thinking *here it comes*, for as he said after the game, "You have to always anticipate Mike flipping that switch and making the All-Star Game into a memorable moment."

All weekend, the voices of the new generation muttered about how it was their moment now. They tried to ignore the Jordan Effect hoping the world—all two hundred ten countries watching—would see the torch, the mantel, the grip on the game passing from Michael to Kobe, Garnett, Iverson and any of the nine first-time all-stars making their debut this weekend. Michael didn't pass it, of course, as much as he fumbled it away, bouncing it off the back rim in an oops-I-did-it-again stupor. The second of his back-to-back fortysome-things two weeks earlier, a third decade of game-winning shots in Cleveland, the MVP talk might be wiped way by a missed dunk that stood now as the memorable moment of the Third Coming.

Michael returned in the third quarter, hit one more eighteen-foot jump shot, missed five others and experienced another moment he never felt at this level. With the East making a mini-run to chip away at the West's one-time twenty-four point third-quarter lead, Garnett isolated on Jordan because "You could sort of feel the momentum starting to shift a little bit," he said, "and I went to my teammates and said, 'do y'all sense the same thing I'm sensing?' I could look at Mike's face and see that he was getting frustrated by the fact that he was getting beat so much." Garnett then powered over Michael for a thirteen-foot jumper. On his next shot, his next miss, Jordan heard the chorus from the song "Time Warp" blasting through the First Union Center. A swan song, perhaps?

The irony of the moment seemed to be lost among the numbers Jordan finished with. His eight points marked his worst All-Star Sunday since the 1985 game when the supposed freeze out Isiah, Magic and George Gervin engineered out of some worry about Jordan grabbing the torch from them held Michael to seven points. The twenty-three minutes he played, however, were significantly more than the twelve he wanted, because as Michael said, "Sometimes, it's tough to drag yourself away from the competitive moment."

To some of his teammates, Jordan appeared to be dragged away kicking and screaming. When asked to account for how the West managed the 135-120 slapping of the East, Paul Pierce reasoned: "Kevin Garnett (at small forward) killed Michael Jordan." Perhaps Pierce and friends were trying to pry the torch from Michael's cold, dead hand. Perhaps they were living the Jordan Effect more than they realized. After all, the only incident to gather as much media pursuit as everything Michael did short of putting on his uniform on All-Star Sunday came when Britney and Justin stepped out for a half-time soda and wound up having to duck behind a bevy of coat racks to avoid the cameras. Not even Ali and Frazier sitting together courtside, rekindling for the first time in more than twenty-five years the confrontation that defined sports in the seventies can create as much of a buzz as a Jordan dunk. A missed dunk.

As Kobe reeled off the thirty-one points that made him the unanimous Most Valuable Player selection, he splashed jump shots and retreated into a familiar backpedal that underlined what All-Star weekend uncovered. The NBA was still a battle to Be Like Mike, and it would take winning championships and hitting last-second shots and overshadowing a historic Ali-Frazier reunion in Frazier's hometown and global impact on both the culture and the economy—a lot more than an alley-oop to yourself—to walk on Air.

WHO'S GOT NEXT?

1

EVEN THOUGH ALL-STAR SUNDAY NEVER BECAME HIS SHOW, THE REST OF
the weekend bowed to Jordan's rule. The double standard that
made Michael's missed dunk as much of a conversation piece as
Tracy McGrady's Playstation jam applied and appalled. Michael, of
course, was the only player who blew off Friday's mandatory availability to the worldwide media. Iverson missed it too, but he said
he was sick and the NBA powers eventually cut him some slack.
Shaq made it, insisting that even though he was injured and was not
playing Sunday he had a responsibility to the league, a comment
many construed as backhanded slap at Jordan. All season, Michael
had been meeting the press on his own terms, and when he did
show for his one pregame appearance of the weekend in the tag-
team setup with Iverson, he made it clear that unless the question
was a term of endearment, he wasn't really interested. Only one
question had hit hard here, that asking Michael if his success of the
past two months proved to all the doubters that he had refilled his
Air supply. He passed on the chance to let out one glorious I-told-
you-so and continued with his standard rhetoric and even made a
few jokes. But then came a submission Michael wasn't going to
stand for.

Allen, can you compare Michael and Kobe and their two games?

"I wouldn't answer that if I were you," Jordan interrupted. A silence abruptly echoed through the room, followed by more than one hundred reporters exchanging is-he-serious looks.

"That's an unfair question," Michael reprimanded the questioner. "Really. Truly."

Unfair, maybe, because Michael couldn't bear to hear the Answer in Kobe's favor? Actually, his warning came primarily from what George Koehler explained as Michael's hardened belief that there was no accurate way to compare players. And if Jordan couldn't stand it when Jerry Krause tried to compare players from the 1960s and '70s to Michael, then how would he feel about players of the new generation being compared to him? This is a man who, when hearing or seeing headlines about Kobe or Iverson going off for back-to-back forty-pointers, always reminded his confidants that he rang up four straight fortysomethings. In the NBA Finals. Yet with all the hype flowing about the high point of the season coming two days after the All-Star Game—the first real meeting of Michael and Kobe in the Third Coming—that Heir Jordan talk stammered nonstop like a community sing doing "Row Row Row Your Boat" in the round.

For the past fifteen or so years, this kind of talk followed every Ron, Nick and Jerry who could get his elbow near the rim or take off from the foul line and move the ball from one hand to the other in midair. Ron, Nick and Jerry—Harper, Anderson and Stackhouse—like Gerald Wilkins, Jimmy Jackson, Kendall Gill, J.R. Rider, Penny Hardaway and Grant Hill stirred up so much hot air about their potential that they could have formed the all–Next Jordan team. And then there was Harold Miner, who had to wear that "Baby Jordan" tag while still in college in the early nineties but when he couldn't make a shot other than a dunk found the label changed to "Err Jordan."

This quest for who's got next became so ingrained in the popular culture that during All-Star weekend 2002 many of the NBA's best appeared in a movie validating the search. *Like Mike* featured Iverson and Kidd and T-Mac, among others, but of course they were supporting actors to rapper L'il Bow Wow, whose fantasy was to be like Michael. Who's got next became so compulsive that it actually turned into a lifestyle in 2002 for Ohio prep basketball star Lebron James, a six-foot-six soaring and scoring star built like Mike, who after spending a few days at Jordan's Camp Comeback in 2001 was projected to be a top pick in the NBA draft. And he wasn't even a high school junior yet. Who's got next turned so desperate that during the summer of 2002 a report spotlighted the play of a thirteen-year-old at a national AAU tournament in Memphis, a five-foot-nine swingman playing for a team from Deerfield, Illinois, who had thirteen points in one game and eighteen in another. This next one went by the name Jeffrey Michael Jordan, the blood heir apparent. Now, the Third Coming seemed to be replaying the pattern from the first two about who had next. Each candidate would make a claim to the torch, and each one seemed to be met with a punch line of a headline.

HEIR TODAY, GONE TOMORROW
BAD HEIR DAY
TO HEIR IS HUMAN, TO BE LIKE MIKE DIVINE
RECEEDING HEIR LINE

Michael, though, seemed intent on picking the Jordan heir himself, just as Larry Bird anointed him by deadpanning the "God disguised as Michael Jordan" line after he put up sixty-three points in that 1986 playoff game, or as Magic did a year later when he said, "Everybody talks about how it's me and Larry. Really, there's Michael and there's everybody else." Jordan would bequeath it to somebody he felt understood how to be the Greatest Player of All Time, somebody who understood that scoring and soaring only scratched the surface. And he would do so in a way nobody might hear about, like in the summer of 1996 when he left a note for a Mr. Kidd to "See Mr. Jordan in Suite 1001 ASAP." Kidd, then a budding third-year star with the Dallas Mavericks, had come to Yokohama, Japan for a Nike promotion when he found the summons from Jordan at the front desk of his hotel. Beyond the flash and splash, Kidd had shown a winner within that Michael knew the next one had to value. But Kidd also had shown a petulant outer layer when he complained publicly about teammate Jim Jackson's selfishness. Kidd heeded the calling from Jordan and knocked on his door. As the *Fort Worth Star-Telegram* described it, "In a scene straight from *The Godfather*, Kidd was told to wait in the corner." Jordan went about his card game, never looking at Kidd. After a fifteen-minute wait, Michael took Kidd into a private room and proceeded with a how-to-be-like-Mike speech in which Jordan told Kidd, "He was the future of the league." Kidd explained it as a wake-up call. "He said he's going to retire pretty soon and that I was one of the ones who would get the torch passed on to him."

Similar statements could be read in between Jordan's lines the past few years. When the Third Coming was incubating, President Michael observed how with two years having passed since he retired, basketball fans were now gasping for some fresh Air. Public opinion was advocating for several rising stars, and in his own dismissal of the idea that any player had begun to approach the Jordansphere, Michael recognized who might get there and how by reportedly saying, "The Kobes, the Vince Carters, I'd love to play against them. It would be a battle of minds." Imagine Michael, the voracious game player, making this who's-got-next thing like playing Clue to reveal who done it someday. (Paul Pierce, with the Game-Seven-winning three, in the Eastern Conference Finals.) The issue is important to him, something he brought up as early in the Third Coming as the news conference to officially announce his return. Remember when he said he was pretty sure the young dogs would be barking and that he wouldn't be barking too far away? "I'm not saying I can take Kobe Bryant. I'm not saying I can take Tracy McGrady. But I'm pretty sure they're welcoming the challenge." (T-Mac, with the garbage can, in the playoff locker room.)

Although Michael said that "If you didn't have this talk, the game would be hypeless," each Coming brought supposed Peer Jordans, one six-foot-six shooting guard who could do the over-the-head slam on the break in nearly every draft since the mid-1980s. And even one or two who seemed to claim more of a right to succession. Harper, Wilkins and Gill joined Mitch Richmond, Roy Marble, Anthony Peeler, Kerry Kittles, LaBradford Smith, Billy Owens and for about a split second Sean Elliott as part of the heir line before Jordan ever won a title.

Owens learned quickly how painful this distinction could be in just his third game as a pro when he brought the hype with him to Chicago Stadium. Michael provided a quick tutorial on the art of being Jordan by stealing the ball from Owens the first three times he touched it. Anderson, Stackhouse, Hardaway and Hill each were treated to the same Jordan for Dummies lessons, but as the heir stylists of the Second Coming, they each also dogged Michael occasionally. By the start of the Third Coming, they stalked Michael like hyenas in the pridelands. Kobe, Iverson, Vince, McGrady, not to mention Pierce, Ray Allen and even Michael Finley were the first generation of players who grew up studying *Come Fly With Me* and Jordan's other videos. Each brought a certain heir-raising ability, more than one even, and thought they had the style to be part of the one-name gang of greatness: Wilt, Kareem, Magic, Moses, Doc, Isiah, Larry and so forth.

"The talent is there in each of those guys," NBC television analyst Steve Jones agreed when joining this discussion right before McGrady was to take his first shot at Jordan in December of 2001. "But if you're talking about separating Jordan from other great players, then who has his ability to impose his will out on the floor more nights on his opponent than other players have?" Michael would find out who was willing, whose bite matched his bark, and by the end of the season bestow his blessing on the next one. Along the way he would uncover the clues as to what made this one the true heir. The one true Air.

2

DOES THE NEXT ONE HAVE TO WEAR CUSTOM-MADE ITALIAN SUITS BOUGHT ON an annual pilgrimage to Europe? Indiana's Jermaine O'Neal contends the NBA is not a suit-and-tie league anymore, that it's gotten younger and that we shouldn't judge what's inside the package by the wrapping. Perhaps O'Neal is onto something. In many ways, the league became more Rodman than Jordan in the three years when Michael went on his second sabbatical. Tattoos, hair braids and a much greater freedom of speech than Jordan ever allowed himself wrap the players hyped as stars in 2002. Maybe that's the Shaq Effect, too, and maybe the search for the next one should end at Shaq, the only one who can claim to rival Michael in his prime as an all-but-unstoppable force and the one who with three consecutive NBA Finals Most Valuable Player awards has the hardware to prove it. Still, Shaq is more Wilt than will, his Hollywood endings have been about clanking enough free throws to keep the game interesting and of all heir heads, he was the one who had the chance to win a championship in the Jordan era and couldn't. Michael always seemed to maintain a wait-in-the-corner-until-I-finish-this-hand attitude toward Shaq because he always saw him as a guy who spent more time working on his sound bites than his game.

Michael was more likely to be impressed with the kind of talk Pierce proliferated. If trying to match Michael's killer trash talk is the key to the kingdom, then Pierce might be the true voice of generation next in the NBA. Pierce had developed a confidence that showed when he answered questions about the honor of being selected an all-star for the first time by saying, "I feel like this is a game I'm supposed to be in," and responding to talk of him being a Most Valuable Player candidate with, "I'm only scratching the surface," or "I'm only halfway to the top." Michael probably liked that Pierce would register at hotels on the road under the name Roy Hobbs, apparently wanting people to know he thought of himself as the Natural.

Remember, Pierce is the one who said he upped his summer work-outs to three times a day when hearing about Jordan's comeback plans, and Michael saw how impressive that workaholism could be when Pierce snuffed his game-winning attempts in the first two Wizards-Celtics meetings of the regular season. Pierce's game is more like the Jordan of the Second Coming: getting so white hot with the jump shot that he could hit twelve in a row and spinning layups out of isolations in the post. Pierce also registered high on the one crucial item on the nextlist: closing. The Celtics swingman led the NBA in fourth-quarter scoring during the 2001–2002 season, and you can just imagine Michael watching Pierce scoring twenty points in Boston's historic fourth-quarter comeback against the Nets in Game Three of the 2002 Eastern Conference Finals and seeing a familiar viciousness.

The playoff poster boy of a season ago, Milwaukee's Allen, has also exhibited a vicious side. Allen has always been known as more like Joe Dumars than Jordan; has always been characterized as having a quiet demeanor. But Ray has also exhibited some of that kicking-over-the-garbage-can impulse, and not just when fussing about Jordan during All-Star weekend. He challenged the Bucks when they trailed Charlotte, three games to two, in the 2001 Eastern Conference semifinals, then led them back by adding to his 27.1 points per game average and 51 percent three-point shooting. In a memorable Game Six of the Eastern Conference Finals against Philadelphia, Allen hit nine of thirteen three pointers and scored forty-one points to lead the Bucks into Game Seven. Prior to this, the only real comparison to Jordan for Allen came with his starring role in the movie *He Got Game*. Both were better ballplayers than actors. Afterward, Ray caught Michael's eye for his desire to grow the Bucks into his team, a playoff-caliber team. Like Jordan did by supplanting Al Capone as the international symbol for Chicago, Allen has made Milwaukee famous for something other than *Laverne and Shirley*. But Allen has also accomplished something Michael never did—

going from a Central Division title one season—2001—to the NBA draft lottery the following year.

Jordan is still a man among boys when he looks at his potential heirs. Truly. Kobe and McGrady have only recently reached the legal drinking age; Carter, Pierce and Allen are still three years younger than Mike was when he hit his first playoff series–winning shot. Surprisingly, Michael started to notice the maturity he felt integral to be a champion in Iverson. Michael knows all about the bad-boy rap album Iverson made and how the NBA wanted to censor him, how the league airbrushed over his tattoos when his picture was on the cover of *Hoop* magazine, the official publication of the NBA. But perhaps Michael is reminded of a young Jordan when looking at Iverson, somebody who plays at full speed end to end and would not be afraid to throw his body into a Pistons triple team if that's what winning demanded. Yes, Michael sees Allen Iverson following in his footsteps and not just because he has won an MVP award or has become the other player in the league most likely to drop forty on any given night.

"His competitive belief as an athlete and as a basketball player, I see traits of me in him in terms of a competitive nature, to overcome any negative outlook from anybody," Michael waxed on about Iverson during All-Star weekend. "People may talk, 'He can't do this,' or 'At his size, he may not be able to do this,' and he's taken it on as a challenge to prove people wrong. Those are things in his heart, and you can see it in the level of his game."

Iverson followed up Jordan's comments with remarks that seemed to come from Jordan's past. "I always said it was unfair that it took me to start winning some games for people to try to understand me. Once I started winning, they started to listen to me instead of just judging me."

"Yeah, that sounded like me in my early days," Michael chipped in. "I mean, we went somewhat the same path. A lot of the critics said, 'You can't lead the league in scoring and win.' We had to prove them wrong. We took that as energy to prove them wrong. That's the type of respect I finally earned, and I'm pretty sure that's something he's going to have to earn. And when you do, it's amazing how they put you in that elite class. Until you win, you just sit in that second tier. And I understand exactly what Allen is saying."

Competitive compulsion, fourth-quarter heroics, vicious energy, scoring soliloquy, bottomless work ethic all formed the best parts of Airudite Jordan. But even Michael recognized the element whoever had next would have to generate. Pierce, Allen and even Iverson couldn't match the hype that accompanied Tracy McGrady's first confrontation with Jordan. On this December 1 night of 2001, college football's major conferences are playing their championship games and the mess about which teams will play for the national championship is about to be sorted out. Yet, NBC has decided to televise nationally Orlando's game against Washington at the MCI Center. Magic coach Doc Rivers notes that one team is 7-9, the other is 5-10 and asks "why the hell are we on TV?" Steve Jones has come to Washington to do the game for NBC, and he knows why the hell he is here: "All I can tell you is that McGrady said he circled this day on his calendar when the schedule came out."

What has been promoted as a showdown of the original *Star Wars* order never actually lives up to the hype. Midway through the first quarter, the master and the understudy are in foul trouble and Hubert Davis matching up against Jud Buechler is not what NBC came to show. When a finger to the eye stuns Jordan and forces him to the locker room in the first half, T-Mac takes advantage to flush a slam that will no doubt lead the *SportsCenter* highlights on this night. Otherwise, the Air raids are limited. Jordan hits a jumper over McGrady to whittle a onetime eleven-point lead to five in the third quarter. Then, with the Wizards clinging to a last chance to make a run, Jordan tries the up-and-under and McGrady doesn't bite. Magic teammate Darrell Armstrong tries to sell T-Mac outscoring Michael, twenty-six to fifteen, as "Maybe the torch got passed tonight." But has McGrady shown he's ready for that? Some who look at his postgame attire, which seems to be made from remnants of a Persian rug, complete with matching fur hat and chain around his neck dangling a gold bar from Fort Knox with his number, 1, on it, might have a different view, might see him more as the anti-Jordan. Rivers says he saw a slight coming-of-age in McGrady. "T-Mac played him. He didn't shy away. And it's easy to shy away from Michael Jordan."

By the time he rises for that alley-oop to himself in the All-Star Game, McGrady seems to have risen to the Jordansphere. Someday, this dunk might be remembered like the high-rise, left-to-right, up-and-under scoop Jordan had against the Lakers in the '91 Finals. McGrady has exhibited an ability to hang in traffic and get his shot off, and he will supplant Jordan as the player who can always find a way to get to the foul line. He even tried another Jordanesque move, igniting his teammates by guaranteeing victory in an elimination game against Charlotte in the 2002 playoffs. His thirty-eight points, however, were not enough to make good on the guarantee, but if he had lifted a team that included Mike Miller going through a sophomore slump, Pat Garrity, an aging Horace Grant and Armstrong to victory, would T-Mac have been considered on his way to being a Peer Jordan?

Michael noted that McGrady does have one aspect to his game that elevates him. "He's one of those guys where you can't go get popcorn and you can't talk to the guy next to you or you just might miss something spectacular." But many people also say this about Vince Carter, and where does he rate on the Air gauge? The player who wants to be like Mike most has become the least like him of all the Heir Apparents. In his two meetings against Jordan, Vince averaged two points in the fourth quarter. Much had been made about his ability to score from anywhere, anytime just like Mike, yet at twenty-four years old, Carter's 25.7 scoring average is ten points less per game than Jordan's at that age. Worst of all, when Carter's Toronto team was tabbed as an Eastern Conference contender for the year of the Third Coming, the Raptors finally made their push to get the eighth and final seed for the playoffs only after Vince went down with a season-ending injury. A Carter teammate has realized what Vince needs to understand if he really wants to be like Mike. "Not just the individual accomplishment, but the team accomplishment," says Raptors center Hakeem Olajuwon. "The quality of a leader. To become a leader like Jordan. That should be the motivation for Vince." Carter might struggle to recover from the 2001 Eastern Conference semifinal series against Philadelphia. On the Sunday morning of Game Seven, he left the team to walk in graduation ceremonies at North Carolina. He returned by game time, but missed twelve of eighteen shots, including one to win the game.

Nobody seems ready to walk on Air, or so it would seem. Jordan hasn't exactly left a note for Pierce or Vince or T-Mac to come to his suite so he can explain how to Be Like Mike. He has been a little more forthcoming with Iverson, but perhaps he knew there was really only one player worthy of inaugurating the next coming.

3

MICHAEL FIGURED THE TIME HAD COME TO HAVE ONE OF THOSE COME-TO-MY-room chats with him, the guy he decided six months ago could become future boy. No note this time; Michael tipped his hand right away, grabbed the young warrior and walked him into the back halls of the arena. He was frustrated, so frustrated he had to hang his head to hide the tears beginning to well up in his eyes. He had just gone through yet another confrontation with the stubborn, unforgiving coach, who told him to sit down and grow up. During the next twenty minutes, he listened to Michael like he was being told the secrets of the ways of the force. And right then and there on this mid-December morning, Kwame Brown received his latest lesson about the air up here.

Eight months ago, of course, Kwame Brown was coming off his

senior prom at Glynn Academy High School in Brunswick, Georgia, when Michael Jordan made him the first pick in the 2001 NBA Draft, the first high school senior to be so selected. When the Wizards won the draft lottery and vaulted to the number-one pick, Jordan called it a wild card and said it gave him, "an opportunity to rebuild this franchise a lot quicker." At that time, he probably had little knowledge of Kwame Brown and less idea about whether he would make him the top pick. But by the time draft night arrived, Michael apparently saw a little something in Kwame to make him believe this could be the next coming someday, a little bit of himself in the young warrior, perhaps. When Kwame worked out for Jordan a few days before the draft, he quickly showed a unique competitive nature, telling Michael, "I'm going to beat YOU one day." Perhaps Michael sensed his own street smarts in Kwame when he flexed such a statement. Jordan knew Kwame had been through greater adversity than getting cut from the Laney High School varsity team. Growing up, he saw his father and two brothers sent to prison and his mother work almost around the clock to support eight children.

Michael seemed to be looking to make the next one his own creation. He had tried this path in his presidential life twice already, trading for two players cut in his mold—Courtney Alexander and Tyrone Nesby—who were proving to be extreme longshots. Alexander seemed to elicit a perception that he wanted to be Michael instead of Michael. Not that Jordan would have responded to being moved in and out of the starting lineup early in the season by pouting as Courtney did. Injuries also stunted his progression, causing him to miss more than a month of the season. But he would supplement the Wizards' success with runs like the three-game stretch in February when he averaged thirty minutes per game and combined to make eighteen of his twenty-eight shots and score at thirteen points per game, then put out body language that asked why the ball wasn't coming to him when the shot clock was winding down.

Not surprisingly, Alexander was headed for a trade, and following a postseason deal that sent him to the Hornets, he vented his feelings for Jordan, saying, "The way things should work out, I will now be the starting two-guard for the team that should come out of the Eastern Conference next season."

Nesby showed the athletic gifts of a young Jordan in spurts during 2001–2002 and Collins liked his ability to handcuff opposing swingmen such as Vince and T-Mac. But talk outside the Wizards' locker room indicated that Nesby's head wasn't always in the game, and the incident from the 2001 season when security had to escort him off the bench after a dispute with then coach Leonard Hamilton seemed to be on his permanent record.

So Michael made it his priority to take on Kwame. Or as Brown characterized Jordan's mentoring: "Every rookie must be broken." During a training camp practice, Brown stopped to complain about being fouled on a drive to the basket. Jordan stopped practice, shot him the glare that maybe only Collins had wrought with the scoring error all those years ago and reportedly exploded, yelling, "You don't get a call on a damn touch foul, you faggot. Get your ass back on the floor and play. I don't want to hear that shit out of you again."

Another training camp day found Brown getting his chance to play Jordan one-on-one and the student made a move that knocked the master off balance. "You reach, I'll teach," Brown said in a fit of bravado his teammates mocked him with all season. Jordan then showed Kwame what it takes to be Jordan, responding, "You reach, and I'll knock you on your ass." Michael then belittled Brown through the rest of the one-on-one, and after beating the rookie insisted Kwame call him "Daddy" from now on.

Michael had tried this same philosophy on the only other player he thought had the skills to play at this level. During Bulls practices, Phil Jackson would pit Michael against Scottie Pippen and Michael would slap him around like a little brother. Eventually, Pip grew to be nearly Jordan's equal from a playmaking perspective—nearly—and he matriculated mentally as well. In that victory at Utah, everybody remembers Michael's final thirty-seven seconds. But lost among the worship over the final shot was Pippen's courage with a back so sore that he couldn't walk. A halftime treatment enabled him to play a vital role defensively in the second half and hit one huge jump hook that ended with a wince on his face usually seen in patients before the dentist applies the Novocain. Perhaps Michael figured if he could Airbrush Kwame this way, that would set him up for next.

When Brown called training camp the roughest two weeks of his life, he admitted that coming out of high school he had no idea what work was. Doug Collins turned impatient waiting for Kwame to develop work habits and frustrated waiting for him to get into NBA shape. He suffered through typical rookie mishaps. A sprained ankle after he blocked three shots in the first half of his first game forced Brown to miss the next four games. Collins tried to play him into shape but grew tired of nights like four rebounds in thirty-five minutes played. Through it all, Brown maintained a relentlessness that Collins said he might have interpreted as an unwillingness to give in, the same stubbornness as the coach, he added. Not that it ever caused Kwame to storm out of practice over a dispute in the score of a scrimmage. But Collins did throw him out before anything like that could ever happen that morning in Houston.

Back in a hallway where nobody could see, Michael explained to Kwame, so broken now that he hung his head to cry, how to handle expectations the rookie had called "almost crippling." Even Michael wanted Kwame to be Kobe or McGrady or Kevin Garnett, but he knew that would take at least three years to develop, roughly around the time when Jordan planned on finishing rebuilding the Wizards. Kwame tried to articulate the pressure of these expectations. Being the first high-school player picked number one overall and being Michael's first number-one pick was suffocating enough. Then they had to go and give him the key to the city the day he left Brunswick for Washington, D.C. So here a kid from one small southern town sat talking to a kid from another small southern town, and Michael realized he really would have to play daddy. How many father-son chats would it take?

Some of those talks included insight about how to navigate the rigors of flying and a plan to eat right. And of course the more Kwame progressed, the more he would have to deal with Michael picking on him like the dad who wanted his son going to an Ivy League school instead of the University of Illinois. Brown had just made his greatest impact as pro, not more than ten days after his coming of age in Houston. Picking up the slack for Christian Laettner's broken leg, Brown had nine points and ten rebounds and one sky-high, follow-up slam that Collins said changed the energy of the game and started the Wizards back from a seventeen-point deficit against Toronto. After the game, Michael served his praise to Brendan Haywood, who had an equally strong inside presence that Jordan said was the benefit of having played four years of college ball—something Michael said a guy like Kwame Brown can learn from.

When Michael comes at you like that, he's looking for a response, for you to stand up like you will need to with the ball in your hands, down one point and two seconds showing on the clock. He knew Kwame had the talent, could see him blow by players like Rasheed Wallace for sweeping hook shots. Would Brown come up with a response to say I got next, something more than a Ray Allen–like, no-more-Michael-Jordan questions he demanded the last week of the season?

He had, to a degree, when the Wizards faced Portland on February 27 while Michael lay in bed recovering from knee surgery. Johnny Bach predicted this would have to be Kwame's night, that after fifty-four games, "The kid would be ready to show us what he's got or he would never be ready." Brown produced what seemed to be an innocuous six points and one rebound, but that move around Wallace, a jab-step-to-the-baseline, spin-back-to-the-lane skyhook that Kwame said he should have dunked prompted Collins to call Jordan after the game and relent, "I think we got the right guy." His averages of 9.1 points and 8.2 rebounds per game the last month of the season started to confirm Collins's assumption. Kwame knew he had been through an heir-raising experience in his rookie season.

After the season let out, Kwame had to wonder if he erased whatever progress he had made in Michael's mind by getting charged for allegedly driving while intoxicated one night in Jordan. Reportedly he was doing better than one hundred miles per hour. The talent was there, but maturity, work ethic and all the other attributes would still need to be developed for Kwame to even think about nudging his way into the heir line.

4

HISTORY MIGHT NOTE THAT MICHAEL JORDAN GLIMPSED THE FUTURE ON Tuesday, February 12 with one minute, nine seconds remaining in the Wizards' game against the Lakers in Los Angeles. Kobe Bryant had spent much of his teens trying to Be Like Mike. One story going around told of a high school Kobe blowing leads in the fourth quarters of games to invent ways to come up with last-second heroics. Another report revealed that as an eighteen-year-old rookie, Kobe couldn't go out clubbing with his teammates so he stayed home and studied tapes of Michael Jordan, back and forth in slow motion, trying to find the intricacies of everything from the bailout to the backpedal.

Now with the last minute of this first Michael versus Kobe of the Third Coming closing in, Bryant had a chance to show just what he dreamed to be. The matchup failed to live up to its marquee value until this point because Jordan spent most of the night playing against Lakers forward Rick Fox while Richard Hamilton took on Kobe. But a pick and a roll has left Jordan switched on to Kobe, standing with his dribble on the left wing, just inside the three-point arc. A one-step takeoff to an up-and-under windmill slam would have been a fitting play here, a symbolic passing of the torch. Michael seemed to expect as much when he backed up on Kobe's hard-step dribble to his left. Then, the Michael of ten years ago flashed before his eyes when Kobe stopped and popped a dagger of a twenty-foot jumper that shredded any doubt the Lakers would win this game. For the record, Michael and Kobe tried to turn this into their game of one-on-one upmanship in the fourth quarter. The jump shots were fired at each other in the last six minutes with Kobe hitting three to Michael's two and each finishing with six points, not that it mattered much with the Lakers having recovered from a twenty-point deficit in the first half to lead by as much as eleven down the stretch.

None of this, however, had much to do with why or how Kobe had become the breath of fresh Air. A game hyped to be Babe Ruth getting one more chance to hit the home run, a game promoted like a prize fight, Kobe passed off as "all business" before it ever started. "If I was going to be stoked about it, I'd say so," he continued. "I can see what all the hype is about. People are going to see this as an individual thing. From the bottom of my heart, I don't see it like that." Whether he did wasn't the issue; Kobe's pregame rhetoric is exactly what Michael would have said. Kobe's approach was the most he could ever Be Like Mike, a sign he was going to play with the same vicious, I'll-beat-him-at-his-own-game-then-have-the-last-word defiance that Michael used to score sixty-three against Larry or throw himself at the Jordan Rules.

Kobe didn't even like Mike when he first saw him. As a five-year-old living in Italy where his father played professional basketball, Bryant didn't get to see any college basketball. He knew the NBA and its leading man at the time, Magic Johnson. In 1984, the national college player of the year led the U.S. Olympic team into an exhibition game against NBA players. Early in that game, the national college player of the year, Michael Jordan, made his first impression on Kobe Bryant. "Magic was my favorite player and I remember him running back on defense and Michael coming down and taking off from God knows where and dunking the basketball on Magic," Bryant related during one of those All-Star Game media briefings in which he spent nearly forty-five minutes answering questions about Jordan. "I didn't like him too much after that."

When he was thirteen and back living in Philadelphia, however, Kobe began his studies in the ways of Michael Jordan. The stories of this pubescence are well-documented: The night in 1997 at the United Center when rookie Kobe used the down time during a free throw to ask Jordan about his fadeaway, and the tale of Bryant trying to create situations in high school games to perform Michael Miracles, and the summer of 2000 when he emulated Michael's voracious work ethic by shooting two thousand jump shots every day. If you watch Kobe walk on the court, you can see Michael's rigid bobbing as if he's winding himself up to play. Michael's machine-gun jabsteps when isolated on a defender, fadeaway with the right leg kicking forward like a Rockette and eyes-as-big-as-hub-caps glare on defense show up on Kobe as if they were passed genetically. Listen to Kobe spew certain words like "basketball court" or "challenge" and it's as if he pulled them off a tape of Jordan like someone learning to speak tourist Spanish.

"When I was with NBC, I'd do an interview and I'd close my eyes and I'd think I was talking to Michael," Doug Collins recalled of the time when his network gig during the three years previous to taking up with the Wizards set him face-to-face with Kobe. "The inflection in his voice, the mannerisms, the way he dresses, the moves he makes on the floor, the way he does things. . . . He has the same kind of approach as Michael, the explosive quickness, the post-up, shooting the ball, going to the basket. He can miss ten in a row and want the next one because he knows the eleventh one is going in." Just like Mike.

Only, Mike wasn't so sure. Let Kobe make all the comparisons he wants. But if you ask Michael, Kobe wasn't the only one shooting the fadeaway. "I see other guys fading away, too," he said. This is Jordan's way of telling the world that no one person has enough yet to compare to the best of Michael. His entire take on the matter of comparing Kobe to Michael came down to a statement that he could only get there over time: "It's a standard of measurement," Jordan reasoned. "Just like I had to go through with Doctor J and Elgin Baylor."

The rest of the NBA seemed to see it a little differently. A up-close perspective comes from the one man to play with Kobe and Michael in his Third Coming, that being Tyronn Lue, who Jordan signed away from the Lakers as a free agent after the 2001 season. And Lue said he saw what has been known as the best part of Michael in Kobe. "Kobe wants to win every drill, every possession, every game. He wants to win at everything he does. Michael is the same way." Kobe still needed to add thirteen points, two rebounds and two assists to his career averages to catch Michael in points, rebounds and assists per games. And until he wins a title without Shaq, he may also suffer the same fate as Magic, who privately admitted a lack of fulfillment over never having won a title without Kareem.

In the end, the true measure of international status still favors Michael. His shoe, the Air Jordan XVII, sells for two hundred dollars, seventy more than the Kobe Two. Kobe figures he's caught Michael in only one arena. The stories about Michael eating twenty-five Chicken McNuggets on the bus ride to the game apparently have nothing on Kobe. "An hour before the game," Bryant revealed, "you can catch me in the back of the locker room with a Coke, a Quarter Pounder with cheese and some fries."

Kobe didn't need this February game of 2002 against Michael to show he had mastered the Jordan rep. Two nights earlier, he cultivated the show of shows for his own scoring aria, running off eleven points in the last four minutes of the first half of the All-Star Game on a combination of driving layups, fast-break dunks and turnaround fadeaways. He had already proven he could do this when it counted, his eight overtime points rescuing the Lakers playing without Shaq in Game Four of the 2000 NBA Finals against Indiana that put them one victory away from winning their first championship. In fact, Michael might have been more motivated in this supposed torch relay game had he remembered Kobe's take a year ago when the comeback talk started. When Michael was in Los Angeles scouting a game, Bryant told him, "Stay right where you are, old man." And Michael seemed to know where Kobe was coming from even before he admitted after beating Michael and his Wizards that he wanted to "send a message."

Some nights in his career, Michael made it his business to send the message and came out in what Johnny Bach liked to call the stalking, predatory mode. He did so in his first meeting with Shaq in January of 1993, scoring sixty-four points in what Collins explained as a you're-not-ready-for-me performance. This night in L.A. seemed to be another one of those nights, with added incentive coming from Michael's first-ever game against former coach and spiritual advisor Phil Jackson. (Maybe this game would finally provide an answer to that burning question: was it Michael or the triangle offense?) He accelerated and ascended off the fast break for a dunk that left a row of fans behind that basket at Staples Center bowing in homage. He threw up the scoop-and-a-hoop in the first quarter and spread out for jumpers from both sides and the top of the key. He even pickpocketed Kobe with fifteen seconds left in the first half, but couldn't muster enough legs to bury a jumpshot at the end of the getaway. Michael had his team leading by thirteen points at the half, a margin that would eventually grow to twenty-five minutes into the third before Kobe found his game.

Collins had observed that if Bryant had truly wanted to morph into Michael, the evidence would come on a night when he would miss ten shots in a row and still call for the ball on the eleventh. More importantly, do it in the final minute, when Michael always asked to be judged with the greatest scrutiny. Kobe's one last shot in this 104-93 defeat of the Wizards gave him twenty-three points and stirred enough postgame blather that it was finally okay to compare him to number twenty-three. But the heir-today-gone-tomorrow debate was about to reach a breaking point. Kobe tried to leave his perspective on the floor during the other time Jordan used to measure Air flow. In the 2002 playoffs, Bryant put forth two memorable fourth quarters against San Antonio in the Western Conference semifinals that seemed Jordan worthy, twenty-three points over the two games that rescued the Lakers after they had lost the first game of the series. In the make-or-break Game Three, Kobe answered a horrific first three quarters by dropping all five of his shots in the final period of a 98-89 win in San Antonio. When all was said and won and he had perhaps come close to a no-more-Jordan-questions moment, Bryant wanted the world to hear his true feelings. Was he ready for a time when he would no longer have to be compared to Michael? "Yeah, like right now. We're completely different people. I think it will go away. It will go away. Me continuing to play will make it go away. Yeah, it's definitely a compliment, but at the same time, I'm Kobe, he's Michael."

It won't go away. Kobe unleashed a defining performance in Game Three of the 2002 NBA Finals against the New Jersey Nets. After the Lakers recovered from a seven-point deficit, Bryant hoisted a twenty-two-foot jumper as the shot clock ran out to run the L.A. lead to four, 100-96. Moments later, he slithered through a double team usually only seen trying to stop you-know-who and hit a turn-around fadeaway with 19.1 left to play that proved to be the back-breaking play in this backbreaking victory. That all came after a dribble-drive right through the Nets' defense ended with a climb-the-ladder, one-handed slam over New Jersey's seven-foot center, Todd MacCulloch. When Kobe finished with thirty-six points he could have taken the starring role away from L'il Bow Wow.

By Game Four the young warrior gave in to the master. Kobe had been wearing a series of vintage jerseys off the court throughout the playoffs recalling superstars from all sports, and he said for Game Four he would be wearing one from the greatest. Sure enough, he strolled the hallways of New Jersey's Continental Airlines Arena prior to the game wearing that Bulls white number twenty-three.

By that time, Bryant and Jordan had already settled this matter on their own. When the Lakers came to Washington in early April, Michael had already rushed back from knee surgery and tried to lead the Wizards on one final playoff push playing on one final knee. Afterward, Kobe shared a conversation with Michael that played out as a Yoda-on-his-deathbed moment. But there was be no passing of the torch, no last rites, no breath of fresh Air. "I know I can't be the Michael Jordan of 1993 or 1994 against those guys," he said. "The realistic look is that they're not going to face me in my prime, and I'm not going to face them in theirs. See, it wouldn't be a fair comparison."

Really.

Truly.

THE THIRD GOING

1

FORGET KOBE. VINCE AND HIS COUSIN T-MAC AND IVERSON AND PAUL PIERCE and Shaq, forget 'em all. Michael Jordan never faced an opponent like this. For the first time in his NBA life, Michael has admitted vulnerability. Imagine Sinatra without the bravado, Gates without Windows. Pat Riley's Knicks never exposed Jordan as so human as Pat Riley's Heat did on this February night that upstaged any of the absurdity in nearby South Beach. Fifty-two games into his Third Coming, Michael had not shown this repertoire yet. He made the locomotive dribble to his left, stopped, kicked his leg forward and with his first shot of the game caught just enough of the rim to avoid the *aiiiiirrr baaaallllll* chant. On his next shot, he pirouetted, hoisted and came even closer to an air ball. He tried the drive, went reverse for the layup and saw a big hand swat the ball so hard it looked like a balloon sputtering out of air.

Such futility had to come from some hybrid of Dumars, Ron Artest and Manute Bol hounding him. But if it were that easy, then Michael could do what he always did, keep jabbing, keep probing, keep attacking until the tormentor goes numb or succumbs to fear. If only this opponent didn't have the same stubborn gene Deloris Jordan passed on to her youngest son, the same no-quit point Magic Johnson envied so much. Finally, word of surrender came out of Jordan, and nobody could remember ever hearing something like this.

"My body can't go the way my mind wants to take me," he relented. With six minutes and twenty-seven seconds left in the fourth quarter and the Wizards trailing 78-74, Michael Jordan foundered into a Lou Gehrig moment, one that seemed to embody as much dejection as that legendary streak of consecutive games played coming to an unexpected yet unavoidable end.

"Michael, do you want me to take you out?" Doug Collins asked.

"Yes, Douggie," Jordan said.

Tendonitis, arthritis, egoitis eating away at his right knee had gutted Michael in a way he had not known since the Jordan Rules. Infections squirting puss like Old Faithful, battered wrists, broken cheekbones, sprained ankles and repeated scratching from John Starks had never kept Jordan from playing through. One night in 1993, he had hobbled out of Chicago Stadium on a sprained ankle so bad he needed crutches after scoring thirty-four points against Milwaukee, then came back to score thirty-six against Utah two nights later. In the playoffs that year, he hurt his wrist so bad in one game against Cleveland that he had to shoot two foul shots left-handed. In the next game of the series, his wrist was still hurting so bad that he took all his warm-up shots left-handed. After the Bulls trailed at halftime, Dr. Hefferon told him to shoot through the pain. He did so to the extent of thirty-six points and a victory.

But now, playing only moments after having had another load of synovial fluid drained from the knee joint—the fourth, fifth, maybe sixth time he had to endure this procedure the past five months—Michael was hurting in a way Collins had never seen before. He had watched Jordan play on one leg before, watched in more anguish than he had ever let on so far this season. But for the first time, the knee was keeping Jordan from executing the most critical part of his game: going out and playing every minute to win. And for the first time, Riley sent up a phrase never attached to Michael Jordan.

"He's not indestructible," the Heat coach appraised.

He thought he was, of course. He thought he could defy the one opponent that had gotten all the other greatest athletes of the century—

age—and that might have led to Michael Jordan's undoing. Just the night before, when the Wizards played Miami at the MCI Center in the first half of this interstate back-to-back, Michael seemed to have the spring in his steps. He hit his first three shots, he set up Rip and Chris Whitney and Jahidi White for wide-open hoops. He even picked on longtime favorite whipping boy Kendall Gill, getting him to bite on the up-and-under and foul Jordan on a three-point shot attempt. In seventeen minutes of the first half, he scored twenty points, the league-leading seventeenth time he had orchestrated a first half with twenty or more points this season. The Heat would have needed the Dumars-Artest-Bol triple team to stop Jordan in the fourth quarter when he drove past Alonzo Mourning for a pair of layups, found his three-point range and hit six of eight shots, the last of which tied the game at 95 with nineteen seconds to play. Had Miami's Brian Grant not hit a game-winning shot with one second left, Michael's thirty-seven points in thirty-seven minutes might have made his greatest hits of this season.

For Jordan there had always been nothing worse than watching somebody else hit a game-winning shot. When Sam Perkins did it to him in Game One of the 1991 NBA Finals, Michael stampeded back with a forty-two point Game Two that included the up-and-under, change-of-hands move he has since called "That One." When Reggie Miller did it to him in Game Four of the Eastern Conference Finals in 1998—pushing off on Jordan to do so—Michael pushed back by igniting a 29-16 first-quarter run and scoring twenty-nine points to win Game Five. But what made this night against the Heat especially painful was not knowing what hurt Michael most: Grant making the shot; Mike not getting one last shot of his own; or the knee that kept throbbing like a thumb accidentally hit with a hammer while trying to nail a picture hook to the living room wall.

As soon as Grant hit the shot, a team of caregivers began triage on Jordan, applying ice, electrical stimulation and maybe even incantation as he flew from Washington to Miami. There were no card games on this flight; no picking on Courtney Alexander. Teammates afraid to tread on his space would confirm later that the most recent Michael Miracle was Jordan lasting thirty minutes in Miami. That he needed to endure the knee being drained right before tipoff in a cordoned-off section of the locker room at American Airlines Arena using the equivalent of a rusty knife and a folding table, granted more validity to the almost twelve-month-old question of why he was here, why he was still here.

"You can see him favoring his leg and not exploding off it and at the same time going out there," Collins began when recalling his take on that night in Miami. "That's the greatest lesson he gave these players in our locker room. When you're banged up, you try to play."

You play. When you are Michael Jordan, you play. You are still here because the Third Coming has reminded you like the Second Coming that Beethoven never stopped playing. Hey, a bum knee is nothing when you have vomited up pizza moments before an NBA Finals game and in a near-comatose state scored a game-winning thirty-eight points. You are here because you know that Cal Ripken hit that All-Star Game home run at fortysomething and Jerry Rice will catch touchdown passes at fortysomething. So as Michael Jordan posted up on this triple team of mind against body, time and mortality, his only worry was what happens if there's not another game.

As one expert noted, Michael was not following a script here, but creating one. He might be disheartened because less than twenty-four hours after creating another one of those masterful scoring solil-oquies against Miami, Christian Laettner has ten points at the end of the first quarter and Jordan has none facing the same Heat. But when Michael said, "This is a sign, obviously, that things are coming to a closure in terms of where my career could be heading," it's really only a sign of how bad the pain had been. Resting, surgery and retirement are among the options he's been given, but after two comebacks Michael Jordan knows he has at least one timeout left. For if injury is going to do what Dumars never did, it's not going to be a gimpy knee but going over the edge at Mach V with his hair on fire.

2

SOMETHING ABOUT PAIN ATTRACTED MICHAEL, EVEN TEMPTED HIM. PAIN defined Michael. Not like game-winning shots or fifty pointers, but in a degree-of-difficulty quotient pain fed his insatiability to achieve. Maybe, dare the thought, Michael missed the pain in retirement. Certainly, he didn't miss the hard knocks of going to the basket or the random finger in the eye from a Darrell Armstrong double team. And flexing a knee that felt like opening a door swelled bigger than its frame with every movement had no allure. But waking up in the middle of the night and hobbling through the stiffness to the bathroom provided a sense of the soreness being worth the ball-fake, spin-around Paul Pierce layup that ended with landing on his backside. Not that the ice packs were like wearing a medal of honor; for Michael that was more like the nineteenth hole after a round of golf. So in the weeks before the game in Miami—months really—talk about the knee never went public. Michael was playing just well enough that an eight-for-twenty shooting night against the Lakers or not being able to get the stop on Kobe in the end was excused as tired legs or old legs, but never really injured legs.

In fact, Richard Hamilton's frailty had become more of an issue for the Wizards. Opposing teams were sending big, physical, kamikaze defenders at Rip, marking him as the one who could be taken out. Hamilton proved to be the Wizards' Achilles' Heel. Before he went down with the torn hamstring thirty-eight games into the season, Rip had not been held to less than nineteen points in any game in more than a month. During the seventeen games he missed, the Wizards went 8-9 and six of those losses were by eight points or less. There were nights like the January 4 game against Chicago, when the Wizards almost blew a twenty-point lead in the fourth quarter, that Collins would comment, "I could see how gassed Michael was out there and just think how much we missed Rip."

Hamilton eventually became the guy who covered Jordan's back. When he returned from the hamstring injury, the Wizards won their next five games leading into the All-Star break, ironically when Michael admitted he was playing his best ball of the Third Coming. Without Rip, Jordan had memorable nights like the fifty-one against Charlotte and the subsequent forty-five points against New Jersey and the back-to-back forty-pointers against Cleveland and Phoenix. But in the seventeen games Hamilton missed, Jordan played more than forty minutes in nine and more than thirty-eight in five others and Collins was left to wonder if that wear contributed to Michael's tear. "He's so competitive that only in retrospect did he realize his knee was never where he wanted it to be," Collins added.

So competitive that if he responded to his failing against Carolina by coming back with a fifty-one, imagine how he would go after the knee. He began putting himself through weight training nearly as intense as Camp Comeback. As regular as Willard Scott in the morning, 8:30 A.M. would come and the rest of the Wizards could see Michael finishing his lifting. One morning he actually thought about foregoing the routine, that being the one after going out to celebrate his thirty-ninth birthday. But he dragged himself out of bed, and these morning workouts were becoming so religious that teammates were starting to take part on the road in what became known as the Breakfast Club. By mid-February, membership in the Breakfast Club had grown to eight teammates and when the Wizards went on their three-game swing through the West Coast after the All-Star break, Hamilton joined the group the morning after he admitted Kobe had manhandled him in L.A. Could this be a sign, then, of the kind of professional commitment Michael had hoped to teach the Wiz kids as part of the Third Coming? He knew this much: When Pip and Ron Harper and others joined the original Breakfast Club in Chicago, it made a difference there.

Still, as it had all season, the age-old question of age was again becoming the underwear creeping up of the Third Coming. Collins continually fought the personal conflict of trying to limit Michael's playing time, the words, "not when we have a chance to win" echoing every time Jordan walked gingerly to the locker room following another forty-minute night. Collins would hear the question of how much Michael actually had left in his legs, then see him top forty minutes in every game of that stretch when the Wizards won seven of eight heading into the All-Star break and worry not so much about the years but the mileage. The temptation of getting on a roll would squelch any suggestion of Michael easing up in the second half of those grueling back-to-back games. What became a pattern of the grimmest night being followed by the most promising part of the comeback happened again and again. Michael would hit the proverbial front rim one night in Sacramento then ride a Phoenix to revival the next.

When the Wizards stumbled into Phoenix the night after losing to Sacramento, the usual pomp and circumstance of venues getting one more look greeted Michael. Tickets behind the Washington bench were priced at fifteen hundred dollars, the most since that Barkley guy was winning the MVP award here and leading the Suns to an NBA Finals loss to Jordan's Bulls. Hamilton had seen this scene so many times. He described it as "people who looked like they were seeing a ghost." Michael always played through the pain for moments like these. His mom and sister Roslyn had become residents of the Valley of the Sun recently, and they were at the game, Roslyn even encoring her singing of the Star-Spangled Banner like she used to do at Chicago Stadium when Pops was still alive.

About twenty-four hours before he turned thirty-nine, Jordan turned back the clock. Nine of his twenty points came in the fourth quarter, when he kept the Wizards in position to win. Tyrone Nesby followed up a Jordan miss to tie the game at 95 with 16.2 seconds to play, and after Suns point guard Stephon Marbury hit only the second of two free throws, Washington had one last shot. "Who the hell did you think was going to take the shot?" Jordan was heard to say as he glared toward the Phoenix bench. Taking the inbounds pass in the backcourt, he pushed forward and. Suns forward Shawn Marion allowed just enough space for Michael to shoot a seventeen-footer.

"That's what they pay me for. That's what they pay me for,"

Michael said after his third game-winner of the season made the fans at the America West Arena feel like they had seen the ghost that beat them in NBA Finals almost ten years ago.

Only these days, the game-winning shots weren't coming without a hefty toll. The Wizards took a day off after the Sacramento-Phoenix junket, and when Michael showed up for practice the next day he related how age had begun to creep up. "Some days, getting up in the morning, it's tough to go down to the gym and do your normal routine after playing back-to-back," he told the *Washington Post*. "Physically, it's been a test because your body gives you signals and I have to listen to it. Mentally, the passion is always going to be there. But you can't go out and enjoy the night and then come in early and try to play the next day. Those days are over and done with."

Those days are over and done with threatened to become the epitaph of this season or, at least, its broken record. Michael seemed to flicker from walking on Air to zero balance like a living room lamp with a short, and Monday, February 18—three hundred sixty-four days from his fortieth birthday—was one of those days. That night, Michael revealed that a two-week old bruise on his right knee had grown into a hornet's nest, and it showed with the third-lowest scoring total of the season in a 102-89 loss to a Houston team not playing much better than the one the Wiz beat to begin its December winning streak. Talk about low points: Michael didn't score in the first quarter, had just three in the fourth quarter and finished with eleven. He had fluid drained from his knee again, after the game, but there was still some discrepancy about how much this slowed him.

The games Michael obsessed over each have one common denominator. Cards—bid whist and blackjack to be exact—like golf, like basketball present opportunities to erase a mistake, a flop, a bad play with instant gratification. No matter how much you're down at the blackjack table you're always chasing to get even. You go bust on one hand, double-down on the next. For every moment in the rough, there's a twenty-five foot putt waiting or the chance to chip in. Even if you took a snowman on the last hole, who doesn't step up to the next par three thinking the tee shot can go right in the cup?

Michael had to see the Houston game as the basketball equivalent of being stuck in the rough. Yes, the knee had become enough of a problem that he sat out a game against Detroit two nights later. Though returning for New Jersey the next night left him busted again with an 0-for-the-fourth-quarter—no points and no shots with Jason Kidd checking him—Michael merely doubled-down against Miami and pulled that thirty-seven. Ever the card shark, Jordan tried to gut his way through the rematch with the Heat, admitting "For three quarters, I was able to disguise it to some degree." Up until this point, the past seven days had reinforced the way Michael always played the game, any games. He came up with bad hands in L.A. and Sacramento, put more on the table and came up with a big winner in Phoenix. He was lost in the rough before finding his stroke against the Heat. But as he walked off the court in Miami, leaving six minutes and twenty-seven seconds of a winnable game in the pot, Michael finally had to consider that the only one who he had been bluffing about how long he could continue to endure the pain was himself.

3

ONE IMAGE OF MICHAEL JORDAN REVEALS SO MUCH OF HOW THE THIRD COMing transpired. Both his knees are wrapped in ice bags the size somebody might buy for $1.99 at the corner store, and it is only ten o'clock in the morning. He hasn't practiced in three days, and tonight he will play a game in which he admits he took about one shot that felt good, one that felt in the kind of rhythm where he got his feet set under him. His shot is rusty. His game is rusty. And his knees are rusty like the hinges on a creaking door. And it is only opening night of the 2001–2002 season. After he missed the three-point shot that could have tied the game with nineteen seconds left, Michael publicly stated that his knee was bothering him a little bit, which as we know now could be anywhere from a little bit to ready for surgery. The mystery of wounded knee has already swelled to the point that every night somebody will wonder if Michael is too old for this game. What will ultimately have the most impact on the knees, though, is whether it's the years or the miles.

Before the season started, before training camp opened, it's a little of both. How much Michael's knees have fallen to the chain reaction that started with the broken ribs becomes evident on September 10, the day before he was set to publicly confirm the Third Coming. For three weeks, he had been going almost at Mach 5 twice a day to regain the shape he had lost when Ron Artest got in up to his elbows. This was the way Jordan used to do it every summer in North Carolina, a crash course similar to Jerry Rice running the hills of Mississippi to get ready for training camp. Back then he would come out refreshed. Now, he comes out of Hoops the Gym to see the only reporter who has chronicled his comeback since the workouts began. Michael reaches out to grab *Chicago Sun-Times* columnist Jay Mariotti by the knee and says, "Hurts right here." And he confided that he feared this was not going to change.

At this point, Jordan was actually lucky. His knee had become afflicted with tendonitis, a weakening condition more than a debilitating one. Weight training could compensate for this, building up muscles around the knee to check deterioration. All Michael needed was to keep his knee out of harm's way, where one bump or misstep could inflame the tendonitis into something more confining. And more painful. When ice packs became part of his regular practice gear during training camp in Wilmington, Michael passed it off as preventive medicine. And nobody had reason to think otherwise. Here he was already playing through the prescription for coming back, not foregoing the second of the daily two-a-day practices, as he said he would. When the knee finally gave out on him that December night against Orlando, Michael backtracked. "Actually, it happened during training camp. I hyperextended it and fluid developed from there." Hyperextension, of course, happens when a joint straightens beyond the natural flex point so it actually bends inward.

Hyperextension in Michael led to hypertension for Collins. The Wizards coach had devised a game plan to keep Michael's playing time in a winnable cycle. Take Michael out around the four-minute mark of the first quarter, get him back in with eight left in the half and shoot for the same plan in the second half. But as the Wizards struggled more and more at the start of games, Jordan's will superseded Collins's scheme. And when Doug tried to impose his will over Michael's, the coach risked inciting a wrath far more fracturing than tendonitis. He learned this in the first half of a game at Toronto when Collins switched Tyronn Lue to guard the white-hot Carter in the midst of his twenty-three point roll. Jordan received the order and shot back a laserlike glare at Collins that could have seared a hole through his heart. Collins gave Jordan the palms-down response as if to say *calm down, let's try it for one play*. One play. And then Jordan switched back to Carter. His knees may have hurt, but Michael was never going to let his ego give into the pain. Pride may have been the perpetrator of this whole ordeal more than any other influence. Even though Michael's best minutes seemed to come fresh off the mid–first half breather, he wanted to play through when Washington was sinking in the first quarter. But missing fourteen of twenty-two second-half shots against Atlanta in November and/or the block party Paul Pierce threw at him suggested that Michael didn't always know best.

Michael, of course, played on. "Michael knows he has to play less minutes," Collins admitted a month into the season, having seen Jordan hobble through an average of more than thirty-eight per game, or six more than the coach had prescribed. "Earlier in the year, I would say, 'Michael you've got to come out,' and he would say 'I want to keep playing.' I did err on the side of letting him play too much." And here is where Michael came up against the antagonist he didn't know how to handle. When he broke the bone in his foot in

1985 that forced him to miss sixty-three games, Michael felt so pow-erless that he developed the response of throwing soda cans at the television when watching his team lose. The pent-up wrath then exploded on the Celtics with that sixty-three point playoff game. Now, the more he played, the more he felt he had to play to get the shot to go down, to ride to the rescue of a team losing nine in a row. When Boston came to the MCI Center on November 24 and the Wizards had a shot at their first victory in twenty-one days, Michael refused to back off. Even though he missed the "last shot," he played through the overtime, grinding to the victory because when your tee shot keeps spraying into the rough, you grind through to make par. But forty-five minutes against Boston put the knee through a grinder that Richtered like fingernails on a chalkboard. Collins knew Michael had gone over the edge, the cycle of destruction becoming ever so apparent. "His knee got sore and it was very difficult for him to prac-tice because he has to rest," Collins continued. "So I don't know how he's going to stay sharp. It's hard for him, because he really has to watch his legs and then come out and try to play when everybody is gunning for you. And if he gets out there every day, his knee is going to swell up, so we have to be careful."

Practice had become limited to running a few drills and then watching his teammates run intrasquad scrimmages while he rode an exercise bike on the side. This caused even more acute pain because practice was where he planned all along to execute his plan of teach-ing the Wiz kids how to play the game. To do so, he needed to be at full speed, and the Wiz kids needed him to be at full speed because practice is what they had heard all about, that this was the place where Pippen and Grant and B.J. Armstrong showed Michael they could stand up to his intensity. The trust to share the ball took so much longer to develop, as a result, and to make up for it Michael would push his knees through forty-five minutes in Boston.

This, to be sure, is not what he planned for. Michael wasn't going to try to fool anybody into thinking he could play forty minutes every night. In his championship years, he averaged slightly more than thirty-eight. But the part of the Third Coming that was failing now floundered because Michael couldn't find his finishing touch. If he was going to show the Wizards how to win, he would need to be playing like ice, not wearing it. His fourth quarters began to show too many four-for-nines in the first month, or worse, the nothing-for-six against Boston that included overtime, and the zero in the fourth quarter against Orlando as the season turned into its second month. Five, six years ago, even three years ago, the line about having Michael Jordan on one leg was better than most guys on two wasn't always a joke. Now, it was sad the way Michael was limping around the fourth quarter, Ground Jordan watching T-Mac steal the air up there.

After the Orlando loss, when he revealed the news about the hyperextension, Jordan conceded, "It's time to pay attention to it so it doesn't linger all season long. If it's not going to get any better other than me just sitting out, then I guess I got to do that." The next day, he made the secret trip to Chicago to see Dr. Hefferon, had the knee put through a magnetic resonance imaging exam, watched more fluid drained and heard the prescription from his trusted medicine man: Cut back on your playing time. Even consider sitting out the second half of some back-to-backs, or you will wind up right back here in a couple months. Or worse.

The test for the Third Coming was never going to be whether Jordan would score. And win. Those who advised against a return or didn't want to see him smudge the greatest legacy in sports preached that the only downfall would come because a thirty-eight-almost-thirty-nine-year-old body—even one with a Secretariat-sized heart—could not withstand the pounding of an NBA season. Every playoff season shows every third player wearing a support on a knee or an elbow, a brace on an ankle or those little pads wrapped around fingers. Twenty-five-year-old joints and limbs wear down during any normal season, so how could thirty-eight-almost-thirty-nine-year-old knees expect to endure?

Fluid gushing from his right knee followed by sitting out the San

Antonio game left Michael facing a dreaded I-told-you-so from the general public, et al. But the Wizards' twenty-one victories in the next thirty games, with Michael averaging 25.2 points, 6.1 rebounds and 5.2 assists, a product of that getting-the-last-word motivation that started this whole comeback, worked more to help the knee than any ice, rest or Advil—or so he thought. Nights when he scored just six points or made just five of twenty-one shots can be considered evidence that his knee occasionally buckled under the duress of Michael wanting to get the last word. But those fortysomethings and winning at a 70-percent rate from December through the All-Star break might be enough to believe Jordan when he said if he could just get his legs under him, he could regain another posture of his former life: ignoring the doctor's prescription. Bad days and better days healed into good days and bad days, and Michael knew that if he could just keep the knee from suffering another hyperextension or any other trauma he could withstand the grind.

Some variables, however, are not in Michael's control even if his two-hour weight-training sessions almost every day worked his body into maximum fitness. When you play in the NBA, you never know when you might cut through the lane and run into one of Karl Malone's elbows. Michael happened upon an incidental contact with teammate Etan Thomas as the Wizards were stunning Sacramento on February 7 at the MCI Center, the last game before the All-Star break. The knee-on-knee bump Michael suffered was so unexpected, it might not have happened if he was slow-dancing with Thomas. The pain from one of these mishaps lasts no longer than a punch to the stomach; you get your wind back and you go on, wondering if there's any further damage and knowing it might not show up for weeks.

The bump and the more worrisome forty or more minutes per night Jordan had played in nine of the past eleven games compelled Collins to suggest Michael pass up All-Star weekend, but the intoxication of riding in once again as the game's greatest miracle worker was too much to pass, not to mention the chance to tell the other stars that his team's 21-9 run was the best in the league the past two months. Okay then, Collins thought, then limit your playing time in the All-Star Game. Michael indicated he only wanted about twelve minutes on the floor, but then the intensity picked up and the same ego-flexing that ignored Collins and Hefferon pushed him to playing almost half the game.

Coming out of the break shooting 38 percent and the Wizards going 1-6 in the games leading up to the Miami doubleheader only made Jordan more desperate with his push. Though Collins observed, "banging knees with Etan bothered him, maybe more than he was willing to let on," Michael would show the knee was not a lingering problem by running amok for thirty-seven against the Heat, an effort that finally pushed him over the edge to precisely where Hefferon told him he would be. When he came out of the back-end of the Miami set with six minutes and change still to play, Michael knew he was facing the kind of adversary he never thought capable of catching up to him. Age, time and injury had him triple teamed. The only option now seemed to be putting the knee on ice. A rest period of somewhere between one game and the rest of his life was coming. This is what Michael contemplated as he heard doctors tell him they believed his injury was an arthritic condition.

Or worse.

4

NO BODY PART IS MORE AT RISK ON THE FIELD, THE COURT OR THE ICE THAN the knee. Tendonitis, arthritis, bumps, bruises sometimes seem like getting off easy for a joint not exactly constructed to be the hinge used to leverage a six-foot-five, two hundred and twenty-pound defender out of the post. The effects of spinning and pushing off, then landing postdunk on the knee can feel like an axe chipping away at an oak tree. Parts of the knee can splinter off almost as easily with every whack. Though all the mileage on Michael's knees—mileage that didn't come at a low level, Collins reminded—didn't necessarily result in this latest grounding, he knew it was coming. The fluid that kept being drained should have been the first clue. All joints produce fluid that keeps them lubricated, but when extra fluid builds up to make joints feel like they are locked, it's often a sign of either an injury or an arthritic condition. Especially if after being drained, the fluids come back. So what may have started out as tendonitis—an inflammation of the tendon at the front of the knee between the kneecap and shinbone—and felt like tendonitis because of the way it limited Michael's mobility probably degenerated into an arthritic condition. Or worse. He could have been dealing with a tear in cartilage—the loose-pebble-in-the-shoe feeling—or a tear to another of the knee's shock-absorbing parts. Or worse.

What was becoming clear to Michael after he left Miami was that a couple of days of rest would not be the cure. Suddenly, he faced the prospect of something he had never known in his basketball life. Surgery was the only option. Exploratory surgery, doctors told him, and Collins, who had endured seven variations of knee surgery during his career, sensed for the first time that Jordan was maybe a little scared. "The whispers are going to start," Collins figured. "That's the way it always works. What he's going to hear is, 'Yeah, we knew he couldn't make it through a whole season' and 'Why did he come back?' Michael wanted to play every game. I was the one who said, 'Michael, please don't play today.' "

So when Jordan consented to have surgery, he finally tipped his hand as to how painful the grinding had become. Giving up what would have been a pretty good shot at winning his sixth Most Valuable Player award—as many as Kareem and Russell—would become easier to digest, especially if the Wizards stayed within three-point range of the playoffs while Michael healed. But the day he decided to have the surgery, Portland came to the MCI Center and not even the temptation of finally getting that one shot at Scottie Pippen, now the point forward and in Michael's eyes the poster boy for the petulant Trail Blazers, could jumpstart him one last time.

Too much anxiety now to think about that as he limped into Sibley Hospital in D.C. on this February 27 morning. He hoped he would leave here this afternoon feeling much better and not just because of the painkillers they would send him home on. They had to find something that was causing this injury to be as much of a pain as Ron Artest had been. Collins confided that when talking to Jordan after the operation, he could hear the sound of hope through the slur of the Vicodin. The exploration revealed a torn lateral meniscus cartilage in Jordan's right knee, which was repaired along with cleaning out some loose pieces and smoothing some rough edges. The lateral meniscus is that bony substance you feel on the outside of your knee where it bends into a right angle. Torn and inflamed, it inhibits the push needed to change directions or get power into a jump. Wizards team physician Stephen Haas, who performed the ninety-minute procedure, said the exploration showed the normal wear and tear an athlete the caliber of Michael Jordan would put his knee through, presuming that normal was gravity-defying torque and reckless abandon. Collins elaborated that Jordan was relieved to know there was a source of the problem and that he wasn't just some broken-down old ballplayer. Collins also knew the toughest part of all this was whether Michael would give his knee time to heal.

As he watched from home on this night, Michael might have had a my-work-here-is-done sensation. Though they lost to the Blazers 105-101, the Wizards scored sixty-one points in the first half, the most they had scored in one half the entire season. Hamilton carried the day with a rejuvenating thirty-one points, steadying the Wiz kids' halfcourt offense with a series of flash-and-catch jump shots. Chris Whitney and Courtney Alexander showed signs of being able to play the Michael Jordan role with nineteen and thirteen points respectively. And if not for what Alexander termed a questionable call that turned a would-be steal into two Pippen free throws with 6.5 seconds to play, the Wizards would have had a shot to win the game. Michael actually perked up at the end of the third quarter when he saw Kwame Brown stare down Portland's Rasheed Wallace and pull off the tornado move around the Blazers' big man for a half hook and a hoop. Jordan joked to Collins earlier on this day to tell Kwame not to drink too much water, a Jordanism for implying that the spotlight shifting to Brown with Michael out might cause Kwame to wet his pants. After the game, Collins called Jordan and when discussing Kwame's drive on Wallace submitted the "I think we got the right guy" comment.

Michael seemed tempted to begin rehabilitating his knee right then and there. Or it could have been the Vicodin talking. The prognosis set the rehab at two to four weeks, with four seeming simply Jordanesque for it would put him back just in time for Kobe and the Lakers to come to Washington. Somewhere in the recesses of his mind he was probably thinking he could come back to fuel a final playoff push against a schedule that included games with contenders Milwaukee, Charlotte, Indiana and Philadelphia twice in addition to the Eastern Conference–leading New Jersey Nets. Or it could have been the Vicodin talking.

Johnny Bach figured a quick recovery was already in the works. He knew Jordan's tolerance for pain was best explained by an incident during the 1992 season. Bulls forward Horace Grant complained of a pregame headache and even asked Phil Jackson about taking the night off. "As he was leaving the locker room, Michael looks at Horace and says, 'Take a fucking aspirin.'" Bach remembered all the times he saw Jordan laying on a table in the closet that passed for a training room in Chicago Stadium, vomiting then coming out and scoring fifty, all the nights Jordan played through colds and viruses and upset stomachs. "He always found a way to play," Bach explained. "I would see him and kid him that he didn't come from this planet."

Sentiment in the Wizards' locker room after the Portland loss indicated that they were prepared to go the rest of the season without Michael. Even welcomed the prospect according to Alexander, who said, "We can take what he taught us and try to use it without him. There's a lot of excitement in this locker room." Across the way, a Portland guard and former teammate of Jordan's talked about how he had the same surgery two years ago when he was thirty-four years old and wondered if the legacy had passed beyond the point where Michael could take an aspirin and overcome.

"It took me three months and I was rehabbing hard every day," Steve Kerr said. "Maybe he's different. Maybe he's Michael."

Maybe.

Maybe not anymore.

ONE LAST SHOT

1

THE FOURTH COMING HAS PASSED THROUGH ITS FOURTH GAME, AND MICHAEL is hearing hauntingly familiar words from Doug Collins. *Don't press the envelope.* Let's see, when did he say that? Last month? Last week? Opening night? Before Michael Jordan ever played a minute of the Third Coming, Collins declared that if he can't control his addiction to try and win the game all by himself, "It will come back and haunt him." Behind the sweat and anger of that catatonic stare, the pounding echoes, *win, Michael, win,* more than ever before as if this 2001–2002 season has become one long round of golf with Richard Esquinas and he is just getting to the point of putting one million dollars on a single putt. Three weeks after having an arthroscope inserted for a cleaning and shaving of his knee, Jordan made the comeback within the comeback. Finishing the job is what he had in mind, seeing if he could help the Wiz kids in one final playoff push, for as former North Carolina roommate and Monopoly and pool adversary Buzz Peterson might say, this was Michael not giving up until he could say he won. In other words, pressing the envelope.

Four games into the Return, Michael is grinding through grueling therapy/rehab work to play the twenty or so minutes per game he has prescribed for himself, enough he believes to add some offensive punch and be on call if there is a victory to close out, a basketball version of Mariano Rivera. It is March 27, exactly one month after

Michael had knee surgery, and the job isn't going so well. Washington has won two of four—the second coming last night—since Michael rushed back, but both those wins came against a Denver team so bad it actually traded away its two best players for Juwan Howard two months ago. The Wizards have a 34-38 record, are sliding quickly out of the playoff picture and Jordan hasn't really helped, making just 34 percent of his forty-six shots since coming back.

Reports indicate that Michael's knee is anywhere from 50 to 65 percent of normal, whatever normal has been this season. And on March 27, Collins drops some more words that draw reaction like they came out of some sealed envelope. "I'd be surprised if Michael played next year," Collins commented when making a guest appearance on the ESPN talking-heads show *Pardon the Interruption*. "I just think the wear and tear . . . I'm not saying he's not going to play, but right now it's up in the air." Collins eventually explained that his assumption was based on post-op thoughts Michael sent up, reiterating what he said last month and the month before that and the month before that. But just when season-ticket holders were contemplating stopping payment on checks to reserve for next year, Jordan confirmed this much about Collins's testimony the day before: "I would be surprised if I'm back playing. If I'm going through the same situation, it wouldn't be wise for me to play."

And while all this is going on, Michael is trying to figure out a way to win the game, though Collins and others are wondering if Jordan has confused what the game is all about and who it is against. Making the playoffs would do it, for he said last month and the month before that and nearly twelve months ago that taking this team to the postseason would be the equivalent of any of those stogie-smoking, champagne-sipping moments with the Bulls. Reinventing his game one more time to become a setup man/on-court traffic cop who can come off the bench, yield to the teammates he has tried to clone, then flip the switch in the final six minutes could allow him to rationalize the season's turn of events. And he could almost certainly do that on one-and-half legs.

But right now Michael needs something more spectacular, the equivalent of dropping fifty with a couple of dunks for a man his age with a recovering knee, something to convince Michael—if not anybody else—that the rumors of the last two days are greatly exaggerated. Doctors may have removed bits of cartilage with that arthroscope, but they didn't take out his will. Perhaps Jordan can recall motivation like this one other time in his career, that being in 1986 when he made his last pass across the injured list. After a fifteen-game playing rehab, a God was born in the playoffs against Bird's Celtics. That outburst had come after Jerry Reinsdorf demanded that Michael's rehab assignments be limited to eight minutes per half.

In the first four games of the Fourth Coming, Collins had similarly been using Jordan off the bench, inserting him into the game with three minutes left in the first quarter and letting him go for eight minutes or so. The score and the Wizards' chances to win became the barometers for Collins and Jordan to figure his second-half playing time, though Collins wishes it were the retreat showing in the tightening of Michael's face every time he pushes off on his right leg dictating things now. This is the one phase of the game Collins has on Jordan, his seven knee surgeries processing just how much pain comes into play. But Michael is ignoring everything, the pain and the coach.

Then, on the night of a game against Milwaukee—the fifth game post-op—Jordan told Collins, "Don't be afraid to put me in. I feel good." Collins called for Jordan at the 6:48 mark of the first quarter, and for the first time since the All-Star break Michael seemed to take the floor with a bounce in his step. The drive was working. The shot-fake was working. He went up-and-under Glenn Robinson and Anthony Mason to hit five consecutive shots in the first quarter. In the second quarter, he seemed to play like a guy recovering from knee surgery, with three misses on his four shots including a layup that the Bucks' Tim Thomas blocked.

But in the second half, disguised as a guy recovering from knee surgery, the old Michael Jordan appeared. Collins again let Jordan go midway through the third and in two minutes he put up seven points that stretched a three-point margin to eleven. When he hit his last shot with 1:31 left in the game, the MCI Center sounded Gary Glitter worthy. A standing ovation accompanied Michael's exit after he scored thirty-four points on twelve-for-twenty-two shooting in a barely sweat-breaking twenty-six minutes. The 107-98 defeat of Milwaukee also gave the Wizards momentary hope of making the playoffs, which was the point of the Fourth Coming. Certainly, a good part of this was personal for Michael. After all those years of proving people wrong, you don't know how to live any other way. And this time, Jordan had somebody new on the I-told-you-so list, himself. For whatever reason, playoff talk now replaced talk about next year and warnings about the cost of winning, and Collins wasn't about to bring up the notion that Michael had once again pressed the envelope.

Five days later, the Wizards were hanging on to a thread of playoff hope as frayed as a tendonitis-riddled knee. Two losses dropped them to 34-40 and even winning their last eight might not have been good enough to make the postseason. The night before, the Wizards had flown to Milwaukee following a loss to the Lakers when Michael promised a playoff run was still possible. Playoffs seemed to be the last concern after Michael sat out the second half against L.A., the lead too big to risk minutes and the knee in a position that caused Collins to send up more watchwords: "Michael, please, I don't want you to play." Michael didn't ignore this time, didn't argue.

As he boarded the team flight that night for a road game against the Bucks the next day, the pain in his knee must have been so great because it was prevailing in the one-on-one with his win-at-all-costs mentality. Michael knew he had gone over the edge of the envelope just by getting on this plane, but when sprained ankles and sore wrists have gotten better overnight you think this will, too. When he awoke the next morning, however, the words in the envelope had come back to haunt him. Swelling in his knee prompted Jordan to check out of the Milwaukee hotel and check out for the rest of the season. The last sight of Michael for the season was him limping into a limousine headed for the airport. The statement the Wizards released reported that Michael was going on the injured list for the rest of the season because it was finally time to let his knee heal properly. The rest of the Wizards officially learned that Jordan was finished for the season when they boarded the team bus at five o'clock that afternoon. "We saw him briefly in the lobby," Tyronn Lue said. "And, then, he was gone."

Again.

2

WHEN HE LAST LEFT THEM, THE WIZ KIDS WERE JUMPING INTO A NEARBY phone booth and coming out in 2003. The day that Michael went under the arthroscope, his teammates found their legs, running to those sixty-one first half points against Portland and their first hundred-pointer since the pre–All-Star break victory against Sacramento. Despite the 105-101 loss, the postgame locker room finds the Wiz kids insisting they have learned to walk and are ready to fly. Kwame, of all people, speaks from the heart of the team when he says that for the first time in a long time, "It was a fun game." He also hits another point of contention by asserting that they can no longer play with eight guys now. "We have to have twelve."

Tyrone Nesby picks up on this thought, adding, "With Mike gone, we will learn more about each other." Collins called this "growing up time" and evoked all the other clichés applicable to finding out about the future of the organization. There are many who believe this is something the coach wanted to find out about what he can do with these young players without them having Michael around to use as a crutch. President of basketball operations Michael Jordan had left them with a interior line of young, mobile hustlers with a discernible upside and a perimeter of young, mobile clones who could run and dunk and shoot. Now the time has come to find out what the playing legend Michael Jordan has left them.

Not much, judging by the first road game of Washington's first post-Jordan era. Ironically, this game came in Chicago, where without Michael Jordan the matchup was pushed back to page seven of the *Chicago Tribune* sports section and where courtside seats that had been fetching twelve hundred dollars a week ago were now down to face value. Courtney Alexander said that the Wizards owed it to Michael to show what they had learned because of what he risked to come back for them. Alexander then let those words come back to haunt him by scoring two points in a 90-81 loss that immediately prompted questions about how the Wizards were no better than a lottery team without Michael. Or worse, no better than the Bulls.

The highest esteem the Wiz kids could pay Jordan at this point was to show they were a team created in his own image. Hamilton seemed intent on carrying out the mission to play Michael, and he nearly pulled off a dead-ringer impersonation by overcoming vomiting and a stomach virus to score thirty points in Chicago. But the one player best equipped might have been Alexander. Even though Michael's ability as a talent evaluator was still in question, he apparently did see something in Alexander when asking for the then-rookie to be part of the Juwan Howard deal last season. Collins fingered Alexander as well, telling him before the Portland game that despite his up-and-down season he could still be the Wizards' Heir Apparent. But this was a last chance for Alexander, who had been offered the part twice already this season. The consensus among the Wizards hierarchy was that this third audition would be his last callback.

With Jordan sitting in the locker room the Sunday following the surgery in his first visit to the team post-op, Alexander gave it one last shot. He gutted through fifty minutes of a 107-102 overtime upset of Orlando that broke the seven-game losing streak. Collins was heard to say, "This renews hope," after Alexander put up a Jordanesque stat line. Twenty of his thirty-two points came in the second half and overtime, and he added seven rebounds and four assists. He even bettered Michael by one-upping McGrady, who had twenty-seven of his thirty points after halftime but missed two of three shots in the extra session.

Brendan Haywood actually called it a blessing in disguise playing without Michael when the Wiz erased the debacle in Chicago by blowing out the Bulls 115-90 two days after the Orlando game. They scored the most points they had all season, they shot a season-best 57 percent from the field, and Alexander even provided a look beyond Michael by following up with twenty-six points against the Bulls. The new Wiz was running and gunning and in what seemed to be a Kobe-esque, stay-right-where-you-are-old-man statement, Alexander looked at the style that had forged the first back-to-back wins since February 7 and explained the difference by saying, "We're not, you know, old." But none of them were Michael, either, especially Alexander in the end. When he could play the fast-break game, he could put up some twentysomethings. But then he would come up with a back-to-back like Utah and Toronto in late March with two and four points respectively. And on a team that Collins called a bad defensive team post-op, Alexander was cast as one of the primary liabilities. The Wizards gave up ninety-five or more points seventeen times in the final twenty-seven games, and of the ten games they didn't, four came during the Fourth Coming.

Losing the next four games while Michael rehabbed by a combined eighteen points indicated there was still some work to be done. But Michael figured the way the Wizards lost could be filed away as growing pains. The two-game winning streak ended against eventual Central Division champion Detroit when the Pistons' Jon Barry made like his father Rick and hit a three-point shot as time expired for a 95-92 victory. The next night, McGrady answered for his failures of the previous week and Orlando needed the last two of his fifty points to break a tie with twelve seconds left in a 99-96 Magic win. Bad shots and bad decisions at the end of the game then caused back-to-back losses to the Celtics, prompting one Boston columnist to sling this at Michael: "His team folds like a house of cards over the final few minutes."

When Collins saw his team quickly fall to a four-game losing streak, he did not hesitate to point out what the Wizards were missing. "In this league, you have to have star players at the end of the game." Hamilton was even more succinct, telling the *Washington Post*, "When MJ was playing, it seemed like the ball always bounced right." Perhaps the entire Washington locker room was now sharing the sentiment of a sign flashed at Boston's Fleet Center during the recent 98-91 Wizards' loss: GET WELL SOON, MJ.

Back when the Wizards were muddling through their we-stink phase, Collins kept telling his team winning would be a bromide. Michael said he tried to extend that thought by preaching that winning breeds winning. And though the only salve for his knee right now would be getting back on the court, seeing his Wiz kids stand up and walk on their own felt like a shot of bromide with a champagne chaser. Collins even began to see the Wizards bristle enough to respond to this challenge, a response he described as, "I think they're wanting to show him: You know what, Michael, we know how to play."

Because of him or in spite of him would become the lingering question this season. The part of the mission aborted early in the Third Coming was Jordan's desire to spread his basketball gospel. After all, the man had invented more moves than any coaching textbook could ever detail. But if the Wizards thought they were going to be studying filmmaking at the hands of Spielberg, they never had enough time on the practice floor with Michael to learn how to break down a defender in the post or how to set up the back-door cut for the layup or when was the right time to dart into a passing lane to make a steal. He couldn't risk putting his knees through the additional strain. Michael did find a few moments to work Rip through the intricacies of the yo-yo fake. And from time to time, Popeye would submit observations on how Michael being so fundamentally sound was helping the rest of the team improve on the basics.

Collins, however, figured that was his job, and that Michael's part in turning Washington from a nineteen-win team to a thirty-seven win team was a season-long process. The coach argued that going into packed arenas every night on the road with opponents playing on a vengeance directed at Michael's Bulls hardened his Wiz kids, and that they would become a playoff team ultimately by using this experience to improve on the twenty-eight games Washington lost by ten points or less. Michael tried to grow these teammates like he had grown Scottie and Horace and B.J., the only way he had ever known. He would make them understand the value of competing by keeping them in a pecking order he determined and continually goading them into trying to fight their way up. He would trash their desire to broadcast rap music through the pregame locker room, and he would refuse to let them sit in the more luxurious back of the team charter flights if he thought they didn't defend well enough to deserve such a reward. Sometimes on the road, he'd challenge the Wiz kids to shooting games for money. How many free throws can you make with your eyes closed? Or left-handed? Or maybe good old-fashioned H-O-R-S-E. And when he won, he would keep their money.

And that's about as close as any of the Wiz kids got to Michael during the Third Coming. Kwame discerned the presence and impact of MJ when he told the *Washington Post*, "Nobody meets Michael. You gotta know somebody who knows somebody before you meet Michael." They came to view him less as a legend mainly because they saw him slip to mere mortal and then human status as the knees gave out. But for the most part, Michael saw his teammates this way: Back when Michael was about ready to come out of Camp Comeback, *Sun-Times* columnist Jay Mariotti said he stood outside Hoops the Gym one afternoon throwing the vagabond and wannabe names from the Washington roster at Jordan like they were playing the lightning round from *Password*. Popeye, Whitney, Nesby, Jahidi, Etan Thomas, Alexander: How was he going to make these guys better? Or more succinctly, how much better could he make them? This from a guy who had done more with less than any player in the history of the NBA. Not that Michael didn't root for them to be better, especially when his knee called time out. In his post-injury grand plan, perhaps Michael figured if the Wiz kids could stand on their own for a while, he could ease into the first few months of the 2002–2003 season, take time to get in shape and then kick into third, fourth, fifth gear—whatever the last gear was now—after the All-Star break with a record still respectable enough to make a playoff push. The ultimate win-win for Jordan would be if the Wizards could sustain the winning. That would be their way of telling him it was time to retire.

But nobody is daring to tell him that now, two weeks after the surgery when Collins noted that Michael's rehab had advanced to the point where he was edgy, picking on everybody again, a sure sign he was feeling better. Collins even talked about Michael joining the team on its upcoming six-game road trip through the West Coast, though he said this was no indication the Fourth Coming was scheduled. In the meantime, what victories Washington did manage came with the Wizards playing Jordan by committee. Lue took his turn at Seattle, scoring eleven of his twenty-six points in the fourth quarter to break the losing streak at five. Two more losses set up what Collins called a win-or-make-early-summer-plans game, and Chris Whitney donned the MJ cape, hitting a three-point shot with twelve seconds left for a 99-96 defeat of Golden State. Winning four of twelve so far with Michael rehabbing, the Wizards were now 31-36. Collins figured ten more wins might get them into the postseason. But with nine of the fifteen remaining games scheduled against would-be playoff teams, the season seemed like it was about to press the edge of the envelope.

3

URGENCY SEEMED TO FLOW THROUGH DOUG COLLINS NOW THAT THE WIZARDS had lost nine of thirteen without Michael. Or emergency. He said Michael could show up any time, and with one win in the past seven games going into Golden State, maybe Collins was wishing more than forecasting. Apparently, Jordan said his knee felt 100 percent better than before the scope, though in two weeks his rehab hadn't progressed beyond some shooting and basic basketball mobility exercises, cutting, pushing off the repaired knee and the like. If the window of opportunity was still open, then it was no more than the crack owners leave when the dog stays in the car at the grocery store. But that's all he needed, all he wanted, all he could endure now. The faintest of hope provided the one last shot Jordan needed this season, the final challenge that could provide one more rabbit test. As George Koehler related, Michael considered that he had more success at coming back than anything else he had done. So here he cultivated motivation for meeting the Wizards in Denver on March 19 with the possibility of playing the next night against the Nuggets coming via some sadly familiar words:

"It's an itch to get back out there with our team in a playoff situation."

Jordan said he turned into a couch coach watching the Wiz kids play so hard yet fail at the moment when he thought he could always make a difference. And even on one leg, apparently he thought he could still make a difference, judging by the vehemence of his return. He said he wouldn't play without getting in two or three practices, and Collins confirmed that Michael wouldn't burst out of the phone booth before the game at Toronto in five days at the soonest. But the morning of the Denver game, there was Jordan pressing the envelope again. A non-contact practice the day before had no negative impact on the knee, so Michael progressed into the shootaround, a workout a team typically uses on game day to walk through plans for that night. After the shootaround, Jordan asked Rip to play him in some get-me-ready one-on-one and after that Michael spent another thirty minutes working on his shooting, repeating a routine he had been using all season, sometimes choosing to work on his jumper early in the morning or late at night so nobody could divulge how many he was making, or missing. Michael had nobody fooled; this was not a practice but a dress rehearsal, and even Denver coach Mike Evans knew it, including Jordan in the scouting report he gave his Nuggets prior to the game.

The start of the Fourth Coming was not going to be just another game, not with this being the first time in 883 games in which he was not part of the starting lineup. But even before he went back into the halls of Denver's Pepsi Center to warm up for the reappearance by riding an exercise bike for ten minutes, this event had become more carnival than basketball game. His return incited a small ticket-buying frenzy the afternoon before the game, and when he came out to warm up fans rushed to the Wizards' side of the court as if they were going to get one more look at the bearded lady. All this scene needed was a clown, and there was Rocky, the Nuggets mascot, wearing a Wizards number twenty-three jersey as Jordan readied himself to play. Truth be told, this is part of what kept dragging him back. How, after all, do you ever get over this kind of adulation? As much as he came back for the love of the game or to scratch an itch or as Air freshener to give the Washington franchise a sniff of winning, the Fourth Coming, like the Second and Third—and probably the Fifth and the Sixth—ignited because he was always looking for one more shot to be the greatest of all time.

Michael, of course, filled his spot on the bill. After missing his first two shots, he splashed a jump shot from the left wing then posted up on Denver's Calbert Cheaney, pulled out the fadeaway, hit the shot and drew a foul that led to a three-point play. As if the trained monkey had just saved his best trick for last, the crowd erupted on the play. In sixteen minutes, Michael scored seven points, missed seven of nine shots and rushed back just in time to help the Wizards survive Denver with a 107-75 victory. On a night when the Pepsi Center wasn't exactly filled to the rim, a group of fans showed up on the spur of the moment after seeing cars in the parking lot and thinking the Colorado Avalanche was playing a hockey game.

Whereas previous Comings had been filled with the Air for the dramatic, this one was passing into the theater of the absurd. What could be worse than trying to play a back-to-back now? What if that back end came in Utah, where some fans were still on their cell phones, still talking about the final thirty-seven seconds of that night in June of 1998? Though his knee stiffened after the Denver game, Michael could have left the Delta Center content with twenty-two minutes and eleven points. A dunk with one minute, forty-seven seconds left in the first half even could have been a show of strength. More positive reinforcement could have come when Michael came off the bench with seven minutes, sixteen seconds left in the game and helped cut a sixteen-point Utah lead in half. But this night only provided the surest sign yet that the legend was fading. The Jazz fended off the Wizards' comeback when Bryon Russell pulled up on Jordan and put a three-point shot of redemption in his face. "I looked at him, sized him up and I just shot the ball," Russell said, noting that the roar of the crowd was the sweet sound of revenge. "Then I got right in his face and said, 'I hope you hear that Mike, on your flight home.'"

Michael's response two days later included a statement about "plenty of time." Presumably, he was talking about Washington's playoff push, for the next two games seemed to indicate anything but. A Sunday afternoon in Toronto playing the Raptors without Vince should have been a three-foot putt. But the Wizards trailed by twelve points with five minutes left in the third when a Jordan jumper ignited a 13-0 scoring run that put Washington ahead. Michael seemed on the verge of fighting off age, time and mortality again by hitting a shot with two minutes left to put Washington ahead by five and another with one minute, fifteen seconds remaining to forge a 91-88 lead.

Then came thirty-nine seconds nearly as telling as the thirty-seven in the Delta Center four years earlier. After Toronto cut the lead to one, Jordan missed a jump shot. After the Raptors missed on their next possession, Jordan seemed to have the game in his hands, holding a rebound when Antonio Davis knocked the ball loose, picked it up and dropped in the go-ahead layup with fifteen seconds left—all of which again left Michael with one last shot. He worked into position from sixteen feet away, eluded the Raptors' Jerome Williams with an up-and-under fake and in one crescendo he would make up for clanking the three-pointer on opening night. "Yes," he could almost hear Marv Albert say as the ball arced almost perfectly into the basket and halfway through. Then, like the three-foot putt pulled just a bit, it rimmed around and out.

Even during the Third Coming, Michael had avoided this, being marked by the plays he wasn't making. After the miss against Toronto, the coming-of-age moment in the next game—Denver's visit to the MCI Center—battered Michael when Voshon Lenard, who had his fifteen seconds of Air Apparent playing with Miami against the Bulls in the 1997 Eastern Conference Finals, blocked a Jordan shot in the first quarter with so much force that he fell to the floor. For all the fourth-quarter failings and five-for-twenty-six nights, this is what nobody wanted to see in the Third, Fourth or any subsequent Coming. The infamous scenes of Gehrig falling off his stool trying to tie his shoe or Mays swinging and missing badly had just played here, Michael hearing the phantom cries of "Are you ready for Medicare?" or "Do you need a walker?"

Michael will always think about the Fifth and the Sixth Comings because of how he picked himself up three days later against Milwaukee. The legend of Michael Jordan will cast this thirty-four point wonder as another in-your-face response, especially with the way he had the up-and-under move working and the range he had his jumper calibrated to. But as Jordan looked at this game and saw an opportunity to trample the Bucks en route to that eighth and final playoff spot, he said to hell with the pain and worry about the knee tomorrow because a win is out there like blood in the water. So press on.

Only there was no tomorrow. Not this season. The biggest weekend of the season started with Milwaukee on Friday and included an NBC game against Dallas Sunday afternoon. At 34-38 and with no margin for error, the Wizards needed one more Michael Miracle against the high-octane Mavericks. They got Michael Mortal. The Mavericks' Adrian Griffin, a slightly older version of Jumaine Jones and Ricky Davis, who admitted he was so nervous the last time he played Michael that he shot an air ball, held Jordan scoreless until fifty-eight seconds remained in the third quarter when he hit two free throws. His first basket didn't come until the eight-minute mark of the fourth quarter, and although Michael kept the Wiz in the game by hitting three consecutive jumpers in the last four minutes, he crashed with two misses as time ran out. On the game. On the playoff hopes. On Michael.

He tried to press the envelope. To know, all you had to do was look at him on that last night of his 2002 season against the Lakers. He came out wearing panty hose. Or what looked like support hose, a synthetic blue legging designed to keep the knee warm and help blood flow like a lubricant to prevent stiffness and locking up. Had it become more painful to play or to watch him play? Phil Jackson made sure his defenders knew to not go for the pump fake, and as Jordan tried to find a shot Phil winced like a father having to spank his child. By the time Michael hopped off the exercise bike and checked into the game, the Wizards were losing by ten points. Three games out of the eighth and final playoff spot in the East with eight to play, Washington was all but eliminated when Michael made his one last shot, a twenty-one foot jumper with ten minutes left in the second quarter. Down seventeen at the half, Collins called game over, the right call to Jackson who said Michael looked like "a shadow of himself." The last line on this season now read a career-low two points in a career-low twelve minutes. Michael pshawed this, saying, "I'm not here to chase any stats. I'm not here to chase anything. Yeah, it's a career low, whatever. It didn't make a difference." He had not been this pissed since catapulting to block Ron Mercer's shot three months ago.

4

AS HE CHECKED OUT FOR THE SEASON, GYRATIONS OF THOUGHTS MUST HAVE raced through his head during that ride to the airport in Milwaukee on this first Wednesday of April. He had never felt pain so deep, the knee barely bendable and so swollen that he felt like he was limping on one big thigh. The limp reminded him that six to eight weeks of rest and then another, more intense course of rehab formed the barrier to another one of those games like five nights ago against the Bucks. But he knew he had another one. At least.

Phil told him he thought he had some good basketball left in him. Kobe also said there was no doubt he could still play. He heard critics who initially defied his egocentric babble about getting the Wiz to the playoffs being as satisfying as winning a title, conceding that the legend had grown by getting this collection of kids, role players and lifelong backups *thisclose* to the postseason, not being officially eliminated until the eightieth game of the eighty-two game season. And he really only felt completely healthy for about a one-month stretch, that run from early December 2001 to January 8, 2002, when the Wizards won thirteen of fifteen games.

He also knew he was still the best game in town, at least one-third responsible for the increase in attendance across the NBA according to Russ Granik, and the pied piper of a 32-percent jump in home crowd attendance, largest in the league. But there was also the feeling of his first failure since Laney High School. Priority One of the Third Coming, he said, was to teach the Wiz kids how to win. They seemed to get it during that 22-9 stretch in December and January. But they went 11-22 after his surgery, which would be roughly a twenty-seven win season, or a meager eight better than the previous year. He knew there was one conclusion he would not face again. He would not walk away with that feeling of knowing he could have played another season. He also didn't want to get to the point where the masses were saying he needed the game more than the game needed him and have it be true.

Flying off into the sunset of this season, Michael knew there was one thought he would not bother to consider. Everybody had been asking the same question for going on two months now. Michael Jordan was not sure if he will play again. He's not sure he won't. *Washington Post* columnist Tony Kornheiser expounded the most basic principle of Jordanology when he wrote, "Whatever he says today, goes for today—but not necessarily for tomorrow. If his knee feels better on a Thursday, he'll want to come back on a Friday. It's his nature."

After checking out in Milwaukee, Michael dropped off into a self-imposed silence, an anonymity that lasted more than three months. While rumors swirled that he would begin working out again in two weeks or that he was having surgery to fix his other knee, the only confirmed sighting during that time put Michael on the scene watching sons Jeffrey and Marcus play for the Rising Stars basketball team, an AAU club that practiced in Deerfield, Illinois, around the corner from the Jordans' Highland Park estate. All Rising Stars coach Michael Weinstein would give up about Jordan revealed that he wasn't one of those parents to scream at coaches or officials. Eventually, he broke his silence, appearing on ESPN toward the end of August. He said he wouldn't play another season in pain and had instructed the Wizards coaching staff to plan for the 2002–2003 season without him. As is the degree of conclusiveness with Michael, however, Collins said the next day that he expected Jordan to put himself through the series of intense workouts he had planned for September and declare himself ready for one more shot.

Whether he was more content to be the family man than the GM planning to play next season still wasn't clear. What was clear was that he had already put the knowledge gained covering his teammates' backs to use. In the end, he realized that his partnership with Hamilton would be more Andy and Barney than Lone Ranger and Tonto, that Rip's physical vulnerability might be too much of a risk for Michael's one last season, that developing his fragile frame and perhaps ego might be too much of what Jordan went through with Pippen. So less than a month before training camp for the 2002-03 season began, Michael and the Wizards traded the twenty-four-year-old Hamilton to Detroit for a four-years-more-mature and North-Carolina-bred Jerry Stackhouse, an upgrade when combined with the offseason acquisitions of Bryon Russell—yes, that one—and Larry Hughes forged a supporting cast that could insulate Jordan in the style he had become accustomed to for one more run. In the 2002 draft, the Wizards grabbed Indiana forward Jarred Jeffries with their eleventh pick, their lottery pick for not making the playoffs. Though power forward–tall at six-foot-eleven, Jeffries had enough inside-out game to play the small forward spot; Michael's spot. With the seventeenth pick in the first round—the one the Wizards received in exchange for Alexander—they selected Maryland guard Juan Dixon, the most outstanding player for the 2002 NCAA champions, a tough competitor and the kind of winner Michael thought the franchise didn't have enough of. Jeffries playing up front with Jahidi, Kwame, Haywood, Etan Thomas, and Stackhouse as the shooting guard would allow Michael to pick and choose his spots to play. More shooting guard for sure. Maybe even some point guard, a role he had talked about with Collins during the Fourth Coming. Or he could even take up the role of supersub that rumored around during the offseason.

Other stops on his summer itinerary seemed to have Michael still looking for a game. Another game. Between Monte Carlo and Las Vegas, he no doubt hit the blackjack tables trying to get back into the win column. Not only did this season end with him on the injured list but also with him not in the playoffs for the first time in his playing career. Yes, he defied logic with scoring soliloquies for the ages and three more game-winning shots, but he didn't defeat it. In the back of his mind, if it had not been for the rib-pasting the previous summer he might have played into this one. Watching the Lakers sweep up the Nets in the NBA Finals, he had to think, *how could this team come out of the East?* If the ribs didn't take a hit, he would not have rushed back into shape, his knees might have endured and on the way to Finals he would have put one last shot over Paul Pierce. No, maybe it wouldn't have been that easy. But he saw Ray Borque lift a Stanley Cup at forty-one years old, Roger Clemens throw ninety-five-mile-an-hour fastballs at forty years old and Barry Bonds hit record-setting home runs at thirty-eight years old. Maybe he could go on Bonds's eat-to-win diet complete with some Creatine cocktails and return stronger than ever.

But from here, no doubt bad days and better days would always be ahead for Michael Jordan. The successes and failures of the Third Coming were conceived from the same source. "No one knows me, like me," he reminded time and again. Nobody tells him what to do. If he listened, he might not have spent so much of the Third Coming fighting to save his knees. And his marriage. The bliss he found, however, came from the preparation, the happiest moments being Camp Comeback or watching tape to figure out how to bark back at the young dogs or rushing through rehab for one more push to the playoffs. He will always be preparing for the next coming, relentless so the last line will never be two points in ten minutes against the Lakers. All he will ask himself is if he can make the playoffs or if he can handle not making the playoffs. Can he be satisfied with flashes of the old Michael Jordan? Or can he handle the nights when nobody cares about him, when a Lakers-Mavericks game generates a bigger story and he has to live with a headline in *USA Today* reading, "Wizards' Jordan scores 22" as if somebody may mistake him for any other Jordan?

In the end, he did settle the two questions governing the entire Third Coming. Yes, he still has it—or he did anyway—for how else to explain thirty-four points in twenty-six minutes less than one month after having invasive knee surgery? Will, determination, heart—mental toughness as he called it—were there on more nights than his legs this comeback season, and that feeling of being in a close game and always having a chance to win with Michael on the floor never faded even if he didn't live up to Heidi Klum's opening-night expectations. As for why, well, that is why the world will never know if Michael Jordan will come back at fortysomething to put one more game-winner in the face of some Cleveland Cavalier. Why is why the man will wear panty hose, press the envelope, bark at the young dogs, why the world will never see a coast-to-coast farewell tour that bestows rocking chairs, sets of golf clubs and gold watches on him. For Michael Jordan, there will always be thirty-seven seconds left and he will always be looking for one last shot.

APPENDIX

October 30
Madison Square Garden
New York
Knicks 93, Wizards 91

ON THIS DATE IN MJ HISTORY

In his one and only regular-season game in Kansas City, he led the Bulls to a 109-104 victory by scoring twenty-six points in 1984, the fourth game of his rookie season.

THE GAME STORY

This shot was a far cry from That One.

Forty months after his final shot gave the Chicago Bulls their sixth championship in eight years, Jordan reclaimed all his hype by sending up a potential tying shot from eighteen feet out with eighteen seconds remaining.

"I guess the difference is I'm a little bit older," Jordan said of the heave that made it only seventeen-and-half feet.

His game looked older, too. He played primarily at point guard, handed out six assists and probably should have had six more.

In thirty-seven minutes, Jordan scored nineteen points on seven-for-twenty shooting, mostly from the perimeter. Knee problems, irritating him for almost a month, already held him below the 32.6 points per game he averaged in 53 previous games against the Knicks.

November 1
Philips Arena
Atlanta
Wizards 98, Hawks 88

ON THIS DATE IN MJ HISTORY

On opening night of the 1986–87 season, he dropped the first fifty of his career in a regular-season game. The fifty points scored the Bulls a 108-103 victory against the Knicks and was the first of six games of fifty or more points this season.

THE GAME STORY

Jordan announced his return with thirty-one points, including eleven in the first quarter. He matched the nineteen in the opener by halftime.

"I know I can play the game of basketball like I'm capable of playing," Michael told the worldwide media still following him. "I know guys will rip me. But I know that when teams double-team, I know I'm back."

He said his legs came back but they still weren't there in the fourth quarter. After tossing up a pair of airballs, Jordan made two free throws for an 88-83 lead with just over four minutes left. On the key play, he drew a double team on the wing and kicked it to a wide-open Chris Whitney, who drilled a three-point shot to seal the win.

Jordan played forty minutes and hit thirteen of thirty shots and added six assists and six rebounds.

November 3, 2001
MCI Center
Washington, D.C.
Wizards 90, 76ers 76

ON THIS DATE IN MJ HISTORY

After seventeen games and a second-round playoff loss the previous spring, he officially began the Second Coming by scoring forty-two points in a 105-91 victory against Charlotte at the United Center in 1995.

THE GAME STORY

In a game hyped to match up the MVP of the past against the MVP of the present, Allen Iverson, Jordan played erratically and Iverson did not play at all, opting to rest his surgically repaired right elbow.

The Wizards outscored Philadelphia 44-10 during one extended stretch. Richard Hamilton played the lead role for the Wizards by scoring twenty-one of his twenty-nine points in the second half.

Jordan scored twenty points on seven-for-twenty-one shooting primarily against Matt Harpring, who said he had trouble handling Michael's moves. A Jordan head fake drew a foul on Harpring and the ensuing three-point play gave the Wizards a 53-52 lead with 4:41 to go in the third period. Washington kept coming and opened a 64-56 advantage behind Hamilton, who scored fifteen points in the quarter.

"He got me on one move," Harpring said. "It was a good move. I'll try to stay down on my feet next time and not take his head fakes."

November 4
The Palace of Auburn Hills
Detroit
Pistons 100, Wizards 78

ON THIS DATE IN MJ HISTORY

After missing sixty-three games the previous season with a broken foot, Michael scored thirty-four points to lead the Bulls to a victory against San Antonio and a 3-0 start to the 1986–87 season. It was part of a streak in which he scored thirty or more points in eighteen of the first twenty games en route to averaging a career-best 37.1 points per game.

THE GAME STORY

Jerry Stackhouse was more Michael Jordan than Jordan, hitting ten of thirteen shots and scoring twenty-two of his twenty-eight points in the first half of a game Doug Collins said the Pistons could have won by fifty.

Jordan scored seventeen points, hitting seven of fourteen shots, in the first half. He finished with nineteen points and a season-high eight rebounds. But in his first back-to-back set of the Third Coming, he left the game at the 7:51 mark of the third quarter and took the rest of the night off.

November 7
The Fleet Center
Boston
Celtics 104, Wizards 95

ON THIS DATE IN MJ HISTORY
In the seven games he played on this date, he averaged 32.29 points per game, but the Bulls were just 4-3 in those games.

THE GAME STORY
The most emphatic definition of the difference between this Michael Jordan and "that one" came with the two Jordan shots Paul Pierce blocked in the fourth quarter.

Pierce swatted Jordan with 5:05 left, but Jordan later scored on a fadeaway jumper to forge an 89-89 tie with just under four minutes to go. After Antoine Walker converted a three-point play to give Boston the lead, Jordan continued to discover that the NBA is a different league now. He drove the lane against Pierce, missed badly and subsequently was whistled for traveling, arguing to no avail.

Jordan made twelve of twenty-six shots for a season-high thirty-two points but failed to help his teammates, registering just two assists.

November 9
MCI Center
Warriors 109, Wizards 100

ON THIS DATE IN MJ HISTORY
Four games into the 1988–89 season—the season of "The Shot"— Michael hit for fifty-two at Boston in a 110-104 victory. He dropped fifty-two more on Philly a week later and another fifty-two a week after that at Denver.

THE GAME STORY
For the first time since the first three games of the 1990–91 season, Michael Jordan felt the dismay of a three-game losing streak. And he was losing his patience.

"I don't think we're playing well as a team," Jordan told reporters after the loss. "I think we're playing as twelve individuals. I don't know if they're trying to impress me or management with their contract situations, but this is not a collective effort."

He tied his season high with thirty-two points, making thirteen of thirty shots. Rip Hamilton had ten points in the first quarter but just six the rest of the way.

If there was any positive statement on this night, it came from Kwame Brown. The rookie came off the bench to score ten points and played thirty-five minutes having recovered from a sprained ankle suffered on opening night.

November 11
MCI Center
Sonics 99, Wizards 84

ON THIS DATE IN MJ HISTORY
Having missed a game-winner in regulation against the Pistons on this night in 1992, Michael needed only overtime for a shot at redemption. With time running out, he pulled up on Joe Dumars and buried a running three-pointer that gave the Bulls a 98-96 victory.

THE GAME STORY
One of the not-quite-as-young dogs treated Michael like a fire hydrant.

Gary Payton helped force MJ into one of the worst shooting days of his career, a five-for-twenty-six embarrassment from the field that included missing his first fourteen attempts. Michael finished with sixteen points, his low for the season to date.

"It was one of those situations where I caught myself laughing because as hard as I was trying, I just couldn't get it to fall," Jordan said. "Even the easy shots, like layups."

Payton, who received help from Desmond Mason to humiliate Michael, added thirty-two points and fifteen assists. Kwame Brown had five points and six rebounds in his first career start.

November 14
MCI Center
Bucks 107, Wizards 98

ON THIS DATE IN MJ HISTORY

The 1986 night conjured thoughts of that game against Boston nearly six months ago. Michael proved the sixty-three pointer the previous spring was no fluke by going off for forty-eight points in this rematch with the Celtics. The big difference this time around: Larry Bird's thirty-seven weren't enough to keep the Bulls from a 110-98 triumph.

THE GAME STORY

This was the first of those nights to send up the how-old-is-Michael-Jordan jokes.

He looked like his old self, scoring sixteen points during the third quarter. Then the punch line came. He just seemed old in the fourth quarter when he hit two of six shots and added three turnovers.

Jordan did finish with thirty-one points on twelve-for-twenty-four shooting, the first time that he hit the fifty-percent mark from the field this season.

A teammate finally answered the call to be Jordan's running mate. Popeye Jones was almost Pippenesque with thirteen points and ten rebounds.

"Hopefully, I can build on that and become a threat because it allowed Michael to get some more open shots," Jones told the Associated Press.

November 16
MCI Center
Jazz 101, Wizards 92

ON THIS DATE IN MJ HISTORY

During the Jordan Years (1984–98), the Bulls played three times on this date without Michael. Orlando Woolridge won the Michael Jordan lookalike contest by scoring thirty-five points in a 1985 defeat of Cleveland with MJ on the bench due to the broken bone in his foot. During the first retirement, Toni Kukoc scored twenty in a 1993 loss to Seattle, and Ron Harper had twenty-seven in a 1994 loss at San Antonio.

THE GAME STORY

John Stockton said Jordan picked up where he left off in 1998.

Michael tied the NBA high for points in a game with forty-four, a mark Nick Van Exel and Tracy McGrady had already reached. He even topped fifty-percent shooting for the first time, hitting seventeen of thirty-three from the field.

Still, another game ended with a that-was-then-this-is-now feeling for Jordan when Quincy Lewis, who wasn't even in the NBA in 1998, emerged as the hero.

Jordan converted two three-point plays during a 12-2 run in the fourth quarter and tied it, 87-87, on a jumper with 5:50 left. The teams traded baskets before Lewis drained consecutive baskets forty-six seconds apart to put Utah ahead for good. Oldies night also featured thirty points from Karl Malone and a season-high seventeen assists from Stockton.

November 20
MCI Center
Hornets 95, Wizards 88

ON THIS DATE IN MJ HISTORY

The fifty-four points he scored against the Lakers on this 1992 night was the first fiftysomething of the season for Michael. The first of just four that season. The Bulls lost this one in overtime, 120-118.

THE GAME STORY

In just twenty-one days this had become the worst season of Jordan's career. The seventh consecutive defeat marked the longest losing streak of Michael's career, and there was little solace for him that only the Chicago Bulls had a worse record than the Wizards at this time.

"It's disappointing more than frustrating," he said. "Obviously, I believe in the team and will continue to do that. We have to be strong through these moments and not point fingers at other people."

Michael had thirty but just four in the third quarter and eight in the fourth. Still, the number that stood out was his league-leading average of 25.4 shots per game. He had scored thirty or more points in five of his past six games, but Rip Hamilton was Washington's only other player averaging double figures so far.

November 22
Conseco Fieldhouse
Indianapolis
Pacers 110, Wizards 103

ON THIS DATE IN MJ HISTORY
Michael was on one of those binges again. He followed up the fifty-four in L.A. in 1992 with forty against Phoenix.

Two nights later, he would add forty-nine at Golden State.

THE GAME STORY
What does Pacers rookie point guard Jamaal Tinsley have in common with Michael?

Yes, both are Brooklyn natives, though when Tinsley was just a babe there Jordan was coming off hitting an NCAA championship-winning shot at North Carolina. On this night, Tinsley was the star of the show with an NBA season-high and team record twenty-three assists.

"I don't know how to put it into words," Tinsley said referring more to playing against Jordan than the record. "He's one of the greatest ever. I just wanted to play hard."

Jordan made just eight of twenty-six shots and finished with twenty-one points and afterward sent up an observation that said a lot about what he looked for in players these days. "One thing I think people are overlooking is that he went to college for four years. I really think that was big for (Tinsley's) development."

November 24
MCI Center
Wizards 88, Celtics 84 (OT)

ON THIS DATE IN MJ HISTORY
In one of the highest-scoring games in franchise history, the Bulls defeated the Nuggets in Denver, 151-145 in 1990. Ironically, Michael didn't top fifty. He didn't even top forty, finishing with thirty-eight.

THE GAME STORY
When Michael finally saw the end of the longest losing streak of his career, he really had nothing to do with it.

Christian Laettner hit the tiebreaking jumper with 8.6 seconds left in overtime, and Richard Hamilton followed with a clutch defensive play, while Michael had just two points during the fourth quarter and overtime.

This was hardly a night to celebrate for Jordan. Paul Pierce slapped Michael around again, blocking three of his shots and drilling a three-pointer over him to bring the Celtics back from a fifteen-point deficit with six minutes left and tie the game with fifty seconds to play.

Postgame analysis fingered Michael as forcing up shots in the fourth quarter and ignoring his teammates, perhaps to settle some vendetta with Pierce. All that did was run his minutes up to forty-five, the most he had played in any single game of the third coming. He waved off Doug Collins' attempts to rest him, and the grind of the victory left Michael feeling his right knee boil up with career-threatening pain.

Jordan hit seven of twenty-four shots to finish with nineteen points and added eleven rebounds and six assists.

November 27
Gund Arena
Cleveland
Cavaliers 94, Wizards 75

ON THIS DATE IN MJ HISTORY

Michael played just four times on this date in his career, but the most memorable November 27th came when he was resting. In 1986, Jordan was in Los Angeles getting ready for not just a game against the Lakers the next night but a run in which he topped the forty-point ceiling in each of the next nine games.

THE GAME STORY

The season-low seventy-five points scored, the second-worst loss of the season and perhaps his own abysmal shooting caused Michael to bubble up with the most famous words of the comeback season.

But it was Doug Collins who had the most profound comments on what caused this loss:

"I knew it before the game," he explained. "Guys messed around getting on the floor. They didn't get out until there were fourteen minutes to warm up. I kept asking them to get out, get out and warmed up. We walked out on the floor and we were twenty points down."

Michael's eighteen points actually led the Wizards in scoring but those came on nine-for-twenty-four shooting. His postgame observations could have been directed at his shooting, which had fallen to forty percent for the season, or at his teammates. Richard Hamilton was equally atrocious, scoring just thirteen points on three-for-thirteen shooting, and Christian Laettner was the only other Washington player in double figures with ten points.

"I think we stink," Jordan announced in what became his infamous and oft-repeated rhetoric. "I just haven't shot the ball particularly well, and I'm not going to sit here and make excuses. I missed layups and I missed easy wide-open shots, but that doesn't mean it should sink our boat. I don't see anyone covering my back as everybody probably expected me to cover theirs."

November 28
First Union Center
Philadelphia
Wizards 94, 76ers 87

ON THIS DATE IN MJ HISTORY

On perhaps the worst night of his career, and certainly the worst night he ever had at Madison Square Garden, Michael scored his New York low of seventeen points in a 112-85 loss to the Knicks.

THE GAME STORY

He hoped there would be more nights like this. He needed more nights like this.

Allen Iverson, three years and one Most Valuable Player award more confident, tried to turn his first meeting of the Third Coming with Michael into a one-on-one, and no one man was going to take down Michael that way. Not yet. Iverson scored twenty-seven points in the first half on the way to forty and jumped the Sixers to an early lead. But Jordan one-upped Iverson by scoring the Wizards' last fourteen points of the first half to cut the margin to three.

Richard Hamilton scored twenty of his twenty-eight points after halftime, thirteen in the third quarter, including eleven during a 19-6 run that helped the Wizards take control.

Michael finished with thirty, hitting eleven of seventeen shots, and collected seven assists, six rebounds and a season-high five steals. Philly coach Larry Brown underscored the difference between Jordan and the player trying to "Be Like Mike" on this night.

"A thirty-eight-year-old is playing basketball the way it's supposed to be played," he said. "Here's a guy who hasn't played in three years and he completely controlled the game. He got Hamilton looks, he guarded Aaron McKie. I can't image anyone taking three years off of anything and playing at a level like this guy is playing."

November 30
American Airlines Arena
Miami
Wizards 84, Heat 75

ON THIS DATE IN MJ HISTORY

He finished the 1986–87 season with a 37.1 points-per-game average, his best in any single year. But ten years later, Michael was streaking just as voluminously. In a 97-88 victory at San Antonio on November 30, 1996, Jordan scored thirty-five points, the second-to-last of an eight-game run during which he averaged 37.5 points a night. He also scored the 25,000th point of his career on this night.

THE GAME STORY

He was used to winning games all by himself, but this was not one of those Classic Jordan moments. Michael scored eight of his twenty-two points in the fourth quarter, and he nearly outscored the Heat, which had nine in the final period.

Jordan was even held scoreless in the third quarter, but the seven rebounds and five assists he added to nineteen points from Richard Hamilton had Doug Collins believing the Wizards were starting something. "This is his calling card," he said of Jordan. "To go into other people's houses and play these kind of games."

Michael scored twelve points in the first ten minutes of the game as the Wizards jumped to a 24-16 lead. He was held scoreless in the third when the Heat built up a thirteen-point lead. But the abysmal fourth caused Miami to drop its eleventh consecutive game. The Wizards snapped an eleven-game losing streak against the Heat.

December 1
MCI Center
Magic 96, Wizards 87

ON THIS DATE IN MJ HISTORY

A 98-97 victory at Golden State in 1987 featured John Paxson leading the Bulls with nineteen points. It was the only time in the eighty-two game regular season when Michael did not lead the Bulls in scoring.

THE GAME STORY

He couldn't tell which was more of a pain: Tracy McGrady trying to turn this matchup into a High Noon, Darrell Armstrong poking him in the eye or the pain in his knee making him feel like a jet plane with one engine burned out. McGrady had looked so forward to his first tête-à-tête with Michael since reaching the legal drinking age that when the season's schedule came out he circled this date on his calendar. T-Mac scored twenty-six points to fifteen for Michael, who missed nine of his last ten shots against McGrady.

"He looks good," McGrady said. "He has a lot of veteran's tricks out on the basketball court. To be thirty-eight, yeah, he definitely looks good. Don't ever underestimate that guy."

But afterward, Michael said he felt thirty-eight. Older. McGrady didn't know the half of his veteran tricks. Michael had been covering up how bad the knee had become since he hyperextended it during training camp. He had been fooling his coaches, teammates and the public. The pain in his right knee had inhibited the lift on his shot so much that he decided to go to Chicago to have Dr. John Hefferon, his personal guru and team physician when he was with the Bulls, check out the problem.

Was he fooling himself?

December 6
Compaq Center
Houston
Wizards 85, Rockets 82

ON THIS DATE IN MJ HISTORY

In the midst of that 1986 streak of nine consecutive fortysomethings, he scored forty-three points in a 106-97 loss to San Antonio. Interestingly, the Bulls went 3-6 during that stretch.

THE GAME STORY

For three quarters, he played like somebody nursing an injured knee that forced him to sit out the game two nights earlier in San Antonio.

And then Michael Jordan was walking on air again.

His decision to play seemed ill-conceived after he missed eleven of fifteen shots through three quarters. But the "Air" for the dramatic returned in the fourth quarter with Washington clinging to a 64-62 lead when Jordan sparked an 8-3 scoring run. Jordan began the stretch with an acrobatic reverse layup and made a fadeaway jumper before feeding Brendan Haywood for a dunk. He capped the burst with another fadeaway to give the Wizards a 72-65 lead with 5:11 to go. After a pair of Rockets free throws, Jordan nailed an eighteen-footer. He made another jumper and assisted on jumpers by Tyronn Lue and Popeye Jones in the last two minutes.

"It's hard to believe that he can still do what he does," Houston coach Rudy Tomjanovich commented afterward. "I think he's the greatest, and he simply elevates the bar in this league."

December 8
American Airlines Center
Dallas
Wizards 102, Mavericks 95

ON THIS DATE IN MJ HISTORY

A game at Atlanta in 1992 is one of the few losses to make it in the Michael Jordan highlights. He had thirty-two points and twelve rebounds, but, in one of his last flights of fancy, Dominique Wilkins provided some fresh "Air" with forty-two points in a 123-114 victory for the Hawks.

THE GAME STORY

Now, this is what he came back for.

Richard Hamilton, the man who would be Michael, and the man who led the Wizards in scoring the past three games, had nineteen points. Brendan Haywood, the product of Jordan's draft-day fleecing, scored another nineteen. And Michael had fifteen of his twenty-one points in the fourth quarter to seal the deal.

Missing his first twelve jumpers had little impact for Michael, which is just the way he wanted it when he made that "We stink" comment in Cleveland.

"You could see it in the last couple of games," he said. "The guys are starting to come out and play aggressive."

December 11
The Pyramid
Memphis
Wizards 91, Grizzlies 81

ON THIS DATE IN MJ HISTORY

This is what happened to the Bulls when Michael Jordan went into his first retirement: In a 1993 game against the Cleveland Cavaliers, the leading scorer was not Scottie Pippen or Horace Grant or any one of the threepeat champions. Steve Kerr had eighteen to lead the Bulls.

THE GAME STORY

Perhaps this was a glimpse of the Wizards of the future.

Rookie Brendan Haywood scored eleven of his seventeen points in the second quarter, and Richard Hamilton soared for thirty, relegating Michael to the supporting cast with sixteen points, nine assists and six rebounds.

Haywood and Hamilton combined for nineteen points in the second quarter when Washington outscored Memphis, 30-14. Hamilton, for one, knew where this type of effort came from.

"Playing with Michael, I'm learning so much," he said. "I think that now we've pretty much got our lineup adjusted."

December 12
MCI Center
Wizards 82, Heat 80

ON THIS DATE IN MJ HISTORY

A date that will live in symphony: In six games on this date, he averaged 35.7 points per game, including scoring forty-one in 1989 against the Mavericks' Rolando Blackman, one of those players cast in the 1980s as the guy who could stop Michael Jordan.

THE GAME STORY

The excitement, the hope, the possibilities resonated through Michael after this victory.

The Wizards survived a potential game-winning three-point shot by LaPhonso Ellis. Afterward, Jordan related the growth spurt that took place during a timeout with 11.3 seconds to play and the Wizards leading 82-80.

"When I brought the guys together with 11.3 seconds left, I said, 'We're on a string.' That means we're going to have to cover each other's tail.'" Jordan said. "The guys did a great job."

Michael scored fourteen of his twenty-five points in the first half and added seven rebounds and six assists.

December 14
MCI Center
Wizards 96, Knicks 80

ON THIS DATE IN MJ HISTORY

This night in 1989 made many wonder about his viciousness. Reggie Theus, the Bulls scoring soloist of the 1980s, returned to Chicago Stadium with Orlando and hit for nineteen points. With Theus guarding him, Michael obliterated the past by doubling down with thirty-eight points.

THE GAME STORY

Richard Hamilton confirmed that Michael was succeeding in his mission to teach the Wizards how to win.

"A lot of guys in this locker room have probably never won five games in a row," Rip noted.

Most of all, Jordan seemed to be having a profound impact on Rip. Hamilton scored twenty-seven of his season-high thirty-four points in the first half and hit fourteen of his twenty-four shots. Jordan recovered from a slow start to score nineteen points. After the Knicks closed to 31-29 in the second quarter, Hamilton and Jordan combined for all of Washington's points during an ensuing 11-1 run that essentially turned the game into a blowout.

This was not a night to celebrate, however, because starting forward Christian Laettner was lost to a broken left fibula early in the first quarter that sidelined him for a month.

December 16
Air Canada Centre
Toronto
Wizards 93, Raptors 88

ON THIS DATE IN MJ HISTORY

The forty-one points he scored to lead the Bulls past New Jersey, 99-98, in 1986 was almost inconsequential. In this season, Michael hit the forty-point juncture thirty-five times.

THE GAME STORY

The game began with Vince Carter trying to show how much he could "Be Like Mike." It ended with Carter realizing how much further he had to go.

Carter seemed determined to show his predecessor at North Carolina that he was the breath of "Fresh Air" in the NBA by scoring nineteen points in the first quarter. But with Jordan shutting out Carter in the second half, a one-time nineteen-point lead for Toronto evaporated under Michael's new reign.

Brendan Haywood and Kwame Brown fueled a 20-3 second-quarter run that helped the Wizards recover. In the third quarter, Jordan hit four straight shots to give Washington control. He finished with twenty-one points, and Rip Hamilton added twenty-seven as Washington won its sixth in a row for the first time since December 26, 1997.

December 19
MCI Center
Wizards 103, Hawks 76

ON THIS DATE IN MJ HISTORY

Coming off a third consecutive NBA Finals appearance, the Lakers were the measuring stick in the NBA in 1989. Jordan conjured another of those when-the-spotlight-is-hottest miracles with thirty-seven points to lead a 93-83 dismantling of Magic, Worthy and company.

THE GAME STORY

For at least one knowledgeable bystander the Michael Jordan of old had returned.

He had twenty-three points in just twenty-seven-minutes and rapid-fired for eighteen in the last seven minutes of the first half. He ended up hitting eleven of nineteen then sitting out the entire fourth quarter.

"It reminded me a little bit of the old Bulls' practices," Toni Kukoc, Michael's teammate from 1995–98 told the Associated Press. "Obviously, that's Michael."

Jordan said this was the best he had felt since early in the season, and the victory gave the Wizards a chance to post their first eight-game winning streak since the 1982–83 season when a certain North Carolina sophomore was tearing up college basketball.

December 21
TD Waterhouse Centre
Orlando
Wizards 93, Magic 75

ON THIS DATE IN MJ HISTORY

When the question came about which player Michael was most like, Julius Erving, Dominique Wilkins and Elgin Baylor were the standard answers. Some also insisted George Gervin. When Michael was out with a broken foot in 1985–86, Gervin understudied for him and on this night scored twenty-one in a 117-114 defeat of Utah.

THE GAME STORY

What did you expect Michael to say after the win streak hit eight, despite him making a paltry three of sixteen shots, missing his first eight and not scoring in the final twenty minutes?

"This is probably the most impressive of the eight," he told the media gaggle. "This is big growth for a young team. It has taken me a while to realize these guys have confidence in themselves. The guys really impressed me tonight."

After Richard Hamilton went down with a groin injury in the first quarter, Hubert Davis responded with nineteen points to lead five players scoring in double figures. Even Popeye Jones' thirteen topped Jordan, who had a season-low twelve.

The Wizards matched their longest winning streak since March 19–April 1, 1983, when the franchise was known as the Bullets.

December 22
Madison Square Garden
Wizards 87, Knicks 86

ON THIS DATE IN MJ HISTORY

Twenty-nine games into his pro career, Michael provided another preview of coming attractions. Against the defending champion Celtics in 1984, Jordan scored thirty-two and added twelve rebounds to lead a 110-85 pasting of Boston.

THE GAME STORY

This will be remembered as "The Shot of the Third Coming."

Jordan was on the verge of deflation again in The Garden. He missed two key shots in the last minute-and-a-half that would have put the Wizards ahead. But with three seconds left, he hit the game-winning shot this time, the shot that would trigger the most memorable week of the comeback.

It was a historical win for the Wizards and not just because it gave the franchise its first nine-game win streak since 1978, the season Washington reached the NBA Finals.

"This nine-game win streak has given us confidence," Jordan said. "We've been playing hard and when you play hard, you get rewarded. That's the only way you're going to change the franchise around. This is an indication of that. I think it's changing."

December 26
Charlotte Coliseum
Hornets 99, Wizards 93

IN THIS DAY IN MJ HISTORY

Like a lot of people, Michael could be a little hung over the day after Christmas—metaphorically speaking. Since NBC inaugurated its holiday game in 1991, the Bulls were part of the entertainment every season through 1997. In 1993, he laid forty-two on the Knicks and that came after dropping fifty-seven on Washington two nights earlier. So on December 26, 1992, he rested and watched Horace Grant lead the Bulls with thirty in a defeat of Indiana.

THE GAME STORY

His Blue Heaven turned to Blue Hell for one night.

The Carolina boy had always played his best basketball here. In thirteen seasons with the Bulls, he was 14-3 in Charlotte Coliseum and averaged 31.7 points per game, his best mark against any team.

But in the fourth quarter, he missed four straight shots and fumbled away the ball when the Wizards still had a shot to stay in the game in the waning seconds. He finished with twenty-eight points, making just eleven of twenty-eight shots.

December 27
Conseco Fieldhouse
Pacers, 108, Wizards 81

ON THIS DATE IN MJ HISTORY

Call this the best day of the season for Michael. Any season. In five games played on this date, he averaged 44.2 points per game, culminating with a high of forty-seven against Atlanta in 1997.

THE GAME STORY

Only Cal Ripken had a more prominent streak than the one that ended on this night.

After eight-hundred and sixty-six games of scoring at least ten points, Jordan was held to a career-low six. He hit two of ten shots and sat out the final fifteen minutes. This was his worst night since scoring eight against Cleveland on March 22, 1986.

With Richard Hamilton still out with the groin injury and Tyronn Lue leading the Wizards with twenty-three points and it being the fourth game in six days, Jordan submitted his own rationalization about the maladies of the evening.

"Everything fell into my lap and no one stepped forward to carry the load," he said. "We had nothing. Our jerseys were there, but our bodies were not."

December 29
MCI Center
Wizards 105, Hornets 86

ON THIS DAY IN MJ HISTORY

His NBA Player-of-the-Week performance in 1997 crescendoed with a forty-one pointer against Dallas, the second half of a back-to-back forty or more, his first of two in the final season of the second coming.

THE GAME STORY

A measure of Michael will always be how quickly he can erase his failings.

He needed two minutes, forty-three seconds to top the six he scored against Indiana and quadrupled that six-pack by the end of the first quarter. If his legacy will be that he was better at coming back than anything else he did, he added to that by coming back from the Indianapolis debacle with a record fifty-one points.

He set team records for most points in a quarter (24), half (34) and became the oldest player to hit for fifty. He scored the first thirteen points for the Wizards and didn't miss a shot until the 8:09 mark of the first quarter.

December 31
MCI Center
Wizards 98, Nets 76

ON THIS DATE IN MJ HISTORY

He never played a New Year's Eve game with the Bulls, that ritual being something Washington introduced to the NBA the past two years to use a game as an opening act for a concert. His best New Year's ever probably was 1992–93 when he scored thirty-nine against Miami on December 30 then came back with another thirty-nine against Indiana on January 2.

THE GAME STORY

"I think you can keep all of those old player conversations down a little bit," Jordan announced. He was feeling young again after following up the fifty-one with forty-five to ring in 2002.

Jordan hit sixteen of thirty-two shots and added that his knees were feeling good, so good that he scored twenty-two consecutive points during a six-minute stretch over the second and third quarters. He outscored the Nets 23-13 during that time.

Doug Collins turned away from the young Jordan versus old Jordan debate, insisting this was a new Jordan. "I think he is more of a surgeon now," Collins said. "I think before he just beat you with just sheer will, skill and energy. Now he slices you. He finds out where to attack, and he just reads it."

January 4
MCI Center
Wizards 89, Bulls 83

ON THIS DATE IN MJ HISTORY
The twenty-seven points he scored at Charlotte were noteworthy only because the Bulls beat the Hornets to add a fourth consecutive win to three previous victories at home. This would eventually grow to an eighteen-game winning streak, the longest of Jordan's career.

THE GAME STORY
His superlatives seem so spontaneous that you wonder if they're pre-meditated.

Michael's comment following his first-ever game against the Bulls—"If we have to step on people to move up, then that's what we do"—might explain the events of this night.

The nineteen-point second quarter in which he hit seven of ten shots would have been enough of an "in-your-face" to his former team. Becoming the fourth player in NBA history to score thirty-thousand points with a second-quarter free throw would have been satisfaction. Then came "The Block," a two-handed smother of Ron Mercer's layup that would have made it too close in the fourth quarter.

"This is special in a sense that we're trying to claw our way out of the basement of losing teams," Jordan said. "I like to think that we're moving in the right direction and Chicago may not be moving in the right direction, and I don't want to be compared with them. I want to show some separation. That's the importance of it more than anything."

January 8
MCI Center
Wizards 96, Clippers 88

IN THIS DATE IN MJ HISTORY
The fifty-three points he scored against Portland in a 121-117 victory in 1987: not even one of his top five that season.

THE GAME STORY
Popeye Jones appeared to be getting it.

With Michael struggling to score but four points in the fourth quarter, Popeye drained consecutive jump shots to hold off the Clippers after they cut the lead to two points late in the game.

"There is a part of me that always says give Michael the ball late in the fourth quarter," Jones told the reporters. "Tonight I just stepped up and took the shot with confidence."

Jones finished with sixteen to supplement Jordan, who had eighteen points, ten rebounds and eight assists. Hubert Davis, filling in for the still-ailing Richard Hamilton, scored fourteen of his sixteen in the third quarter.

January 11
The Bradley Center
Milwaukee
Bucks 105, Wizards 86

ON THIS DATE IN MJ HISTORY
The best he could do in five games played on this date was thirty-two points in a 110-86 dismantling of Houston in 1997.

THE GAME STORY

Ray Allen and Tim Thomas played their own game within the game to see who could be most "Like Mike."

Allen made the greatest claim on the court, scoring eight consecutive Milwaukee points in seventy-two seconds of the second quarter. Thomas challenged Allen's twenty-seven points with twenty-five of his own and some choice words.

"Tonight, I was better (than Jordan)," Thomas told a media horde postgame. "But I wish it had happened when he was in his prime. It's still a great moment for me. Hopefully someone in my family was rolling a tape on this game so I can show my kids someday."

Jordan had two points in the first quarter and fourteen in the second but finished with twenty-two on ten-for-twenty-four shooting. He also committed a season-high six turnovers.

January 12
MCI Center
Timberwolves 108, Wizards 100

ON THIS DATE IN MJ HISTORY

He went one-on-one with Larry Bird in 1988 and lost. Actually Michael outscored Larry, forty-two to thirty-eight. But the Celtics defeated the Bulls, 104-97.

THE GAME STORY

Michael always had this thing about challenging the players who wanted to claim his "Air space."

So he went at one of those guys, Kevin Garnett, scoring twelve points in the first quarter and fourteen more in the second on six-for-eight shooting. Garnett had his own solo, scoring thirteen of his thirty-one points in the second quarter, but in the end he needed twenty-nine points from Chauncey Billups to offset Jordan's thirty-five for the night.

"I'm in the wonderful world of Michael's land here," Garnett said. "I've definitely been keeping an eye on him and I know he definitely has the ability to heat up, so I was just trying to be aggressive myself. It was fun."

January 15
MCI Center
Spurs 96, Wizards 91

ON THIS DATE IN MJ HISTORY

If only he could make Washington this good again, so good that even with forty-six from Michael on 1996, the Bulls struggled to *hold off* the Bullets, 116-109.

THE GAME STORY

At least Charles Smith didn't throw up. Unlike the night when Indiana's Dan Dakich found out he was going to guard Jordan in an NCAA Tournament game, Smith held his dinner—and Jordan—down.

Michael made five of twenty-one shots and was held to just eleven points during the first three quarters before rallying to finish with twenty.

"I thought about it all day," Smith told the *San Antonio Express-News.* "I just said, 'Well, I'm going to be in awe for a minute, but once the ball tips up, I have to defend him and do my job.' And that's what I did."

Jordan helped by missing six of sixteen foul shots. Afterward he sent up some familiar words.

"You've got to give our guys credit," Jordan said of his fellow starters who each scored in double figures. "They played their hearts out. Me, I stunk it up."

January 16
Continental Arena
New Jersey
Nets 111, Wizards 67

ON THIS DATE IN MJ HISTORY

Michael greeted Orlando's Shaquille O'Neal in his first visit ever to Chicago Stadium with sixty-four points in 1993. This turned out to be one of the most embarrassing nights for Jordan. Despite his scoring brilliance, his turnover late in the game contributed to the Magic forcing overtime and winning, 128-124.

THE GAME STORY

In a season of first-time-evers and never-befores, this was the first time ever Michael had been beaten this bad. He had never before lost a game by forty-four points. The previous low was a 112-75 debacle in New York on November 28, 1992.

New Jersey's first sellout crowd of a season in which the Nets were the surprise success story of the NBA came to see Jordan and saw him for less than a half. The Nets built as much as a twenty-seven point lead in the first quarter, and Michael sat out the entire second half after scoring ten points in the first.

January 19
The United Center
Chicago
Wizards 77, Bulls 69

ON THIS DATE IN MJ HISTORY

The battle to rule the "Air space" between Jordan and Dominique was always a one-on-one. In 1988, Michael thought he had him by scoring thirty-eight only to have Nique lead Atlanta to the win with forty-one. Two years to the date later, Jordan outscored Wilkins, 36-26, to lead the Bulls to a win.

THE GAME STORY

Following the prolonged standing ovation that greeted Jordan's first game in Chicago and almost brought him to tears, the game had nowhere to go but downhill.

And it went fast. He had nine turnovers and missed fourteen of twenty-one shots. The only saving grace was that the Wizards victory tied their win total of last season while the Bulls lost for the two-hundredth time since Jordan retired in 1998. The Bulls were so bad, they missed their first thirteen shots and didn't score a basket until the 5:56 mark of the first quarter.

By game's end Michael probably echoed the thoughts of the entire crowd, saying "I'm very glad it's over with."

January 21
The Target Center
Minneapolis
Timberwolves 105, Wizards 101

ON THIS DATE IN MJ HISTORY

One of his better days, he averaged thirty-nine points in eight games, including a season-high fifty-one against the Knicks in 1997 and a season-high fifty-three against Phoenix in 1989.

THE GAME STORY

Minnesota guard Anthony Peeler noted Jordan was back into his "Mike mode," quicker than he had been when the teams played nine days ago.

But not in the fourth quarter. Michael hit only one of eleven shots in the final period, the one being a bail-out three-point fling that barely beat the shot clock. Jordan finished with twenty-nine points and a season-high fourteen rebounds, but he made just twelve of thirty-four shots. After he scored twenty-two points in the first half, Minnesota used the bigger, stronger, quicker Kevin Garnett to slow down Michael in the second half.

January 22
MCI Center
76ers 91, Wizards 84

ON THIS DATE IN MJ HISTORY

The Bulls nineteen-point blowout of defending champion Houston in 1995 epitomized their inconsistency without Jordan between the First and Second coming. In the nine days prior to this victory, the Bulls lost to two woeful teams: Sacramento and Washington.

THE GAME STORY

Jordan had one of those nights that Allen Iverson described to reporters afterward this way:

"When a guy is hitting shots like that, it really don't matter what type of defense you have in front of him."

For one half, anyway.

Jordan scored the first six points of the game and hit nine of fourteen shots in the first quarter when he scored nineteen of the Wizards' twenty-three points. He had twenty-eight points by halftime. But in the second half, he hit just one of eight shots, that coming on a dunk with five minutes left in the fourth quarter.

January 24
MCI Center
Wizards 94, Cavaliers 85

ON THIS DATE IN MJ HISTORY

With the Bulls losing this 1993 game in San Antonio badly, Jordan huddled the team around him in the second half and uttered words to come back by: "Let's run," he said. Michael finished with forty-two points, but he was no Rockne. The Spurs won 103-99.

THE GAME STORY

After Jordan hit three of twenty-three shots combined in the second half of the past two games, old jokes were making the rounds again. But his twelve third-quarter points and fourth game of topping forty this season seemed to give Michael the last laugh.

"A lot of people have been saying that I am physically tired and I don't think that is the case," Jordan said. "I just think that the teams we have been playing—Minnesota and Philadelphia—made adjustments at halftime, and I think we hadn't been able to adjust to their adjustments."

Jordan's forty points also enabled the Wizards to up their record to 20-20 and top their win total of the 2000–2001 season.

January 26
MCI Center
Wizards 112, Suns 102

ON THIS DATE IN MJ HISTORY

A sign of the times came in 1985 when Jordan dropped forty-five on Atlanta. It was the third time he scored that many in his rookie season yet it wasn't even his season high.

THE GAME STORY

Before the second game of the season, Jordan had announced publicly we would see things similar to what we're used to seeing.

We are. On the night he was re-elected as a starter for the NBA All-Star game, Michael authored his second back-to-back forty-or-more of the season. Spreading forty-one almost equally over two halves, he led the Wizards to finishing the first half of the season with a winning record (21-20).

He was averaging thirty-five points per games during the past four games.

"Physically, I'm feeling good," he said, "and if I continue to feel good, then you'll probably see those numbers."

January 29
MCI Center
Pistons 89, Wizards 86

ON THIS DATE IN MJ HISTORY
In a 120-93 defeat of New Jersey in 1988, Jordan had thirty-two points and a career-high ten steals. He was in the process of becoming the first guard in NBA history to have more than two-hundred steals and one-hundred blocked shots in two consecutive seasons.

THE GAME STORY
Will the Wizards find somebody besides Jordan to make that one last shot?
Michael brought them to the brink of victory by scoring fourteen of his thirty-two points in the fourth quarter, including eight in a 12-0 run that catapulted the Wizards back into contention.
But trailing by two points in the final five seconds, Chris Whitney and Hubert Davis each missed potential tying shots. Doug Collins said confusion on the last play kept Jordan from getting the ball for the last shot.

January 31
Gund Arena
Wizards 93, Cavaliers 92

ON THIS DATE IN MJ HISTORY
Perhaps this is when the Pistons "Jordan Rules" began to develop for in a 104-98 overtime victory, Detroit held Jordan to twenty-one points.

THE GAME STORY
Just down the road from where Chuck Berry, Mick Jagger, the Beatles and so many others are enshrined, they might want to start the Shock and Roll Hall of Fame.
He added to the "The Shot" and the other "Shot" by hitting a game-winning jumper from the free-throw line as time expired. This one might have been more hairy than any previous shot, considering Jordan had all of 1.6 seconds to work with. Afterward, Michael compared his latest string music to the first one by saying, "Either way you look at it, it's a win."

February 1
MCI Center
Wizards 97, Hawks 90

ON THIS DATE IN MJ HISTORY
In the two-hundred and forty-six regular-season games of the Second Coming, the Bulls lost by more than ten points just six times. This night in 1998 was one of the worst. Despite thirty-one from Jordan, the Lakers defeated the Bulls 112-87, their third-worst loss of the Second Coming.

THE GAME STORY
The supporting cast continued to grow.
Tyrone Nesby scored a season-high twelve points and made a clutch defensive play in the closing seconds. Courtney Alexander scored twelve of his fourteen points in the first half. Etan Thomas provided a surprising lift by collecting season highs of nine points and ten rebounds.
"They have been waiting their turn," Jordan accentuated after scoring twenty-eight points. "Waiting for when they can get on the court and show they deserve to be on this team."

February 3
MCI Center
Wizards 109, Pacers 89

ON THIS DATE IN MJ HISTORY

He scored forty-four points in this 1990 game at San Antonio but one or two more would have avoided a 112-111 loss. Still, this was one of twenty-two times Michael topped the forty-point mark in 1989–90.

THE GAME STORY

Perhaps Jordan wanted to make one thing perfectly clear in the Third Coming: He wasn't going to back down.

So when Indiana's Jalen Rose tried to turn this matchup with Jordan into a hockey game, Michael merely absorbed the shoulder check, went nose-to-nose with Rose and watched the Pacers guard get ejected after picking up his second technical foul for the roughhousing.

"I said: 'If that's the way you want to play the game, then let's play the game that way,'" Jordan told the media afterward. "I just want to go out and play straight up, but if that's the way he wanted to play it—with anybody—I'll play it that way."

You had to figure Jordan would hang tough on this night considering he was held to six points in the last meeting with the Pacers. He scored seventeen of twenty-three points in the second half. The better news for the Wizards was the continued progression of Richard Hamilton, who had twenty-one points in his third game since returning from a groin injury.

February 5
MCI Center
Wizards 99, Raptors 94

ON THIS DATE IN MJ HISTORY

He apparently developed a thing for Boston early in his career, scoring forty-one on this night in 1985. In five games against the Celtics during his rookie season, Jordan averaged 33.8 points.

THE GAME STORY

Vince still had not learned to "Be Like Mike."

It was Jordan who shined in the end, overcoming a dismal first half to score twelve of his twenty-three points in the fourth quarter and dished out of a double-team to Popeye Jones for the key basket with nine seconds to play.

Vince Carter apparently was in need of some more heir brushing after scoring just four points in the fourth. Michael overcame one-for-five shooting in the first half while Carter hit just ten of twenty-three shots.

February 7
MCI Center
Wizards 108, Kings 101

ON THIS DATE IN MJ HISTORY

Enough, Michael said with forty points in a 1996 win at Golden State. You can imagine his wrath, the Bulls having suffered a two-game losing streak, their only losing streak of the season that came after an eighteen-game run of victories.

THE GAME STORY

If there is one game Jordan will look back on as having done what he said he would do in the Third Coming, this might be the one.

Richard Hamilton scored thirty-three points, Popeye Jones hit all eight of his shots for a season-high eighteen and the Wizards scored a season-best thirty-five points in the first quarter to beat the team with the best record in the NBA.

Oh yes, Jordan added twenty-five points, nineteen in the first quarter to go with Hamilton's eighteen. Washington had won all five of its games since Rip returned from injury, and going into the All-Star break with 26-22 record—that coming with an eight-game losing streak—had Michael giddy.

"This is the type of emotion I always envisioned about this team, where the young guys just feed off each other," Jordan said. "We've got a good chance of putting our-selves in a good predicament, which all along I felt like we could. In some ways you want to think greedy, but nut-cutting time is starting to come."

February 12
Staples Center
Los Angeles
Lakers 103, Wizards 94

ON THIS DATE IN MJ HISTORY
When Detroit coach Chuck Daly coined the term "Astro Points," he might have been thinking about 1985 when Jordan scored his rookie-season-high of forty-nine in a 136-129 overtime defeat of the Pistons.

THE GAME STORY
Did Kobe beat Michael at his own game? Did the true "Air Apparent" intend the Lakers to recover from a 63-43 deficit three minutes into the third quarter?

"It was fun coming back from twenty down," Bryant said.

Kobe had ten points when the Lakers came back with a 34-11 run to close the third quarter. He finished with his first triple-double of the season: twenty-three points, a career-high fifteen assists and eleven rebounds.

Michael had twenty-two points but fizzled in the fourth quarter when the Wizards went a period of more than eight minutes without scoring a basket.

February 14
Arco Arena
Sacramento
Kings 109, Wizards 93

ON THIS DATE IN MJ HISTORY
Jordan missed his first fifty-pointer of the 1990s by one point, scoring forty-nine in a 135-129 overtime loss at Orlando in 1990.

THE GAME STORY
At the All-Star Game a few days back, Sacramento's Chris Webber told Jordan he would get revenge for the loss in Washington earlier this month.

Whether that was his motivation or anger over media scrutiny of his relationship with supermodel Tyra Banks, Webber joined Kobe as one of the few players to com-mand the spotlight from Jordan. He scored nine of the Kings first seventeen points en route to a twenty-point, fourteen-rebound, nine-assist domination.

Jordan hit six of eighteen shots in his worst performance since the disaster in Chicago nearly a month earlier.

February 15
America West Arena
Phoenix
Wizards 97, Suns 96

ON THIS DATE IN MJ HISTORY
Believe it or not, the thirty-two he scored against Detroit in 1996 actually dragged down his points-per-game average. Michael was in the midst of one of his mid-winter binges in which he averaged 35.7 points over seven games.

THE GAME STORY

He had missed a potential game-tying shot with sixteen seconds to play. He had missed his previous five shots. He had scored seven points since the start of the second quarter. And with two-tenths of a second left and the Wizards trailing by one, Michael Jordan said he felt, "no fear."

With perhaps the whole world expecting not just his shot but the headfake to set it up, Jordan went through the motions and netted his third game-winning shot of the Third Coming.

"When you feel like you can do something, go out and do it," he told a mass of media afterward. "There is no fear, there is only two things you can do. Make it or miss it."

Jordan played the hero while Richard Hamilton again played the star with twenty-nine points. Michael added twenty-two.

February 18
MCI Center
Rockets 102, Wizards 89

ON THIS DATE IN MJ HISTORY

The forty-four points he scored in 1996 against Indiana—twenty more than Reggie Miller—were gratifying. But no moreso than exactly one year later when Scottie Pippen, the player Jordan had banged heads with for so many years in practice to get him to be more like Mike, registered his career high of forty-seven.

THE GAME STORY

To Doug Collins, the season-high eleven assists from Jordan was more of a telling sign than his eleven points.

The Wizards coach could tell something was wrong the way Michael looked to pass the ball rather than shoot. He had not practiced for two days and for now they were calling this injury a bone bruise in his knee. And he had turned thirty-nine years old the day before.

Postgame, there was talk about Jordan taking a game to rest his knee. Even more than a game. "The competitive nature is sometimes to gut it out," he said. "But if you're looking at the long haul, you have to kind of use your head a little bit."

And his agreeing to consider as much was telling to Collins about how much Jordan was hurting.

February 21
MCI Center
Nets 93, Wizards 82

ON THIS DATE IN MJ HISTORY

For a change, he didn't give Cleveland the back of his hand in a 113-111 loss in 1991, even though Jordan scored forty-six points at Richfield Coliseum.

THE GAME STORY

Sitting out a game the night before in Detroit indicated his knee was getting bad. And if Jordan not taking a single shot in the fourth quarter on this night wasn't enough explanation of how bad, he added the detail.

"You lose your lack of mobility and you limit your game to jump shots," Jordan said at a postgame media briefing. "When my game becomes limited to one option, I'm easy to guard."

Sitting out the loss to Detroit did little to heal the bruised knee. Michael scored sixteen points and missed ten of seventeen shots. The Wizards fifth loss in their past six games dropped them into a tie for the eighth and final playoff spot in the Eastern Conference.

February 23
MCI Center
Heat 97, Wizards 95

ON THIS DATE IN MJ HISTORY

By this point of the 1993–94 season, the Bulls finally found their man to replace Jordan in his first retirement. Pete Myers scored twenty-six points to lead a 123-100 defeat of Golden State.

THE GAME STORY

These are the nights that might keep Jordan coming back until he can't walk.

Two days after a no-show in the fourth quarter, Michael scored thirteen of the Wizards final seventeen points. He hit a game-tying turnaround jumper with nineteen seconds left, and only a deflected pass kept him from getting his hands on one last shot to tie the game again.

"These are the type of games character is built upon," Jordan surmised afterward. "Winners and losers."

Miami's Brian Grant hit two shots in the last sixty-five seconds to upstage Michael's thirty-seven points. Jordan, however, might have perceived this game as a setback only because Richard Hamilton failed to score in the fourth quarter.

"I can't do it every night," he added.

February 24
American Airlines Arena
Miami
Heat 92, Wizards 80

ON THIS DATE IN MJ HISTORY

Portland's Isaiah Rider had been one of those Jordan wannabes. Earlier in the 1996–97 season, Jordan showed Rider how to be by going off for thirty-six points. Michael gave him another lesson on this February 24th night by dropping thirty-seven on Rider.

THE GAME STORY

His best move in this game was walking away.

Three minutes into the fourth quarter, Jordan left the game and said afterward that his right knee was so bad he might consider going on the injured list for the first time since the broken foot put him out in 1985.

After having fluid drained off the knee right before the game to ease some inflammation, Jordan made just four of thirteen shots and struggled to score nine points. The diagnosis for the moment ran the gamut from lingering stiffness to an arthritic condition.

After the game, Miami coach Pat Riley presented a notion that few had ever considered about Jordan until this season. "He is not indestructible."

March 20
The Pepsi Center
Denver
Wizards 107, Nuggets 75

ON THIS DATE IN MJ HISTORY

With about a month until the playoffs and a run at a threepeat, Jordan put on a post-season flurry by scoring forty-seven in a 126-101 win at Washington in 1993.

THE GAME STORY

Twenty-one days after having arthroscopic surgery to repair torn cartilage in his right knee, Jordan returned and played about as badly as the night he hobbled away. Seven points, this time, on two-for-nine shooting.

Even now perhaps it was hard to comprehend what Doug Collins was saying after the game.

"Michael isn't going to come back too early and set himself back because he wants to finish out the season."

Jordan said he came back so soon for one last shot at a playoff run. The Wizards went 4-8 in his absence, falling off the playoff pace, so here's what Michael had planned.

"I can come off the bench and give some good minutes and go against some of the other teams' second players."

If Richard Hamilton could score thirty every night like he did against the Nuggets, maybe the plan would work. Maybe.

March 21
Delta Center
Salt Lake City
Jazz 94, Wizards 79

ON THIS DATE IN MJ HISTORY

By the time he put up forty in a 112-97 win at Sacramento, Jordan had scored forty or more against every team in the league during the 1986–87 season.

THE GAME STORY

This was progress: Jordan dunked. With 1:46 left in the first half, his slam tied the game at 46.

The Wizards didn't score again until the second half. Michael ratcheted his game up to eleven points in twenty-two minutes, but he and Richard Hamilton combined to make just six of twenty-three shots.

Jordan returned to the Delta Center for the first time since the legendary finish to Game Six of the 1998 NBA Finals, but otherwise the night packed nothing special. Especially to Karl Malone.

"I've been doing it for seventeen years," Malone told the Associated Press, "and played against him a lot. It doesn't do anything for me."

March 24
Air Canada Centre
Raptors 92, Wizards 91

ON THIS DATE IN MJ HISTORY

One of the better dates of his career, he averaged forty-one points per game, topping out with fifty-six in 93-91 victory at Philadelphia in 1987.

THE GAME STORY

Rushing back wasn't totally a lost cause for Jordan did get another last shot.

This seventeen-foot fadeaway, with time running out, went in and out, a miss that might have been the Wizards one last shot at getting back into the playoff race. Jordan also was hit with the turnover that enabled Toronto's Antonio Davis to score the go-ahead basket. Michael even cried foul after the play.

"Yes, obviously (it was a foul), they were fouling all day long," he said in his usual postgame media conclave. "The ref let it go and it couldn't be more obvious. I had the ball, I had the rebound and the ref was right there."

Jordan finished with fourteen points while Hamilton led four other Wizards who scored in double figures.

March 26
MCI Center
Wizards 103, Nuggets 87

ON THIS DATE IN MJ HISTORY

Eighteen months after retiring the first time, he was back to his old life having to answer questions about another Michael Miracle. The night before, just four games into his Second Coming, Jordan's length-of-the-court run to a jumper from the top of the key as time ran out gave the Bulls a 99-98 victory at Atlanta.

THE GAME STORY

On a night when Etan Thomas scored a career high, even Jordan had no problem driving through the Nuggets for a spinning layup.

Michael had nine points in twenty minutes played, not that he was needed in either capacity as Washington took a 61-33 lead into halftime. Richard Hamilton and Chris Whitney each scored twenty-two in a game the Wizards had to win to stay in playoff contention.

Still, at 33-38 they were two-and-a-half games off the final playoff spot with ten games still to play against teams headed for the postseason.

March 29
MCI Center
Wizards 107, Bucks 98

ON THIS DATE IN MJ HISTORY

Exactly four years ago to the date, Jordan hit Milwaukee with thirty points in a 104-87 victory.

THE GAME STORY

There was hope.

Hope for Jordan, who hit twelve of twenty-two shots and scored thirty-four points in twenty-six minutes playing on a knee Doug Collins said was no stronger than fifty percent of healthy.

Hope, too, for the Wizards, who beat one of the teams they looked up at in the Eastern Conference standings. Richard Hamilton added twenty-four points in a victory that put Washington, now 34-38, two games behind Indiana for the final playoff spot.

March 31
MCI Center
Mavericks 110, Wizards 103

ON THIS DATE IN MJ HISTORY

In one of his last great duels with Larry Bird, Jordan scored thirty-seven in this 1991 game at the Boston Garden. But Bird had one last shot for Michael, thirty-four of his own to lead the Celtics to a 135-132 victory in double overtime.

THE GAME STORY

He had missed all seven of his shots through the first forty minutes, and a guy named Adrian Griffin had been the designated stopper.

Still, Dallas point guard Steve Nash observed: "You can't really give Mike a chance to win the game."

He didn't get that last chance. Jordan responded by scoring eight of his ten points in the fourth quarter, including a reverse layup that tied the score at 96-96 with 2:26 to play. But eleven seconds later Nash hit a three-point shot that the Wizards, and Michael, never recovered from.

The most telling statistic on the state of Michael at this point: He didn't even get to the foul line in the fourth quarter.

April 2
MCI Center
Lakers 113, Wizards 93

ON THIS DATE IN MJ HISTORY

Jordan averaged thirty-five points per game in five April 2nd games, peaking with a forty-four point outburst against Orlando in 1991.

THE GAME STORY

Did Michael stay around too long?

This season, it seemed so.

This two-point effort in ten minutes with Phil Jackson and Kobe Bryant there was being called the worst game of Michael Jordan's career. But after playing just ten minutes and sitting out the entire second half, this should be recorded as a surrender more than a game played. Less than twenty-four hours later, he gave up on the rest of the season, his right knee in too much pain to continue. He sat out the remaining eight games.

The epitaph included such rhetoric as Jordan ended the season scoring less than ten points five times. In thirteen years with the Bulls, he did that once.

Perhaps it all just caught up with him.